Searching for New Sunrises

Around the World without Wings – the sequel

George Williams

Copyright © 2018 George Williams
All rights reserved

ISBN-13: 978-1984302069

Table of Contents

Table of Contents 3
Sector 1 –Southampton to Dubai 1
Sector 2 - Dubai to Singapore 83
Sector 3 – Singapore to Sydney 125
Sector 4 – Sydney to San Francisco 183
Sector 5 – San Francisco to Southampton 281
Other books by the author 372

Introduction

Five years ago, Deb and I experienced one of those life-changing moments. And it was a very positive life-changing moment.

In 2012 we spent three months sailing around the world on a cruise ship, and we saw so many things that opened our eyes and our minds to new experiences. We visited some of the glitziest cities in the world, and then saw the simplicity and poverty of ramshackle villages in the middle of a forest. We saw wide variations of landscapes: the barrenness of deserts, the raw power of volcanoes, the massiveness of rivers and major canals, and the sheer isolation of sailing across the oceans.

Our world circumnavigation left us gobsmacked at what the world has to offer an enquiring mind, and we wanted more.

That winter adventure, as we lived a luxurious life aboard a beautiful cruise ship, was to celebrate our retirement at the end of 2011. It was supposed to have been a special one-off 'dream come true', and used up a major chunk of our retirement money. When we returned in April 2012 we just couldn't simply forget the thrills, and almost immediately we looked at our bank balance to see if we could stretch ourselves to another similar adventure.

Yes, we could.

After many Saturday evenings watching the DVDs we had brought back, we decided that we had to spend some time at home before going again. A tentative plan was put in place to repeat the experience in 2017. Our friends and family were bored with our stories, and amazed that we were even considering a second such cruise, and to be honest there were a lot of times when we also had our doubts. But we were growing older, and our health was about to take a couple of hits that convinced us to do it before it was too late.

The itch to board a ship and sail away towards the horizon remained, so we continued having summer cruises to keep our addiction under control. But the stream of mail shots from P&O and the adverts in the newspapers were becoming far too much for us, and towards the end of 2013 we went to the cruise show in Birmingham, and booked a world cruise for January 2015.

With the deposit paid, we sat back and began the wait, but those health issues crept up on us and our plans took a bit of a kicking.

Firstly, I was told I needed a new hip, but the NHS is far from being rapid and it took until the middle of 2014 before I was even considered suitable for the surgical waiting list. Then Deb had a cancer scare just when we had to commit to paying the cruise balance in October 2014.

The 2015 cruise was cancelled, and a new booking was set up for 2016.

Well, Deb was given the all-clear and in 2015 my hip was satisfactorily replaced, but I now had a niggling pain in my groin. Eventually this required some more surgery. I had a mesh inserted to sit over my stomach muscles to strengthen and reduce my susceptibility to minor hernia problems.

This decision to have this operation was made at the October balance payment point, and yes, we had to cancel once again.

So, the world cruise booking was transferred for a second time, and we were rescheduled for January 2017 on board the Aurora for a 15-week trip circumnavigating the globe again.

Early in 2016 I had the operation to my groin, and then the pair of us refused to go to a doctor unless death looked likely. P&O had advised us that no more changes could be made without our initial deposit being affected, so Deb and I really made sure we stayed as healthy as possible.

By October the balance had been paid, and visas and travel insurance organised and purchased. We had sufficient prescription drugs and supplements to last us the journey, and a lot of new clothes had been bought. We had a bundle of currency for the USA, Australia and New Zealand, and our bank account had enough to cover any likely demands while we were away.

During the autumn months our garden was dug over and de-weeded as well as we could. Any minor work needed to the house was completed, and visits made to see, and bid a temporary cheerio to our families.

Finally on the 8th January 2017 we handed over the house keys to our neighbours, packed the car with eight large suitcases plus hand luggage, and set off for

Southampton. We had booked an overnight stay at the Holiday Inn in the city, and by mid-afternoon, with our room looking like a luggage showroom, we looked out of the hotel window towards where Aurora would be docked the next morning.

In the evening we had a meal and a large glass of wine in the hotel, and then we went to bed with our minds buzzing in anticipation.

The final words in my previous book ("Around the World without Wings") chronicling that first world cruise were:

"There's a lot more world out there to see"

Now this new adventure was about to begin, and we hoped to see and experience a little more of the thrills and magic that the world has to offer.

What would our cruise offer us?

A full world cruise has two options, either to sail westwards or eastwards. In 2012 we sailed from Southampton and went west across the Atlantic Ocean towards the Americas. This time Aurora would turn left at Gibraltar and sail eastward cross the Mediterranean.

Aurora's 2017 World Cruise was billed as something special. It was 180 years since a P&O ship set off on its first commercial voyage. Our cruise was a celebration of this long maritime history, but more importantly it was to recreate what was the beginning of regular commercial voyages between Britain and Australia.

That first trip was made by the Steamship Chusan which left Southampton on 15th May 1852, arriving 80 days later in Sydney on 3rd August. Its primary purpose was to initiate a regular mail service between Britain and Australia, but it was also the beginning of a maritime connection offering scheduled passenger traffic.

The Chusan was seriously different from Aurora. She was a mere 699 tonnes, with a steam powered engine creating 80hp that could achieve 9knots. She had the assistance of a considerable amount of sail in what is referred to as 'barqued-rigged', which increased her potential speed to 14knots. This little ship was under the control of Captain Henry Down and at that time with pirate activity in the Java Sea, Chusan was armed with a quite frightening array of cannons and guns.

Aurora is over 70,000 tonnes, and has an equivalent engine power of around 80,000hp enabling a much quicker voyage of some 50 days. She has no visible gun-power, but sadly still faced potential threats from pirates in the Indian Ocean.

There was one significant difference from the Chusan voyage. The Suez Canal hadn't been built in 1852, so the Chusan had to sail around the south of Africa. Aurora would have a much shorter route into the Indian Ocean.

Anyway our adventure was advertised as a 'Heritage' cruise with special events to celebrate the history of P&O. There were going to be traditional deck games, and tours that offered Heritage Walks around the significant ports that P&O has made regular calls over the decades.

Let the adventure begin.

Sector 1 –Southampton to Dubai

The countries we visited:

- Malta
- Greece
- *Transit of the Suez Canal*
- Jordan
- Oman
- United Arab Emirates

Monday 9th January 2017

As usual, our night in the Holiday Inn Southampton wasn't full of sleep and rest. I can never get comfortable in a strange bed and stuffy atmosphere. But there were other reasons for my insomnia. There was the usual element of excitement about what was to happen, and serious concern about what we might have forgotten to do, or to bring with us.

Eventually daylight peeked through the curtains, and it was time to get up for an early cup of tea.... plus a look out of the window to spot Aurora.

...yes, she was there waiting for us.

Breakfast was a very quiet affair, which confirmed our thoughts that the hotel wasn't very busy. The downside of an empty hotel is that with only a few people eating, some of the cooked bits become a little crispier than expected. As we sat quietly I couldn't help looking around the restaurant wondering if any of these people would be joining us later on the ship.

With breakfast over we washed, and then turned our attention to the luggage. A few items were swapped from one case to another to balance the loads, and other final bits were tucked away in corners. Apart from one left open for anything we might still buy, our suitcases were secured with cable ties, and we were ready to go.

Unfortunately, it was only 9:30 and there was still a couple of hours to waste yet.

We carried some of the cases down to the car, and then went across the road for a stroll around the West Quay shopping centre. There was only one item on my *'to get'* list and that was a memory card reader for my laptop. I quickly found one in Curry's, and then we looked around the John Lewis Store and took a walk outside to some of the shops in the streets. The morning was rounded off with a cup of coffee before returning to the hotel.

Back at the hotel, our purchases were stored away, and the rest of our cases fitted back into the car. We were using a company called *'Parking 4 Cruises'* to look after our car while we were away, and it was now time to give them a ring, and let them know we would be at the port just after midday.

It was time to go. As we walked towards the car, we realised it was raining, but that wasn't going to dampen our adventure.

Within seconds of pulling up at the Mayflower Terminal, a smiling porter appeared and piled up his truck with our mountain of luggage. He quickly pocketed his tip and made his way to the hole in the wall. Before going into the terminal building we drove to the nearby short-stay car park, where we handed over our car to the *'Parking 4 Cruises'* rep. It was a smooth operation, and hopefully all would be well when we got back in April.

Our official boarding time was supposed to be 2:30, and it was still only a few minutes after 12:00, but after strolling (quite excitedly) back to the terminal, we were surprised to be welcomed by the 'meet and greet' team and immediately funnelled through to the priority booking lane. There was already a short queue of seasoned and suite cruisers, but it only took about 20 minutes for details to be checked, passports taken away, photos taken, and cruise cards handed over to us. Boarding had already started as we looked for a seat to wait for our call. Deb just had time to stop at a rack and pick out a few free magazines before the public-address system announced that we could begin the real embarkation, so we walked around the departure lounge and straight to the security check area.

For the first time in several years I managed to go through the scanner without any *'beeps'*. OK so I had already taken off my belt, and had to temporarily hold my trousers up, but the machine was beaten.

Deb and I were on the ship by 1:00 and headed for the Alexandria restaurant for our Caribbean loyalty level buffet and drinks. Two other couples joined us at the table, who were also going all the way around the world. We chatted for almost an hour with a couple of glasses of fizz to begin the relaxation.

By 2:00 we were in the cabin and beginning the mammoth task of squeezing far too many clothes into a very limited amount of wardrobe and drawer space. That took well over an hour, but it was the last time we would have to do this for 15 weeks.

...well, so we thought at the time, anyway.

It was time for a cup of tea in the buffet and a brief stroll around this very familiar ship, but the afternoon was passing quickly and 'muster drill' beckoned.

And by the way, it was still raining.

Our muster station was the theatre and almost every seat was filled by the time we listened to the chat from Captain Andrew Hall before watching the very familiar life jacket demonstration. We have sat through these more than 25 times since we began our maritime adventures in 2000. We don't rebel, and just accept it as a necessary moment of our time.

Back to the cabin and it was shower time before waiting for sail-away. Our plans were to watch the firework display sending us on our way from Southampton. Sadly, the fireworks were not due to happen for some time, and first sitting of dinner beckoned.

We had a table for eight at the back of the Alexandria Restaurant with a window where we would stare out at the spectacular ship's wake for the next three months. There were three couples with us, and they were also on the full circumnavigation. One couple was very late as they had stayed on the decks to watch the fireworks. We just about managed to catch a glimpse of the display through the side windows of the restaurant.

The meal was delicious, with a new menu since our last cruise. The eight of us had a happy chat, and names were exchanged, but as usual it would take me a day or two to remember them.

After dinner we went to the opening show in the Curzon Theatre with an introduction to the entertainment hosts, and some taster songs and dances from the Headliners. There were just five hosts in the team (plus Mickey the manager). I was already thinking that this was shorthanded for a cruise of this nature, and certainly less than we had in 2012. Part of the show was also a chance to be introduced to the guest speakers for the sector. This was quite a good idea, and allowed us a brief overview of the talks, dancing lessons, and crafts available over the next few weeks.

From the show we went to Masquerades for a general knowledge quiz with host Danny. We saw him on Aurora in June, but he had now grown a rather *'ZZ Tops'* beard. I'm wasn't sure about this.

Oh, we won a bottle of wine for being the *'clever clogs'* of the evening.

It was time for bed. Unfortunately, the sea was getting really lumpy, and I hoped my little sea-sickness pill would see me through the night.

Tuesday 10th January

Oh dear, what a horrible night.

The captain had warned us of a 3-4 metre swell and that the ship would be moving around a little.

... *A Little!* - Why do these seafaring people underestimate the state of the sea so much?

I felt as if I had spent the night in a washing machine being tossed around. The ship rolled and pitched and creaked and crashed throughout the night. As the sleepless hours passed I began to feel queasy, and then downright ill, before eventually it was light enough to get up.

The little pill successfully got me through the night, but I really wasn't feeling very well, and refused a cup of tea. I simply curled up on the bed while Deb went to breakfast.

All too soon the inevitable defeat of my stomach and head happened. I began a horrible couple of hours being sick. By this time any food I had eaten yesterday had been digested, so my vomiting was merely an automatic body response that produced nothing more than a little bile, plus a lot of serious pain and discomfort.

Deb brought back a bread roll from the buffet to tempt me, but it remained untouched on the plate. I did manage to get dressed, and we went for a walk to give our steward a chance to clean the cabin. We sat in Anderson's, and while I quietly stared at any stationary object, Deb worked on her diary. After about 30 minutes of nauseous concentration, Deb decided my pale and greenish face meant it was time to go back to the room.

I lay on the bed, and that is where I stayed for the rest of the morning.

Deb wasn't fully happy with the movement herself, but managed to go to the first of the Port Talks covering Valletta (Malta). We always try and listen to these talks to get ideas for a tour, or places to go to by ourselves. Today, the only important thing in my life was being horizontal with my eyes closed.

Deb continued a busy morning by going to the Art Class in the Crow's Nest. She was a little late arriving because the Port Talk overran, meaning she had to sit a long way from the instructor. This made it difficult to hear and see what he was doing. She still found it enjoyable and would continue with it, but get there earlier in the future. From that class Deb went to a coffee chit-chat session with some Facebook forum cruisers, and gave my apologies, before making an early exit herself.

It was her lunchtime, and this time she brought back cheese and biscuits plus an apple from the buffet to join my lonely bread roll. Once more I declined the food and stayed horizontal.

At about 1:00 I finally began to get some interest in life once more. The nausea was subsiding and I found I could lie on my back. I started to look around, and perhaps about half an hour later I spotted the apple. It was delicious, and that led to the bread roll being nibbled at. Finally, I made a cup of tea so that I could take my daily prescription medicines, plus another one of the sea-sickness pills. I lay still for a little while longer and then my head and stomach declared all was well, and I could become sociable again.

Deb had been quietly watching my recovery and asked if I would like to go to the theatre and listen to a guest speaker. It seemed a good idea so off we went and found seats where I could make a quick exit if needed. The guest speaker was called Terry Brown, an ex-policeman, who helped to introduce the 'PRIDE' method of interviewing suspected criminals. Now retired, he gives talks on the subject, and also has a mock Murder Mystery roll-play game where people are either suspects or detectives. The idea is for the detectives to interview the suspects over a number of days, and decide who they think is the guilty person.

He was one of the best speakers I have ever heard on a ship. He didn't use a script, and managed to complete his session within a minute or two of the advertised finishing time. He was amusing as well as being informative and I would thoroughly recommend going to his talks.

Both of us volunteered to be suspects in his murder story, but so did a lot of others so we had to wait to see who he picked. We didn't get selected, but were encouraged to take part as detectives.

Hey, I stayed awake through the talk, and the sea-sickness seemed to be finally clearing up. The sea continued to be angry outside, and a lot of people were looking rather sheepish about being very far away from a toilet.

With my body feeling significantly better, I suggested going for a cup of tea in the Horizon buffet. Easily tempted, and rather hungry by now, the hot drink was accompanied by a toasted tea-cake with butter and jam.

My stomach and brain had reset themselves and I was finally at peace with the Bay of Biscay.

There was no rush that evening as it was casual dress for dinner. This meant we had time to go to the first Individual Quiz in Champions Sport's Bar. It was hosted by Coral who we saw on the ship in the summer. She must have been in a bad mood as her questions were a real test for everyone. I only managed five correct answers, and Deb wasn't too far ahead of me.

What a disaster, and such a comedown after the successful Masquerade challenge the previous evening.

There were only three couples at our dinner table tonight. The fourth pair had requested Freedom Dining, and managed to sort out a change during the day. They never reappeared at the table, although we did occasionally meet them as we walked around the ship. The remaining six of us chattered through the meal, and it was becoming much friendlier as we began to get used to each other a little. I was relatively careful not to eat too much, but at least my stomach had something inside it again.

After eating, Deb and I spent half an hour in the cabin because the show didn't appeal. It was the comedian Micky Zany who we had seen before. He is quite amusing, but just not for us tonight. Later we returned to Masquerades for the quiz again, and we were joined by Richard and Angie from our dinner table. They seemed quite amazed at our knowledge (well Deb's really) of TV Comedy Shows and we won our second bottle of red wine. It was decided to share it at the dinner table sometime in the next few days.

It was bedtime again and we returned to the cabin with great hopes of a sleep-filled night. While Deb was having a read we could just about hear an announcement from the captain on the corridor speakers. I opened the door to listen to it and it was to inform us that the ship was diverting to Vigo for an emergency medical evacuation.

This was so sad that someone had become ill, and worse still, was being rushed off the ship before we had even got to our first port.

I hope everything went well for them.

Goodnight.

Wednesday 11th January

We had another night without sufficient sleep.

It was made worse by the early morning arrival into Vigo with all the docking noises and procedures. As we went to breakfast at 8:00 we saw the ambulance taking the poor soul off to hospital.

Our stop in this Spanish city was very brief, and within a matter of minutes Aurora was unhitched from the dock, and we were heading back onto our course down the coast of Portugal. The sea was less annoyed with us, and there was even a hint of sunshine during the morning. There was still a cool breeze that kept many passengers indoors, but Deb and I took the opportunity for a brisk mile-long stroll around Promenade deck.

Then we went to Raffles for a cup of coffee. This is the main Costa outlet on the ship and we bought the first of our cards to get a tiny price reduction.

Later in the morning we went to another talk by Terry Brown, who was discussing the techniques used by police detectives to identify if a suspect is lying. Once again it was an amusing and interesting 45 minutes.

After lunch there was a chance for a nap to try and overcome the lack of sleep during the night. It wasn't for long, as I had an appointment in the theatre for a talk by Eddie 'the Eagle' Edwards.

What a character he is. He is so recognisable, and quite a good speaker. His first of several talks was well timed as the film of his memorable exploits had been shown in the Playhouse cinema the previous night.

It is amazing that this little man is so famous for coming last in the Olympic Ski Jumping competition. He was the first, and apparently is still the only British Olympic ski jumper. He had a serious round of applause to show how special a place he has in British hearts.

While I was enjoying his story, Deb went to a Salsa class for some exercise, and followed that with her art class. Today the subject was a small penguin, and her rather good effort took pride of place on the cabin wall.

With Eddie the Eagle's talk over, I returned to the cabin and relaxed while I waited for Deb to come back from her painting session. There was a knock on the door and our steward gave me our 'Round the World Cruise' gifts. These are quite special gifts and I am sure they will remind us for years to come, of what this voyage would bring.

Deb was quite late back from her painting, and had to rush just a little to change and be ready for the *'Welcome on Board'* Cocktail Party in Carmen's. Tonight was the first of 26 (I think) formal nights on the cruise. Deb was still ready in time to ensure we were almost at the front of the queue to get into Carmen's. We spotted an officer and chatted to him with a free glass of wine (or several) until the Captain gave his speech.

Dinner time broke up the party and soon we were chatting with our new friends again.

The evening entertainment was a female singer. I know that a lot of passengers enjoy vocalists, and I am sure that many of these singers are very good, but we like our entertainment to be a little more varied than a series of songs. So, we tend to ignore these acts.

Instead we had a rest in the cabin for a while and then returned to Carmen's for a dance. It was good to have a chance for a waltz, cha-cha, quick step, and a couple of sequence dances.

We rounded off the first real day of our adventure with a nightcap in Anderson's. The sea was much calmer, the wind had dropped, and surely this would be a night when sleep returns.

Tomorrow we would enter the Mediterranean.

A couple of surprises

We were only two days into the cruise, but we had already discovered a couple of surprising things.

Firstly, we were quite shocked to see a lack of bacterial gel dispensers, and asked the head waiter in the restaurant why. He said that the new policy wasn't to have them.

.... WHAT?

On our first world cruise on Aurora, the ship was suffering from norovirus when we boarded, and it took almost three weeks before the bug's progress was halted. During much of those three weeks we had various measures in place to reduce the spread of this horrible illness. Although not very effective, the gel squirts were a constant reminder for passengers to maintain their hygiene. Now we were being greeted and waved straight through into the dining room.

Our head waiter's explanation was that people put too much trust in the gel and don't bother with the more important and successful hand washing routine. So, by taking away the gel, and advertising the need to wash hands regularly, it was believed that the result would be a generally better level of hygiene. They still have the gel at the buffet entrances because it is still seen as a good idea, but the served restaurants no longer have it.

Apparently this has been the routine on Aurora for several weeks, and they were norovirus-free.

He continued by suggesting that it was going to become company policy for the fleet, but being out of contact with our forum links, we were not aware of what was happening elsewhere.

The other bit of news was that fewer than 400 of the passengers on Aurora were going all the way around the world. Even more surprising, 900 passengers are only on the Southampton to Dubai sector. Perhaps this is why this is likely to be Aurora's final circumnavigation. P&O's customers prefer their winter cruise adventures to be shorter, and spending more time exploring a single continent.

I felt rather sad that so few people will have the experience that a full circumnavigation provides, especially those people like me with a phobia of air travel.

Thursday 12th January

We woke up with the southern coast of Spain near Cadiz at the end of our garden. The temperature today rose to 18°C on our balcony.

I had a much better night's sleep, but only after I had overcome a bout of cramp in my leg. I had a suspicion that after being ill, and probably dehydrated, I had possibly become a little short of salt. I planned to get some crisps from the shop later today.

The balcony door (and the glass panel next to it) rattled, so this was reported to reception. We wanted to get every little annoyance that disturbed our sleep sorted out as quickly as possible.

For breakfast I just had a bowl of fruit and a single piece of toast (oops with jam). With so much food available on a cruise, I have to make an effort to control my food intake.

Our morning routine was beginning to sort itself out now. After our post breakfast wash, Deb and I regularly went to the area outside of Anderson's, known as Charlies, for half an hour. This was what we called our office, where I worked on my blog entries, and Deb updated her diary, as we watched the ship comes to life.

After that our plan was to walk a mile around the open deck on as many sea days as possible. This morning it was noticeably warmer on the sunny side, and the walk raised my pulse rate a little. As a reward for our efforts, it was time for a cup of coffee, and a delicious apple and cinnamon muffin.

Just before 10:00 we were sitting in the Curzon Theatre ready to listen to a port talk from Crystal, an Australian who was our port guide. Today her talk covered Heraklion in Crete. I just about stayed awake and absorbed a few useful facts and tips about the island, but then there came a chaotic few minutes.

The ship would soon be entering the pirate zone, when Aurora will move up to a higher security level, and hence the crew needed to be ready. Part way through Crystal's talk, the decision was made by the officers to have a bomb scare exercise.

'Bing Bong'

The public-address system cut in and switched off the theatre sound to alert crew of the bomb scare exercise.

This only took a couple of minutes and the talk quickly resumed.

Five minutes later there was another **'Bing Bong'**

Once again Crystal's talk was interrupted, this time with an announcement for the crew to go to their muster areas as presumably the bomb had now been located. Of course, some of the crew were assigned to the theatre, and as they entered behind us, it caused a little concern among the audience.

Very quickly an officer arrived to let everyone know that we could remain seated and not to worry about the intrusion, and Crystal resumed her talk again.

'Bing Bong'

Five minutes later another announcement interrupted us again, and this time it asked that all passengers return to their cabins to look for an imitation bomb. As we all stood up and began to leave, Crystal said that she had almost finished anyway.

'Bing Bong'

This time it was an apology, as the previous message hadn't been intended for passenger action!

For those who hadn't already left the theatre, Crystal completed her talk and we finally had all the information we were going to get about Heraklion.

Reading always plays a major part of our sea day activities, and for the rest of the morning we sat in the Crow's Nest with our books and the glorious views.

This venue is a popular spot with many passengers throughout the day and evening. Early in the morning passengers will be up there to capture the new sunrise, or watching a sail in to the ports around the world. On sea days it is still a magnet for people to simply stare at the sea as it changes through the day.

After breakfast the Crow's Nest fills quickly as a place to sit and let the world slip by, or to look for passing ships. The window seats are the most sought after and their occupants will sit with a book, or grapple with a daily puzzle whilst keeping an eye on the ships progress with the same view as the captain has below them. It has a relaxing effect and within a few minutes a number of the passengers will doze off. This is more often than not the men, and their wives will keep an eye on them and quickly poke them if they snore.

On our cruise the scene changed a little mid-morning with the art class that was fronted by Easa Ali. He had morning and afternoon sessions on sea days with a very good following of passengers new to art, as well as many who were more experienced. Easa concentrated on a small number of water colour subjects to give people a chance of mastering some really superb pictures. They were rarely complicated but the interpretations of a Kingfisher were amazing, as was the Asian woman's head and shoulders with just the eyes revealed from under her black hijab.

There was a steady service of coffee and tea for the passengers, but as lunch neared the number of people in the Crow's Nest reduced as they went to lunch, although some settled for a pint of beer before going in search of food. With lunch time over, the favoured seats would be snapped up again and books quickly became too heavy, and eyelids closed once more.

Late in the afternoons there was a noticeable change with people coming into the venue with tidier clothes to match the evening dress code. Rather than beer the popular drinks were cocktails and wine as little groups of friends gathered to chat over canapes. On most days there was a pianist, or one of the combos playing background music that usually received a smattering of quiet applause between songs, or tunes.

On the four or five evenings each sector when there was a cocktail party, the Crow's Nest was one of two venues for the formal Captain's or loyalty events. The waiters and waitresses would do their best to keep the passengers supplied with drinks for the 30 or 40 minutes of the party. There were officers available to chat to as well as the speech from the master of the ship. These were quite short events but many passengers (like ourselves) did our best to make the most of their favoured free tipple of wine, gin and tonic, or the ever sought out champagne(ish).

After dinner the Crow's Nest would be a truly social place with intimate chatter of couples, or more raucous discussions within groups. Many enjoyed the evening cabaret musician or group, but we liked the more peaceful moments when they were on their breaks. Although on the World Cruise the venue would quieten down around midnight, the Crow's Nest can often be a busy place into the early hours.

Let's return to our day in the Mediterranean Sea as we sat reading in the Crow's Nest. The morning art class session was going on and Deb decided to skip her planned session this afternoon with no enthusiasm to paint a flower head. She likes to paint landscapes rather than objects, but this art teacher didn't seem to like to paint them in the classes.

It was time for lunch and by now our midday routine was usually to eat in the Horizon Buffet rather than the formality of the dining room. I was continuing to control my eating with just a bowl of soup and a bread roll.

...what a pity about that muffin earlier

We returned to the Crow's Nest where Deb read some more while I caught up with my blog. It was very pleasant in the sunshine watching our progress across the Mediterranean, and as we had just passed Gibraltar, it really did feel like a holiday at last.

The lofty Crow's Nest lounge was getting quite crowded so Deb and I moved to the Crystal Pool. Even with the roof closed it at least felt a little bit more open. Yes I know it is just a glorified greenhouse when the cover is on, but it does give the impression of nearly being outside.

Deb couldn't resist the almost deserted pool, and changed for a swim.

I ignored any such energetic ideas, and after dropping my kindle reader a couple of times, I gave in and had a doze.

When Deb came back to me I rewarded her efforts with a tub of ice-cream. It was just a single scoop each, so surely that won't do any harm…will it?

Back at the cabin Deb had a short bath to rinse off the swimming pool residues, and I read some more. Outside the sea was now a gentle wallowing scene, and so much nicer than the dark grey boiling pot we had had so far. It was still a little windy, and with our balcony now on the shaded side, it was a bit too cool to sit out there at the moment. The coolness of winter was particularly obvious, as in the distance we could see the snow-capped hills of southern Spain.

The afternoon was clear of talks and Salsa classes as the Headliners were putting on two early shows in the theatre. This new matinee show idea supposedly gave us all more chances to see the shows. Today it was 'Destination Dance' that we both enjoy, but we prefer the more traditional evening performances, and suspected there would be plenty of other opportunities to see it during the cruise.

Instead we went for afternoon tea in the Horizon Buffet. I had a toasted tea-cake to make up for not eating too much at lunch.

As I said earlier, we were building up our sea-day routine, and the afternoons usually ended with the Individual Quiz. Today was a much better effort than the previous afternoons, and Deb's score was respectable. But she didn't win, as someone managed to get the all 20 questions correct.

How did I do?

…. well I got into double figures.

The evening meal was a good laugh, but Deb and I were considering a request for a different table to somewhere away from the noise at the stern of the ship. The noise made it quite difficult to hear conversations, and this would be our table for another 15 weeks. We didn't want to leave our new friends so decided to give it a few more days before making up our minds.

Once again, I was careful with my food and avoided the *'daily ice-cream sundae'* and just had a piece of cheese in place of a pudding.

The main show this evening was the second one by Mickey Zany but we had a doze in the cabin again. He is really very good and our dinner mates thoroughly enjoyed his shows but we just didn't want to see it so soon after seeing him in the summer.

We rounded off the evening by meeting up with Richard and Angie in Masquerade's for the late quiz. The questions were about TV Comedy again and this time DJ Martin was in control. This was a high-scoring quiz and a tie-break was necessary to separate the top teams. We were very close but missed out by two questions.

As Aurora continued across the Mediterranean Sea, we said goodnight to our friends and made our way to bed.

It had been a quiet, but good day, and I was quite pleased with my efforts to reduce my food intake

...pity about the muffin, ice-cream, and tea cake!

Oh, and as well as attempting to reduce my food intake, we decided today was an alcohol-free day, and at least we successfully accomplished that.

Tomorrow (Friday) would be our final sea-day before arriving at the port of Valletta on the island of Malta.

Friday 13th January – Sea Day

We were sailing across the Mediterranean quite close to the North African Coast. The balcony temperature at 8:00 in the morning was 16°C and the sun was breaking through the clouds. The sea wasn't calm but certainly quite comfortable for Aurora to sail through.

We had both had a wonderful night's sleep and were settling into our winter home.

I spent a while in the office while Deb braved the swimming pool. When she reappeared we prepared ourselves for a busy morning in the theatre. First there was a port talk about our visit to Jordan, where over 800 of the passengers would be going to Petra. The long journey to get there, and the long walk around the area would have been just too much for my legs, so we needed something else to do.

Aurora would be docking at the Jordanian port of Aqaba where there appeared to be a few things to see but which wouldn't occupy much of our day. The talk gave us several options and eventually we decided to go on a tour that would take us around the city of Aqaba before going to the Wadi Rum Valley. It seemed a pleasant way of spending the time in Jordan, and included lunch in a Bedouin camp. So, tour number 18 was booked.

Following the port talk we had a quick coffee in the Horizon Buffet before settling down again for the third talk by Terry Brown and his police interviewing techniques. Once again it was a wonderful session and he had the audience in fits of laughter on a number of occasions.

At 12:00 midday the clocks went forward.

So suddenly it was an hour later and we were late for lunch. Well to be accurate the majority of the ship's passengers decided they were late for lunch and descended on the various eating venues like a herd of hungry hippos. The situation was made worse with a talk due in less than an hour from Eddie the Eagle. It had been a busy morning and lunchtime, so having already satisfied my curiosity about Eddie the Eagle, I simply returned to the cabin and relaxed. Meanwhile Deb had a Salsa session followed by her art class.

While all this was going on, the weather deteriorated from what had been a promising warm day into a more typical winter storm with pouring rain. The sea was fighting all those sailing through her, and we were bobbing up and down and rolling again. The wind was whistling through the ship from any partially open doors, and even through the shut ones on the port side. Our balcony door was allowing a horrid rush of wind through its aging fittings and there was no way of stopping it.

These conditions continued until early evening when the weather, and the sea, began to reduce its anger a little.

By late afternoon Deb and I were back together again. We had our showers and went to the Individual Quiz which was from entertainment host Abbey this time: everyone did rather well with mainly quite simple questions. There were two people who scored 19 out of 20, and the winner (after a tie-break) was the same person as yesterday. I was quite pleased with myself as Deb only beat me by one point.

After several evening meals in the main dining room we decided on a change and ate in the Sindhu restaurant. I am not over-keen on Indian food, but it was mild, very tasty, and an enjoyable meal. Sadly, it involved far too much food and we were both feeling uncomfortable by the time we finished.

Deb and I crawled back to the cabin and lay down for a while to relax our stomachs. After an hour dozing it seemed pointless to consider doing anything else, and both of us were tucked up in bed and heading for sleepy-land before 10:00.

Tomorrow we would be arriving in Valletta around midday for our first visit to the island of Malta.

Saturday 14th January – Valletta, Malta

The weather today began cloudy and cool. It rained early in the afternoon but then there were occasional sunny spells with a top afternoon temperature of 16.4°C in the back garden.

We had another restful night and I was up feeling quite bright at about 7:30.

Our watery garden was a grey colour again with quite a slow-moving swell of perhaps 3-4 metres. But Aurora was giving us a smooth ride as the direction and speed of the swell wasn't affecting her very much.

After breakfast and 30 minutes in the office we joined the large number of passengers walking meaningfully around the promenade deck. Some were strolling, but the majority of us were striding out to give our bodies a bit of a workout. As we walked down the starboard side of the ship we could see the coast of Malta quite clearly.

Deb passed on the art class and we went for a mid-morning coffee.

We were back in the cabin just before 11:00 when the approach to Valletta harbour began. The port lecturer (Crystal) was giving a commentary and soon we were darting in and out to the balcony to look at and photograph the stunning buildings. The walls and buildings looked as if they had been made with Cotswold stone: a magnificent sight. Just after we entered the harbour the midday cannon boomed out and the sound echoed around the city walls.

Before long we were tied up to the dockside and preparations were underway to allow the early birds to get off for tours or simply doing their own thing around Valletta.

We were doing our own thing later, so had a relaxing lunch in the Horizon Buffet.

It wasn't too long before we were also ready to leave. Our plans for the afternoon were to simply look around, but as Aurora was staying in port until late in the evening, we were also seeking out a possible place for an evening meal. As we walked towards the lift to the upper level of the city it began to rain. I had my waterproof coat but Deb had been confident about the captain's weather forecast for a dry afternoon - and got wet. Fortunately by the time we came out of the lift the rain had stopped.

Almost immediately we saw a tourist sign for the 'Wartime Tunnels' and that's where we headed.

For 15 Euros each we had an almost two-hour tour with a very entertaining and knowledgeable guide. In that time we only managed to explore a little of the extensive tunnel system that has been opened up for visitors. The tunnel system dates from the St John Knights in the time of the Crusades, and has been extended and developed through the centuries for the various conflicts that have affected Malta.

Most of what we saw was for the 2nd World War, including the secret war rooms where intelligence was received and acted upon. There were also earlier areas where the explosive black powder had been stored, and outside on the battlements there were examples of the cannons that were used to defend the island.

By the time we came away from the site, my legs were severely tested from walking down and up hundreds of stairs and I was in quite a bit of pain. While walking towards the shopping area we sat in a square for a rest, before exploring the different statues and unusual art work. We moved on to investigate the shops and cafes, but although Valletta is a charming city, we never found anywhere appealing to sit with a coffee on this rather cool afternoon. Instead, we bought our first fridge magnet of the cruise, a new sunhat for Deb, and a guidebook of the city, before turning back towards the ship.

After a cup of tea on board we returned ashore to look at the restaurants and souvenir shops on the dockside. There were plenty of places to eat, but the menus were not that exciting so we decided to eat on the ship again.

There was plenty of time to have a shower, rest my legs, and a little snooze before dinner.

'Bing Bong'

An announcement echoed around the ship to tell us that the Beatles tribute band, who were the main evening entertainment, hadn't been reunited with their instruments so their show tonight had been postponed, and replaced by another female vocalist.

So we avoided the show again, and simply relaxed in our cabin after dinner.

We did go out later in the evening and went to Masquerades for the 9:30 quiz. As we passed by the theatre we heard the singer, and our decision to miss her was a good one. This lady probably has a very good voice, but like the lady who has already been on, jazz appears to be a common theme. I fully accept that many people really enjoy singers but our tastes are different.

The quiz was quite unusual, and based on album and book covers. Scores were surprisingly high, but we were quite a way behind the winners.

After exercising our brains, we went to the Crow's Nest for a late-night drink…well late for us anyway. It coincided with Aurora setting sail from Valletta, and as we chatted and sipped our prosecco we watched the beautiful city buildings gliding by. This had been a late departure from a delightful city, and a place we hoped to return to one day, but maybe in the summer next time!

The Crow's Nest entertainer for the evening had come into the lounge to begin her singing. She is one of a growing glut of low cost entertainers who sing to a backing track, but she enhanced it by occasionally playing a saxophone. I forget what the song was, but she had decided to make it a Jazz rendition. Why do these people tamper with a perfectly good song? Polite applause rippled through the room when it was over, and she began another song which was Country and Western. In the space of just over five minutes she managed to find our two least-liked musical genres.

Time for bed!

Tomorrow would be a sea-day as we made our way to Greece for a chance to visit Athens, and Heraklion in Crete the following day. Then we would start to make the journey south to warmer waters and hopefully a bit of sunshine as well.

Oops!

We had been on board Aurora for five days now, and most of us were getting pretty used to where the pointy end was, and how to decide which way to turn for our cabins, but this wasn't always the case.

I was in a lift with a frail little lady. Her deck stop was before mine, and as she prepared to leave the lift for her cabin, I heard her start to repeatedly chant…."***Leave the lift and turn right***", she even had her right arm gesturing which way she was preparing to go.

Unfortunately her mind must have been playing tricks, and as she walked out into the lobby she turned left. To make matters worse she was still chanting her instructions, and her right arm continued to point in the correct direction.

The brain is an amazing thing, but sometimes menacing little messages in the naughty part of our head trigger uncontrollable instincts to do the exact opposite thing to what our brains are telling us.

Hopefully she quickly discovered her mistake and maybe even laughed at the error.

Sunday 15th January – Sea Day

My normal early morning routine as I got out of bed was to fill and switch on the kettle for an early cuppa, followed by opening the curtains to look at the weather. I also checked the thermometer we had positioned on the balcony to get an idea of what the day would bring.

It was 8:00 on Sunday morning, the sky was cloudy but there were a few breaks for the sun to perhaps peep through later. Our garden appeared to be reasonably flat, but the water was an uninviting grey colour, and the temperature was just a chilly 13.9°C... brrrr!

I could only hope things would get better later.

Aurora was sailing east and then north into the Aegean Sea today for our planned arrival in the port of Piraeus tomorrow morning. From there a vast number of the passengers would be setting off to the Greek capital of Athens.

Breakfast beckoned and we soon discovered just how chilly it really was as we walked across the open deck towards the Horizon buffet. Once our tummies were satisfied, we went down to reception where Deb picked up a copy of the 'Horizon' newspaper and a couple of Sudoku sheets. I asked for a cabin statement so that we could check how our spending was going.

This was the beginning of a weekly housekeeping session.

We always store our receipts in a box, and once a week (usually), they are checked against the statement to ensure we have not been charged for anything incorrectly. This also makes us aware of how the spending is going. At the moment we were working our way through a significant amount of on-board credit. Satisfied we had been suitably frugal, we moved on to refilling our daily pill pots from the 'chemist' – a case stored under the bed. Over the fifteen weeks this suitcase would slowly empty of drugs, shampoo, conditioner, deodorant, toothpaste, and various other bits and pieces. Hopefully the eventual empty case would be available to take home our souvenirs from around the world.

Then it was time to go to the office, but this morning we were unfortunately a little late and our usual office space was busy, so we had to find another temporary one. A table tucked away in a window by Champions seemed OK, but it wasn't as good as our little work area in Charlies.

Our new office was fine for 15 minutes but then it became a bit of a nightmare trying to concentrate as someone began to play a slot machine in the casino directly behind us. What a racket these machines produce as they eat money. Alongside the meaningless *'bleeps'* as the different buttons are pressed, there are annoying repetitive tunes that indicate the reels are revolving, or when they have stopped. Sometimes a different sound tells the user they have won something but at the end of most little clips of tunes there is a short silence that tells the player it is a **'Hah, hah, you lose!'** moment.

It was time to give up on clerical activities and go for a walk in the peace.

Out on the promenade deck it was chilly but a fair number of people were strolling or striding out on the teak deck to work off a few calories. Most go in the same direction but there are always rebels who purposely go against the tide. Every ship with a promenade deck has two narrower sections of the walk at the extreme stern and bow ends. These are always the places that you catch up with someone who is blissfully unaware that a queue of faster walkers is building up behind them, and many insist on keeping very much to the middle. Promenade decks are a shared resource for every passenger, and I appreciate that we all have different speeds of walking, but sometimes (perhaps wrongly) it can be frustrating that a number of people live in a personal bubble, and have no awareness of others around them.

Sadly, there is a distinct probability that one day I will join that *'land of bubble'* and frustrate others.

After the walk Deb went to her art class and I sat and read my book in the cabin for a while. I then tried to find the new memory card reader I bought in Southampton, and searched every box, drawer and shelf for it. Eventually I got to my bedside drawer and after taking everything out, I finally found it. The first 85 photos from Valletta were then transferred to my laptop. There are a number that will end up being discarded, but for now they can stay.

The clocks went forward again at midday and we were now at GMT +2. This time we were ready for the time-slip and grabbed a table in the buffet before it was opened to get a quick start before the afternoon's activities.

Replenished once more (just a salad for me and soup for Deb) we returned to the cabin for a read and then Deb went to Salsa.

This was a very quiet afternoon with just a short break out of the cabin for a cup of tea. The weather went downhill as the day progressed and the ship was rocking its way towards Greece.

Formal dress tonight, and I wore my white tux with a red bowtie to match Deb's dress. As I put on my trousers a button made a bid for freedom, but there was no time to make a repair now. I quickly sought out the other pair of formal dress trousers leaving the first pair, plus its escaped button, to be repaired tomorrow.

It was the full house of six at the table this evening and we shared the bottle of quiz wine from a few nights ago. There was a lot of happy chatter as well while we caught up with each other's adventures.

After dinner Deb and I went to the theatre for a different sort of show. As the Beatles Tribute band were still instrument-less, we had the resident band, Caravan, performing a tribute to The Eagles.

It was sensational.

We have always liked Caravan but this is the first time we have had a show from them on the theatre's stage. Apparently, they have three tribute shows that they normally perform in Carmen's but they had the vacant theatre this evening. When they finished, several members of the audience were on their feet to appreciate the talent in this band.

From that delightful show we went to Carmen's for some dancing, and we danced more this evening than we had done for some time. I was exhausted by the time we left.

The sea had calmed down again, as we closed in on the Greek mainland.

Monday 16th January – Piraeus, Greece
Today's maximum temperature on our balcony was 18.5°C

Our arrival in the port of Piraeus was well under way at 7:30 when I woke up. Docking was a noisy and long-drawn-out affair dominated by the sounds of side thrusters which continued for what felt like ages. Eventually it fell quiet and Aurora was still.

We had arrived at the first of our rearranged stops in Greece. The cruise was originally scheduled to include two ports in Egypt, but the political situation meant this was potentially unsafe. We'd been told months ago that Aurora would instead be calling here in Piraeus, and Heraklion on the island of Crete tomorrow. I met a man in the lift during the morning who said his main reason for booking this cruise was to visit the Valley of the Kings in Egypt. Greece wasn't seen as a very acceptable alternative, and his wife had actually refused to come on their cruise from Southampton to Dubai.

I think that was a pretty extreme response.

Anyway, as I looked out through the cabin curtains I could see a ship across the terminal from us called the Celestyal Olympia. It appeared to be deserted and out of service for the winter, except for the occasional person with tool kits. Later I discovered another of the Celestyal Cruise Line ships was similarly idle in the next berth over from us. This Greek cruise company has three or four small ships offering all-inclusive holidays around the Mediterranean and the Caribbean.

Many hundreds of Aurora's passengers would be away to Athens today, but we have been there before, and although it is an amazing city we decided not to bother on this occasion.

We had other less exotic plans…it was washing day.

I would like to say that **WE** did the washing, but in reality, Deb did all the work and I simply carried the odd armful of clean clothes from the laundrette back to the cabin. It appeared that a good number of the passengers had also decided to avoid Athens as the laundrette was busy with the usual queue waiting for machines to come available. Once the process had started, Deb set up camp in the little room guarding the washing, and ironed the dry bits. That gave me plenty of time to sew my trouser button back on, without Deb telling me how clumsy I am.

A couple from our table recently had a major mishap in the laundrette. They started their washing and went to a talk in the theatre. An hour later, they returned and found their clothes had been taken out of the washer and put into a dryer. The clothes were not dry yet so they put the dryer onto another cycle and went to lunch. When they came back this time, the dryer was empty and there was no sign of their clothes.

They reported the incident to reception perhaps thinking someone had taken them there but no, they had been taken away by someone. They described the clothes and feared they might have to go and urgently buy replacements, but fortunately most of the items were located and returned to them…but not all!

Anyway, that wasn't going to happen to us. By 10:00 our drawers and wardrobes were full of clean clothes again. Between transferring armfuls of clothes, I had even enjoyed a few minutes on the balcony with the rather lovely sunshine making it feel pleasantly warm.

It was time for a cup of coffee now so we made ourselves comfortable in Raffles.

As on many port days while the ship is almost empty, there was a crew exercise. It was a simulated fire in the crew area that eventually progressed to the point when a lifeboat was launched. Passengers like us swanned around Aurora as normal, oblivious to the "incident", while the crew went through a full test of their skills.

We sat in comfy chairs sipping a cup of coffee, watching the activities with mild interest, but without breaking into a sweat.

Deb was getting slightly bored by now and suggested we went ashore. It seemed only polite to at least step onto Greek soil…well concrete actually. It also meant we could have a photo taken against a Greek background for our collection.

The terminal building was as far as we ventured, where we found half a dozen souvenir shops to explore. Our total spend was 4 Euros on a keyring with a small

Greek Urn that will make a perfect Christmas tree decoration. The return walk took us through the Duty-Free shop but nothing else appealed. Less than 30 minutes later we returned to Aurora, but only to collect our laptops as we had spotted a free WIFI spot in the terminal building. So, we caught up with emails as well as updating my blog and Deb's diary online.

That was enough of Piraeus and it was lunchtime. We spoilt ourselves with a plate of fish and chips in the almost deserted buffet. On the way back to the cabin we had a chat to a dinner table waiter who recognised us from our last cruise in June. It is so amazing that these guys remember us amongst the hundreds that they serve through the months.

The temperature had already begun to drop by now so rather than sitting outside on deck for an hour, we sat by the covered Crystal Pool instead. We both took our books to read, but I discovered mine became far too heavy, and after a chapter I put it away and had a doze. My hopes for a little sleep were unfortunately disturbed by someone snoring, and continually waking me up...

Oops that would have been me then!!

As the temperature dropped even more we moved to the Crow's Nest where we had a drink and I read the daily news-sheet. This was also a chance to look around at the port area.

The city of Piraeus is built on a hill with mainly commercial buildings across the road from the dockside. These glass-fronted banks and shipping offices are nine or ten storeys high with very little architectural thought given to make them visually attractive. Behind them there are several long straight roads going up and away from the harbour area, with residential blocks of apartments and flats on either side. There are no villas, no marble pillars, no olive trees - this is where ordinary people live, and the buildings appear almost utilitarian. The dwellings are rectangular blocks of concrete going up seven or eight levels, and while they do vary in design, they are close together producing a scene that looks like an unplanned scattering of grey concrete boxes. Inside of course they may be beautiful, and comfortably luxurious, but to the visitor it doesn't tickle the visual senses.

The sky clouded over as we headed towards the end of the afternoon. It was getting progressively cooler, and looked as if there might be rain before we sailed away from mainland Greece.

Casual dress code tonight meant a relaxed period leading up to dinner, and an opportunity for us to have a bath before the Individual Quiz. Dinner was a chance to share news of what we had been doing for the day while we enjoyed the rather interesting new menus that had recently been introduced across the fleet. I was finding too many fish options, and this didn't suit me as I am someone who doesn't enjoy fish…unless fried inside a layer of batter. Fortunately there were always enough meaty choices to suit my taste buds.

As we finished eating, the six of us promised to meet up at 9:30 for the evening quiz in Masquerade's. In the meantime, Deb and I went to the theatre to watch the first evening show from the Headliners. Titled 'My Generation' it featured music from the 60's. Yes we had seen it many times before, but it was still enjoyable.

Onto the quiz and the six of us put up a superb fight on the subject of television quiz shows. We managed to be equal first and it went to a tie break. The question was to guess the weight (in pounds) of the heaviest snake ever discovered. We went for 452lbs while the other team went for 460lbs. It was actually over 500lbs.

So, no wine for us tonight, but we had a good laugh.

Back at the cabin we realised the wind had increased and was whistling through our balcony door which continued to rattle and bang. This didn't bode well for a good night's sleep.

Laundry Protocols, and NVQ qualifications

After our use of the laundry today, I am proud to announce that I had attained the first and second level NVQ qualifications.

Deb is fully qualified but, as a man, I have to go through various stages of basic and advanced training before being allowed to be more than just an unwanted visitor to the room.

The initial level 1 NVQ was rather simple to get, and allowed me to enter the laundrette and stand quietly giving moral support to Deb as she fed the machines.

Level 2 was also granted by the esteemed examining board of experienced washers after I successfully demonstrated my ability to collect dry and pressed clothes, and return them to the cabin.

Over the next few weeks I would have the opportunity to advance my qualifications through the three higher levels:

Level 3 – To be able to stand around unsupervised for short periods, but not to interfere with, or respond to other people around me who might be chatting and spreading gossip.

Level 4 – As per level 3 but also allowed to use the iron - as long as I accept any advice, without dispute, from the examining team, when I am deemed to be doing it incorrectly.

Level 5 (fully trained) – After accepting ridiculous amounts of unnecessary advice – and showing multiple successful demonstrations of my abilities - whilst being laughed at, teased repeatedly, and not responding to being talked about – I will be permitted to perform all functions of the laundry room and (more importantly) interact with other people.

I never got past a provisional pass in Level 3

Tuesday 17th January – Heraklion, Crete

Balcony temperature at 8:30 was 15.5°C and at midday it was over 20°C – wonderful!

As I suspected it was a noisy night and I only slept fitfully. In the early hours the wind dropped a little, and I enjoyed some decent sleep before waking as the thrusters announced our arrival into the port of Heraklion. It was just before 7:30.

Our back garden today was an expanse of concrete. We were docked in a busy commercial port with containers, bulk freighters, and ferries. Our cabin overlooked the main container area where there were hundreds of coloured metal boxes that have travelled 100,000's of miles around the globe. What stories they could tell of the oceans they have crossed, the continents they have visited and their loads of the latest iPads, or fashionable clothes, and maybe even scrap metal that they have carried.

Later in the morning I watched a bulk freighter offload its cargo of grain into a fleet of lorries. It took less than a minute for a crane to grab a scoopful in its huge metal jaws, and then dump it in the waiting lorry. Within ten minutes the lorry was full and on its way, and while the next scoop was being picked up, another lorry took its place. Each of those scoops would carry enough grain for several thousand loaves of bread and cakes.

Let's go back to our view from the cabin. We were facing to the south so the sun was saying hello from a delightful blue sky. Further away across the docks and the city beyond there was a ring of snow-capped hills, many of which were partly covered by fluffy clouds. Even allowing for the containers here, we would see far uglier docking points than this one over the next few weeks.

After breakfast we prepared ourselves and jumped on the shuttle bus taking us to the dock gates. From there we walked along a yellow painted line that guided us to the city centre. I had a jumper on, but soon the exertion from the walk and the warm sunshine made me doubt it was needed. Our target was the Koules Venetian Fortress on the waterfront across the bay from where Aurora was moored.

This very old fortress cost a mere 1Euro each to enter, and it kept us occupied for well over 30 minutes. Such very good value, but we wondered how this could possibly pay the wages of the people looking after the site, let alone the cost of the historical building's upkeep.

From there we crossed over the main road towards the main shopping area of the city. Very quickly we spotted the first of many souvenir shops, and it kept us happy with plenty of local treasures at wonderful out-of-season prices. The lady behind the counter was very helpful, and although she didn't know it, she was the only one to sell us anything but a cup of coffee for the morning.

Even the lady trying to sell me a rather tatty red rose, and a little boy who insisted on letting us hear him practicing his scales on an accordion, were ignored and went away with nothing to show for trying to disturb us.

The sun was gloriously warm as we strolled back to the ship where I sat on the balcony (topless in January!) while Deb had a swim. There was no need to walk a mile around the Promenade deck today as we had been walking for over two hours already.

It was time for lunch, but we were doing well and kept it to a salad.

Yes alright, Deb had cheese and biscuits afterwards, and I had a bowl of fruit salad.

After lunch we went out on the decks to enjoy the sunshine, but just like the last few days a chilly wind was getting up. We settled in the Crystal Pool greenhouse again for an hour of reading. You will not be surprised to hear that I had a snooze, but that invisible person snoring kept waking me up again.

As the afternoon turned to evening the temperature cooled down, and soon Aurora's passengers were back on board and preparing for dinner before we set off again. This time we would be heading southwards and leaving Europe through the Suez Canal towards Asia.

Coral was hosting our individual quiz session – another difficult one. Everyone struggled, with scores around the room being the worst I can ever remember.

Dinner chatter was full of stories from our table-mates of where they had been on the lovely Island of Crete, but our thoughts are turning to Jordan in three days' time, and the other destinations coming up before Sector One ends in Dubai.

We avoided the evening theatre show as it was another singer (male this time) called Roger Wright. Our primary evening entertainment so far has been one comedian, two female singers, one male singer, and a Beatles tribute band who never played a single note. They got off in Heraklion where they found their instruments waiting for them at the airport. Then they boarded a plane on route to join Ventura heading to the Caribbean.

Somehow I think we have been hard done by on Aurora!

Before bedtime we went to Masquerade's and challenged ourselves to a quiz about musicals and films. It hadn't been a good day for the brain cells as we struggled to come up with any meaningful answers. The problem was common amongst the majority which meant much laughter at the silly answers being suggested around the room.

Back in the cabin we had a read.

The sea was feeling quite calm tonight, and the captain had promised much warmer temperatures for the next couple of days. Tomorrow it should be officially near the 20°C mark and then higher still as we begin our trip along the Suez the day after.

Maybe we can spend some time in the sun on the open deck tomorrow, and hey, I might even have a swim.

Wednesday 18th January – Sea Day towards Suez Canal

Balcony temperature today reached 17.5°C late in the afternoon.

The sun was shining when I got up, and our back garden was looking quite smooth, with perhaps just a hint of a brighter colour. The early temperature on the balcony was 16°C so quite promising. Our breakfast in the Horizon was rather quiet, and I suspect many passengers were having a lie-in after a couple of busy days.

It was time for a spell in the office followed by appointments beginning with a port talk in the theatre about the first of our stops in Oman, before Deb moved on to her art class. The afternoon's schedule included Salsa for Deb, and I planned to go and watch the first cricket session. I really wasn't sure if I should join in, but I knew the temptation might be too much.

The talk on Salalah confirmed we have booked a suitable tour of this Omani city. Deb left the talk early for her art class, but came back almost immediately as she wasn't interested in learning how to paint a cow. Unfortunately the moment she left the theatre, a man took her seat next to me. Deb and I spent the last ten minutes of the talk several places apart.

From the theatre we went for coffee. We finished using our first Costa loyalty card, and I think we had saved a few pence by buying the card for ten cups of coffee.

While drinking our coffee we had a chat to another couple on the full world cruise. Technically they weren't cruising all the way due to a mix up with the visa for India. They had organised e-visas, but only discovered later that they needed a more comprehensive visitor's visa. To overcome their problem, they would have to leave the ship in Dubai, and then fly to Mumbai where they will stay in a hotel until Aurora arrives a few days later. The couple then qualify to be able to use an e-visa. This was an expensive mistake as a result of the complicated rules that India had for tourist visits.

Of course, if they had read my Blog about planning for a world cruise, they would have saved themselves a lot of money!

Coffee over, we went for a mile's walk around the Promenade deck. It didn't feel as warm as yesterday but still a pleasant temperature for a stroll. The sea was so calm that it looked as if we were sailing across a huge sheet of silk that was being gently fanned by a breeze. There weren't any waves; just little lumps like sand dunes slowly moving around. Sadly just 30 minutes later this smoothness changed as a breeze got up, creating a more rolling sea-scape.

It was still extremely calm and gave us a quiet and gentle ride.

At midday the 'officer of the watch' updated us on our position. We only had about 150 miles to go until we reached the beginning of the Suez Canal. Aurora will be there at about 10:30 in the evening and will anchor in the approach lake. Early in the morning all the ships going south will gather in their assigned positions within the convoy before beginning the passage through the canal. Captain Hall announced that he hoped to be given a position near the rear of the convoy to allow us more of the passage during daylight.

After lunch Deb went for a swim while I read my book - sorry dozed off for a few minutes.

When I went to watch the cricket there was really no way I wouldn't join in. In fact, I was the first person to bowl in the warm up session.

Martin (the DJ) was in charge of the cricket sessions, and this was the first of the cruise because the nets had been replaced. He explained the rules and checked that we were all wearing suitable footwear. Then he told us that this was only a game, and not competitive, so we didn't need to run around and get too excited.

This was a moment when about 16 aging men decided not to listen to the messenger.

It was a game, and there would be a winning side and a losing side.

This **was** competitive!

...but I was careful (ish)

It was a lovely hour. I thoroughly enjoyed giving my body a workout that hadn't involved DIY or gardening. Yes my legs ached a couple of times when I moved faster than at any time in the last five years. Yes my arm, and more especially my hand, throbbed when I bowled as the blood was forced down into my fingers with the effort of getting the ball to the batsman. But it was terrific to be actively involved in sport again.

It was a couple of months less than five years ago that I fell over during a cricket session on the 2012 world cruise. The little niggling injury I received to my leg eventually directly (or indirectly) resulted in my new hip, and playing the game again really completed the circle of that chapter in my life.

Dress code tonight was formal, and nominated as the Black and White evening. The ship looked so wonderful with the majority of the passengers dressed accordingly. The cabaret in the theatre was Suzanne Godfrey who plays instruments including the flute and saxophone. She is probably very good but we wanted something to capture our imagination rather than simply a series of songs or tunes. After reading for an hour we went to Carmen's to have a dance at the unusually titled 'Arabian Ball'. We happily careered around the dance floor until we were exhausted.

We rounded off the night with a chat over a glass of wine in Anderson's before getting back to the cabin at 11:00 for a read.

Aurora was at anchor near the entrance of the Suez Canal. There were several other ships nearby that would form the convoy tomorrow morning. The captain posted a message on the TV channel saying that unfortunately we were going to be near the front, so there will be an early start in the dark. We would begin the transit at around 3:00am ... but I didn't expect Deb and I would be getting up to wave cheerio to Europe.

Thursday 19th January – Suez Canal

The temperature on the balcony rose to over 18°C during the afternoon.

I woke in the night and heard the sound of the anchors being pulled up. It was 3:00 and Aurora was about to begin the transit of the Suez Canal.

I went back to sleep.

The clock said 7:00 when I finally got up and took a peek out through the curtains. There was a hint of the sun trying to make an appearance but it was foggy, and this was blocking any chance of looking at the canal. It was also rather smelly with an aroma that I couldn't identify, but it perhaps reminded me of a council refuse dump where waste was being burnt…. Yuk!

Things looked different in the Horizon buffet, with most people wearing long trousers, jackets and hats. Deb and I were in shorts and tee shirts. It was cold but we were not letting that influence our holiday apparel. On the way back, we were joined in the lift by the ship's doctor who looked at our clothes and asked if we had come in to warm up. The little chat was a shock as I discovered she comes from my home town of Helston in Cornwall. We had a six-year age difference as she started at the town's grammar school the year after I left.

What a small world.

Back in the cabin Deb decided to go for a swim, so I didn't bother going to the office this morning and updated the blog material at the cabin table where I could keep an eye on what was happening outside.

It was 8:45 and the sun was shining through the window as the fog began to lift. Aurora was already about a third of the way through the transit. I temporarily forgot the blog, and stared at the scene from the balcony. My view was of the eastern bank of the canal, and the water shimmered in the morning sunshine. The desert sand dunes of Sinai were not that inspiring, but I knew from our previous visit that that would be the case. While I surveyed the vast expanse of desert, we passed by a statue above a huge message on the sandy bank welcoming us to Egypt. There were a few people fishing and they occasionally whistled or shouted a welcome…. or perhaps it was an insult! The only other life on view was several long necked black birds sitting on most of the canal markers. I suspected they might be guillemots, but my bird recognition is pretty poor.

As the captain had said earlier, we were the second ship in the south-bound convoy, with just a car transporter ahead of us. It was still so foggy that there was no sign of this ship, or any of those behind us.

The canal had changed since we were here five years ago, and now has a two-way section in the middle where the north and south convoys can pass. In 2012 the south bound convoy had to anchor in the Great Bitter Lake in the middle, while the north-bound ships passed by. We started to see the ships going northwards in the new canal section from about 9:45, and the last I saw went by at 11:15. By then the fog had completely lifted and the balcony thermometer was registering 14.5°C. Sadly the sun had already gone from our side of the ship, so we were not benefitting from its glorious warmth.

At 11:30 we entered the Small Bitter Lake – or should it not be Less Bitter, or Slightly Bitter?

The captain announced that we would be completing the transit and leaving the canal at around 2:00.

During the morning Deb and I spent time viewing the scene from different areas of the ship, and also took a look at a number of stalls set up in reception, manned by local Egyptian traders who had come onto the ship with the pilot. They were selling leatherwear and various souvenir bits and pieces. We spent a total of 10 Euros on a leather card wallet, fridge magnet and two pens. We could have bought similar things from the ship's own shop which had stalls on deck selling *'stuff'* left over from previous cruises to various parts of the world. The difference was that a fridge magnet from the ship's shop cost £7.50, while at the Egyptian stall it was 2 Euros.

There was a barbecue on deck this lunchtime, and it was busy with people grabbing the sizzling bits and pieces for a change. Deb took advantage, but I am not a fan of barbecue food, so had a salad in the buffet instead.

At about 1:30 Aurora was passing by the city of Suez and leaving the canal. Our voyage would continue south down the Gulf of Suez before turning left towards Jordan and the port of Aqaba that we would be visiting in two days' time.

Finally Deb and I stopped gazing at sand and had our first sun worshipping session. We went up onto deck 14 above the Crow's Nest at the front of the ship and stretched out in the beautiful sunshine. It was glorious and there was a lot of flesh on view up there, and in fact all over the ship.

And this was still January!

Salsa and cricket then demanded our attention to give our hearts a bit of exercise. I was much more careful today to avoid taking risks with my legs, but bowling was still causing me severe pain. I was sure it would get better with time. Oh, and the team I was playing with won today.

Of course it's only a game and not competitive…. **not much!**

While our thermometer on the balcony registered that the temperature in our garden was 18.6°C, it was a lot hotter, yes I said hotter not warmer, up on deck.

Our dinner times were becoming lively events with lots of chatter across the table. The six of us had gelled into a superb group of friends. The two couples who shared our winter with us were Robin and Rosemary, and Richard and Angie. Even our waiter (Adison) and his helper (Cyrus) joined in with our fun at times. Edison was efficient but regularly played a little game. The six of us were rarely paying attention as he served the food, and seeing this he would announce an incorrect choice as he laid the plate in front of us. We would turn to him to tell him of his error and then see the smile on his face. Looking down we realised we had exactly what we had ordered, and then we all laughed. He never made a mistake. He also liked surprising us with unordered scoops of ice-cream. This game was extended to any of the temporary dinner guests we had, much to their surprise, and of course to our enjoyment.

This evening it was smart casual dress code, and in Carmen's there was a 60s/70s party night. In the theatre Helen Wilding was back for her second singing show …yes you guessed - we didn't go. In fact none of us were interested in the show, so we agreed to meet up in Masquerade's later for a game of 'Trivial Pursuit'.

This passed two hours of amusing answers, some ridiculous answers, and occasional correct ones, but all interspersed with roars of laughter. Each day we found out a little more about each other, although as usual, for those of us in our prime of life (or past it) medical issues were a common topic.

Anyway with the 60s/70s party using all the entertainment hosts, there was no quiz and by 10:00 we were the only ones in the bar except for a waiter, but even he eventually gave up on us and we had a security officer guarding the bar. It wasn't long before we took pity on her and bid goodnight to each other, and the security officer.

Deb and I were still on a bit of a high from the evening of fun, so popped into Carmen's to see how the party was going. It was well packed with slightly senior dancers remembering the music and moves of their youth. Sadly only two passengers had made any effort to dress up. We had wondered about this earlier, as we brought our fancy dress kit with us, but when there hadn't been an invitation to dress up in the programme, we decided to check it out first. Looks like we won't be an aging hippy with his Abba(ish) girlfriend on this cruise then.

We didn't stay long, and made our way back to our cabin for a read.

Goodnight.

Friday 20th January- Sea Day to Jordan

The balcony temperature this morning at 8:00 was 21°C, and rose to 25° during the afternoon.

Now that was warm!

I had a wonderful night's sleep that was probably due to slightly more red wine than usual the previous night, but also because I had now properly relaxed into the cruise.

Aurora was sailing south-east from the Gulf of Suez, passing the Egyptian resort of Sharm El Sheikh, and later turned more towards the north into the Gulf of Aqaba. Tomorrow we would be stopping at the port of Aqaba in Jordan. We had a tour booked there going to go to the Wadi Rum.

This seemed an unusual name for a pub, and someone stupidly suggested it is something completely different.... **WHAT?**

The garden this morning looked a little lumpy, as the sea made some haphazard movements as if slightly confused. It was certainly not rough, and our floating paradise gently purred along at a relaxing speed of 11.5 knots to get us to the port of Aqaba tomorrow morning.

While I caught up on the blog, Deb went for an early morning swim.

At 10:00, Deb and I then went to the theatre for a port talk about Muscat. We still hadn't booked a tour for here, and nothing jumped out at us from Crystal's presentation. Hopefully there would be a shuttle to the market (known as a Souk), but it seemed the shuttle had to be called something else, "Muscat on your own" for example, to avoid the local taxi drivers getting the hump. If this wasn't to be available we would stay on Aurora that day.

There was only a short break after Crystal had finished, before the final talk from Terry Brown about Police interviewing techniques...superb again.

That took us up to lunchtime.

After a bite to eat we made the most of the sunshine and relaxed for about 45 minutes, before it was time to prepare for Deb's salsa class, and my daily dose of cricket.

My cricket session was looking like it would be a success. I was chosen as one of the team captains, and we kept the opposition's score down during their turn to bat. We were still doing well after the first couple of our own batsmen did their bit, but then it all went wrong. Many of the later batsmen failed to score, and were 'out' several times giving five runs to the opposition each time.

I ended up as the losing captain.

Ah well, not a problem as it's only a friendly game...

... NO IT ISN'T!!

As dinner time approached, Deb and I were amazed at how early it got dark that evening. To be honest I think it was earlier than back at home.

Our table mates were having an early night because they were on tours to Petra tomorrow, so would have to be up very early. We went to Masquerades to watch the game show "Less is More'" based on BBC's "Pointless" programme. We didn't get chosen to take part, so watched eight of the other passengers try to win a bottle of wine. The hosts were Abby and Danny and the competition were well planned and followed the "Pointless" show very closely.

The winning couple found a pointless answer in the final and won a bottle of house wine each.

That was enough excitement for us and it was time for a read and bed.

Unfortunately, our balcony door decided to bang and boom as bad as I'd heard it, and I didn't expect to get much sleep.

Saturday 21st January – Aqaba, Jordan

The balcony temperature was 14°C at 8:00 and rose to 25°C maximum during the day.

The weather this morning was rather good with a clear blue sky, and bright sunshine.

As expected it was a noisy night, and I was deprived of sleep again. I reported the rattling balcony door once more, and was promised that something would be done about it.

Captain Hall parked Aurora with our side facing away from the docks. The initial scene making up our garden today was across the waters of a bay. There were the usual views of industrial and commercial activities, as well as different sorts of housing, but more pleasing were the beaches and hotels in the distance. We had the amazing sight of three different countries: Jordan, Egypt and a small area of Israel.

The backdrop behind the thin strips of built-up areas consisted of a range of hills and mountains. The colour of these imposing mountains ranged from shades of dark brown through to almost white sand. We were to discover later that the built-up area is only a thin strip of land of a few hundred metres before the mountains begin.

Of course the busy port area of Aqaba was noisily unloading cargo throughout the day, giving us the familiar crashing sounds and constant hum of a commercial harbour.

Looking down onto the dockside we saw 20 coaches for the trip to Petra lined up to accommodate the 800+ passengers making this amazing trip. Shuttle buses were also available to take passengers to and from the city centre of Aqaba, but we had a tour to the Wadi Rum. We weren't leaving until 11:00 so we had plenty of time for a leisurely breakfast, and a mile's walk around the deck before our coaches would be waiting for us.

Deb and I also did a bit of housekeeping and checked our account with a cabin statement. Everything looked fine and we weren't bankrupt yet.

Very quickly the ship felt deserted with so many people already on their way to the major *"must see"* location of this sector. We had nearly two hours to kill before we left Aurora, so after our walk we had a cup of coffee, and indulged ourselves with a little cake each to keep our stomachs happy for the journey to come.

At 11:00 we set off for the Wadi Rum: what a wonderful experience today would become.

Our guide had a few local sights within the city of Aqaba to show us first. There was a square (or Plaza) dedicated to Sharif Hussein Bin Ali, who led the Great Arab Revolt in the early 1900s, and who is seen as the founder of the modern and successful country of Jordan. The square is dominated by a 137-metre-high flagpole supporting a huge flag which measures some 40 metres by 20 metres. Although very similar, this flag is different to the Jordanian flag which has three horizontal stripes of black, white and green from the top, plus a red triangle pointing from the left with a white star. This special vast flag fluttering above us was created to honour The Great Arab Revolt, and has a different design with no white star in the red triangle, and the white horizontal band moved to the bottom.

From where we stood in this Plaza, our guide described the waterway in front of us. The city of Aqaba made up most of what we saw, and then he took our gaze to the left where Egypt sat. There followed a truly heart-felt sad comment that in between these two Arab nations, there is a stretch of land that is little more than a handful of kilometres along the coast of the bay.

This tiny sliver of land is a part of Israel.

He pleaded for common sense to allow the two Arab neighbours to be joined together, and I think many of us understood his sadness.

We re-joined our coach and set off through the streets of the city. The streets of Aqaba are not pretty, and shops don't have shiny glass frontages. There is dust everywhere, and several run-down areas where rubbish is dumped. The only *'wow factor'* came from the hotels which are huge and designed to attract visitors with lots of money. The complexes of International hotel chains are totally different from what the local people can afford to live in.

Soon we were climbing out of the city into those hills we had seen earlier. This was the beginning of our hour-long journey to the Wadi Rum Visitors' Centre. The road was dual carriageway, very straight, and generally of a good surface. Strangely, even with a clear view of the straight highway disappearing away into the distance, there were occasional sleeping policeman traffic calming humps.

The mountains to the side of the road were an astonishing sight and reminded me of the volcanic landscape of Lanzarote- only this was even more spectacular and went on for mile after mile. We now had a close-up view of the multi-coloured landscape that we had seen from the ship. Our guide explained that the base rock was granite with a lot of basalt, but the upper areas were of softer sandstone and had been weathered to create abstract shapes, holes, and crevices that resulted in many gigantic sculptures. Of course sometimes there were more open areas where the sand had been whipped up by the wind to produce the more traditional desert sand dunes and ripples of golden dust.

After a while we passed through a customs point marking the end of the region of Aqaba, and soon we turned off from this main highway from the south to the north of Jordan and beyond. We were now on another quite reasonable road that would take us along the Wadi Rum Valley towards our destination.

The name Wadi Rum means *"Valley of the Romans"*, although the local people refer to it as *"Valley of the Moon"*. It is a huge valley cut naturally into the sandstone over many centuries, and runs from Saudi Arabia to the south going north through Jordan and then on into Syria. It has been used for centuries as a camel trail route: it took three days to complete the Jordanian section by these animals. Today it is used by motorised transport although many Bedouins continue to make their journeys in the traditional way. There is a British connection to this area, as Lawrence of Arabia spent time here and an oasis is named after him.

Alongside our road was a single-track railway line that criss-crossed our route at unmanned level crossings. This was designed to bring pilgrims from as far away as Istanbul to the holy cities of Saudi Arabia. We only saw one train during the day and that had an old steam engine at the front, with a diesel locomotive at the rear.

It was obvious by now that our guide was really getting into the swing of his description of Jordan and the Wadi. His voice was getting louder and louder through the coach's PA system, and there was no way of stopping him, and letting us simply enjoy the views.

On a more positive note, it was on this stretch of road that we finally saw camels. There were several groups of them, but in one field there were perhaps thirty of them, young and old, in differing shades of camel brown.

Now I knew we were really in a desert.

Finally we arrived at the Wadi Rum Visitors' Centre and could leave the coach and get closer to the amazing sights we had passed. Our 20 minutes here allowed us to capture photographs of the really sensational mountain scenery. The weathering of the sandstone had created what looked like pillars from the mountain, and one artistic masterpiece is known as the 'seven pillars of wisdom'. It was one of hundreds of wonderful views on offer.

This was also a chance to use a toilet. They were clean but neither the male or female toilets had any paper to dry our hands afterwards. We all came out performing the hand drying dance, but the hot desert air did a good job to speed up the drying process.

There were a few souvenir shops at the site, but what was on offer was very artisan, and hence very expensive. I'm not sure that much was purchased, and there were very few bags brought back onto the coach.

It was time to move on.

We had a ten-minute drive now to the *"Captain's Desert Tourist Centre"*. This was our lunchtime stop, and like so many things today, it turned out to be rather good.

There were two large Bedouin tents. One was the kitchen creating all kinds of local dishes, while the other was larger, and where three coach loads of us sat in comfort on cushioned benches. We were all given a welcoming glass of sweet and hot local tea, with dates and a grainy biscuit to eat as we waited for the food to be cooked. It was about 15 minutes later that we were instructed to queue up to help ourselves to the hot delights.

On offer were kebabs, barbequed chicken, different curries, freshly baked flatbread, pickled vegetables, and upwards of 20 bowls of different dressings, rice, and olive dishes to accompany the hot choices. For pudding there was a Jordanian sweet cake, sticky sweet fruits, and fresh tangerines and plums.

A couple of stubborn people refused to even try the food and sat on their own sulking, and expressing their disgust at this 'foreign' food. The rest of the 120+ passengers tucked in and tried almost everything with a smile on our faces as we celebrated having the opportunity to sample the local food. It was a little spicy for my personal taste, but I'm always willing to try anything that is offered in the countries we visit.

After a few minutes to photograph yet more mountain scenes and to look at the Bedouin tents that are available for visitors to hire, it was time to begin the trip back to Aqaba and Aurora.

On the drive back, we had another toilet stop at a shop and café complex, which also included a much better range of souvenirs than we saw before. There was jewellery and pottery that was beautiful, but a little expensive for our taste. Luckily there were also a few fridge magnets that were on offer at 1$ (US) each. That was our total spend that day, except for the actual tour cost.

We were back at Aurora by 4:30 and we were exhausted.

There was no time to go to the quiz, so we both had showers and Deb put on a small load of washing while the machines were quiet. For dinner we simply had a main course, as the Bedouin lunch had been far more than we are used to at that time of the day. Then it was back to collect the washing and have a rest in the cabin.

With all the passengers back on board after their tours, Captain Hall announced our departure from Aqaba just after 8:00 in the evening.

The ship would now be at sea for four days while we sailed south down the Red Sea before turning left to go past Yemen, and our arrival in Oman at the city of Salalah on Thursday.

We completed our day with a quiz compered by DJ Martin on events and music through the decades from 1950s through to 2000s. We were doing well until we came to the 1990s and then crashed and burned failing to get anywhere near the winning score.

That was enough and we returned to the cabin after a wonderful day. Jordan had been the second new country we had visited so far, and was certainly a delightful tick on our boxes of places seen.

Oh, and a man had been to repair our balcony door and believed he has improved it this time. Only time will tell, but I hoped he was correct.

Goodnight.

Sea Days to Oman

Sunday 22nd January

We were moving south towards the warmth, and today it peaked on the balcony at 25°C, but the captain said it was hotter up on deck. The wind had dropped, the sky was blue with glorious sunshine, and our garden looked quite smooth with just a few white horses running around.

This was the first of four sea days from Jordan to Oman.

Deb started her day (after breakfast) with a swim while I updated my memories, and then we both lay in the sunshine for an hour. Goodness it was hot! I took my music player out of the box for the first time on this cruise. To me a hot sunny day with my iPod, reminding me of so many years of my favourite music is the absolute definition of pleasure.

Being Sunday, we had to visit the under-bed chemist and restock our day boxes with our pills for the week. This didn't take long so we were soon away on the mile walk around the deck. The Prom Deck was always busy with walkers in the morning and again later in the afternoon. Most people adopted a protocol of walking anti-clockwise, but a few passengers were either rebellious, or maybe unaware, that they were going against the grain. And we always seemed to meet them at the narrow sections of the deck.

The deck was now fully armed with water cannons and the detection systems for the pirate waters that were coming up. Security guards scanned the sea with their binoculars, and the ship would be joined by a Royal Navy escort tomorrow as the risk increased.

The clocks went forward at midday making us GMT +3. That meant we had travelled about an eighth of the way around the globe.

During the afternoon Deb had her Salsa and I played cricket (badly) before we rested to catch our breath before the Loyalty Cocktail Party. That meant formal dress code tonight plus posher-than-average menus on the dinner table.

On our way down to Carmen's for the cocktail party we passed Michael Buerk on the staircase. I was looking forward to listening to his talks.

We had a nice chat with an Italian electrical engineer at the party, and the captain made his usual promotion speech for P&O. We didn't win the loyalty raffle, and after 17 years of cruising without winning, we don't expect we ever will. To be honest the free glasses of wine and chat are all we want.

After dinner we went to a show in the theatre. It was a double bill which started with a comedian/magician called Mark Shortland. We had never seen him before and the comedy was fresh, and I have always loved magic. Putting the two styles together made a really pleasant change.

Then a singer /comedian called Bernie Flint took over the stage. We had seen him before, and the act was identical to the one we had already sat through. His act is based very firmly on the fact that he won the "Opportunity Knocks" TV talent show of the 60s/70s. His opening song was Simon and Garfunkel's "The Boxer" in a style Deb detests, and then a patter of jokes followed where we didn't detect a single new one. Never mind, at least it was only 25 minutes long, and I am sure most of the audience were new to it. We wouldn't be rushing to his second show.

The Masquerades quiz was another disaster. The questions being used at the moment appear unusually obscure, and were receiving groans from many of the passengers.

It wasn't late when we left Masquerades, but I was suffering from a headache that I put down to dehydration in the sunshine. I was very happy to get to my bed.

....

Monday 23rd January

Today it was warm from first thing, with a temperature on the balcony of 27°C in the afternoon.

I was rather reluctant to get up this morning but my head soon cleared and I was ready to face another day. There was just a gentle breeze, and the sea was calm. Mr Sunshine was burning off a few stubborn clouds and that didn't take him very long.

Aurora was about half-way down the Red Sea, with Sudan at the end of our garden to the east, and Saudi Arabia on the other side of the ship to the west. We were expecting the Pirate Drill this morning at 10:00 so there wasn't time to do very much initially. I did a bit of blog work and then we set off for the port talk on Dubai to see if another tour triggered our interest.

After that it was back to the cabin to wait for the captain to announce the beginning of the drill. When the alarms sounded we all sat in the corridor for 15 minutes while the cabin stewards checked for rebels who refused to comply. Captain Hall eventually thanked us for our cooperation, and let us get up and play again.

Deb and I decided it was time for our walk around the deck. We set off as usual but found the deck was closed on one side. Our response was to go to deck 13 so that we could walk around up there, but the sunshine and warmth changed our minds. We grabbed a couple of recliners and took it in turn to go and change into sun-worship clothes – plus getting a layer of protective sun screen on.

There was just enough of a breeze on the very top deck to take the edge off the heat and we stayed there for an hour. My ears were filled with the music from my iPod and one of my all-time favourites came on for the first time this cruise: ELO singing "Mr Blue Sky".

Lunch was beckoning so we said a temporary cheerio to the sun, dropped our towels off in the cabin, and went to the Horizon Buffet. Tomorrow we would be having a change of lunchtime food at our first 'Around the World' lunch.

The post-lunch rest time took us back to the cabin, but at 1:30 Deb turned to me and said that the ship had almost stopped moving. She was right, and I realised that Aurora had met up with our Royal Navy escort vessel that would be shadowing us through the possible pirate waters. I dashed down to look out on the starboard side and there was a quite small, and far from bright and shiny little ship. It was the Centurian I believe, and they were loading equipment onto Aurora from a little inflatable boat.

With that excitement captured on my camera, it was time to go to the theatre and listen to Michael Buerk. I hoped he was worth it, as I had given up cricket for his talk. Deb decided to miss this excitement, and went to Salsa instead.

The theatre was packed for Michael Buerk's first talk. There was a line of passengers standing on the side, and some even sat on the side areas of the stage. He is a very good speaker, and he is open and honest with his opinions. Today it was all about the dumbing-down of news reporting, but there were also several amusing anecdotes of his time as a TV news presenter.

To be honest I was thoroughly enjoying him, but as he relaxed and began to stray from the script a little, I began to feel uncomfortable with some of his views. The trouble was his belief that the vast majority of the British public are not sufficiently educated to know what they are voting for. This was all about Brexit, but he made it world-wide by adding the USA decision to vote for President Trump. He on the other hand, along with his news-casting peers, is far more aware of what should happen in the world, and important decisions that shouldn't be left to the public.

Where does that leave democracy?

Tomorrow the subject of his talk was to be Islam and its role in the troubles around the world. This could also be rather controversial. I wasn't sure I wanted to listen to him again.

It was time to meet up with Deb and have a cup of tea…and a sausage roll.

Following on from what we heard at the port talk this morning, we went to the tours desk and asked about a possible trip in Dubai. Called *'Delightful Dubai'* it would offer morning tea at the 'Burj Al Arab' luxury hotel, followed by a catamaran sail around the 'Palm Jumeirah' area. The advert said that if the weather conditions were unsuitable, an alternative form of transport (to the catamaran) would be provided. Well, after the dust storm five years ago, we knew the view can be wiped out, so asked if a refund was possible if the boat ride was cancelled. She rather bluntly told us that this wouldn't be possible.

I am afraid paying £140 each for a trip featuring a catamaran sail around the Palm Jumeirah, wasn't good value if they changed the transport for a coach. This wouldn't give us a satisfactory view of this spectacular feature of Dubai.

We didn't book it.

Our four table mates were quite subdued this evening because they had eaten their 'Around the World' lunch today, and a further large meal was just too much. We would hopefully be in a similar digestive situation tomorrow.

This evening we had a relatively new show from the Headliners called 'New Romantics'. Unfortunately, there was also an interesting show in Carmen's from a boyband called The Base Tones. We would have to be creative with which we see first.

We decided to miss the Headliners' show and relax a while, before going to Carmen's to get a good seat for the cabaret from The Base Tones. They turned out to be quite unusual and sang a number of songs in close harmony from several decades ago. There was a little bit of comedy as well, so the show was quite a success.

The captain had earlier warned us that the wind was going to get up again as we approached the end of the Red Sea.

On a brighter note, temperatures were due to increase further, and top the 30°C point very soon, as Aurora turned towards Oman for Thursday, and then Dubai at the end of the week.

………………………………………………

Tuesday 24th January

Warmer again today with a hot and rather sticky maximum of 29°C on the balcony.

It was a noisy night as our balcony door continued to rattle, bang and crash, but certainly not as bad as it had been. The maintenance engineer definitely managed some improvement, but hopefully he can do something more to give us peaceful nights.

By the time we woke the ship was jiggling along in the slightly angry sea, but it wasn't upsetting my stomach. The temperature was already a delightful 27°C on the balcony.

After breakfast we went for a walk which completed our 6th mile of the Prom Deck, plus an extra half a lap. My intention was to complete one of the longest duration marathons ever, spread across the three major oceans around several continents. So far it had been the Atlantic Ocean around Europe, and now the Indian Ocean as we sailed by Africa and the Middle East.

Yes I know it was a stupid idea!

The clocks went forward once again today at 12:00 noon. This put us at GMT + 4 hours. This time-slip upset our day as it meant the Around the World lunch would start at 1:00pm ship's time. Hence the talk from Michael Buerk, and Deb's Salsa class would be missed.

During the day Aurora sailed down to the end of the Red Sea, passing Eritrea and Djibouti on the starboard side, and Yemen to port. There were some splendid small islands visible from our balcony just before lunch. They had typical pointy mountains and looked very reminiscent of what children produce when asked to draw a picture of an island. They didn't look very populated and there was little sign of any golden beaches.

Well, our lunch was very nice with a good menu, and lots of chatter with the other people at our table. It was hosted by the tours office lady who upset me yesterday over the Dubai tour. I'm afraid I ignored her for much of the meal.

The wine was smooth and crept up on us, so when we left the dining room we headed for the cabin, and a snooze.

Just after lunch our floating home arrived in the Gulf of Aden meaning we were now entering the Indian Ocean. This also meant we were in pirate waters. The ship made its way into the recognised 'safe passage' channel where naval ships patrol and look after the hundreds of commercial ships in the area. Aurora speeded up from a gentle 17-18 knots to more than 20 knots. At this speed we could outrun all but the most determined pirates.

One of our regular dinner table friends (Robin) was in the Aurora choir that had been practicing since Southampton, and today was their show. Deb and I woke up slightly late, but galloped to the theatre and found seats just as they began. The 30-minute performance was delightful, and accompanied by the Headliner singers, the choir created a really wonderful sound.

Deb and I were both tempted to join in on the next sector.

It was time to prepare for dinner, so I had a shower hoping it would clear my head before embarrassing myself in the individual quiz. Neither of us really wanted to eat very much at dinner so after a simple bowl of soup, we both surprised our dinner mates by just having a plate of chips. Oh, and a small portion of sorbet for Deb, and ice-cream for me.

Nothing interested us from the entertainment choices that night, so we took to the cabin again before completing the evening with an hour in Masquerades. It was an interesting quiz tonight based on 50s and 60s pop music. With the age profile it was no shock that almost everybody had a good score. Yes, we lost again.

It was time for bed. The ship was in pirate-avoidance mode now for a couple of days and nights. Curtains were drawn everywhere to avoid lights attracting attention, and the Promenade Deck was out of bounds to allow the security teams to do their job without being distracted, or frightening the passengers.

....

Wednesday 25th January
Not quite so hot today, with a maximum of 26°C out in our back garden.

This was our final sea day before arriving in Oman tomorrow. We woke slightly later than normal and the first look outside showed a delightfully calm sea. It was already warm out there (25°C) and felt a little humid. Sadly the wind was still blowing, and as we went to breakfast it was obvious that the wind was going to reduce the number of passengers camping out on the open decks early today.

After a light breakfast - we really were getting very good here - Deb went for a swim and I came down to the office in Charlies. By 9:00 the shops were bringing out the sales tables to block the corridor in an attempt to extract more money from the passengers. They only had four days remaining to wring the last pennies from those leaving in Dubai.

I think it would really be a good idea if an alternative company made a bid for the shopping franchise on the ships. The current company has had an easy ride for many years using the *'price it high and sell a few'* retail method. The mark-up they put on day-to-day items is ridiculous, and the clothing is very exclusive, with price tickets to match. Let's be honest, P&O's quality and service has noticeably dropped in recent years to keep their prices relatively low, and this has resulted in a changing passenger profile. Hence the on-board shops are struggling to sell as much. Sadly, rather than finding products that the majority want, or can afford, the current franchise has taken the commercial option of increasing prices even higher. The continual daily round of so-called sales achieves little more than reducing prices to *'not quite so ridiculously expensive'*, and the majority of passengers continue to walk past or through the obstructions with looks of astonishment at the price tickets.

This morning I watched two of the army of sales people stand around the tables beside Charlies for 40 minutes. They sold absolutely nothing.

My office work was over, and it was time to get ready for a 'Round the World Coffee Morning'.

This was the first time we had experienced such a coffee morning, and was another chance to chat with total strangers who have parted with vast sums of money to see a little bit more of the world. The captain came into the Alexandra Restaurant and said hello to us, and we said goodbye as he would be getting off in Dubai to return home to Devon.

For the rest of the morning we sat out on D deck at the stern and enjoyed the sunshine. There weren't many people out there, which was a surprise when so many were packed around the other poolside areas.

As we prepared ourselves for lunch, the officer of the watch came on the PA system at midday for the navigational briefing. We were still in a convoy going through the piracy protected shipping lane, and our position was south of Salalah where we were due tomorrow. Weirdly, we had to continue eastwards in the convoy for another 100 miles before being able to leave it, and then use another protected route to get back to Salalah. This was one of these moments where the journey time is increased in order to maintain safety.

After lunch, with nothing else to do today, we relaxed out in the sunshine again for an hour. Unfortunately the clouds began to gather, and gave the impression that we might be getting some rain soon.

Tonight was the last formal night before Dubai, where this first sector would end. Time to wear my final formal shirt, and tomorrow the bundle of used shirts was destined for the laundry to have them cleaned and pressed. Maybe an expensive option, but it saved Deb the onerous task of ironing the fancy shirts.

The Headliners put on another afternoon matinee show ('We'll Meet Again') which didn't appeal, and in fact has never appealed since we first saw it several years ago. Deb decided to go to the cinema to watch a film entitled "Suffragette" and I had a soak in the bath. For some reason my knee had been very painful for the last couple of days, and I hoped the soak might do it some good.

Deb only managed 10 minutes at the film, and was back in the cabin before I had even filled the bath.

Entertainment tonight featured a second show from the comedic magician (Mark Shortland) followed by the second show from The Base Tones trio of singers.

Oh, and it was a Burns' Night themed dinner with a Parade of the Haggis piped into the restaurant.

The officer we had a drink with at the 'Welcome on board' party paraded in with the haggis, bottles of whisky and a sword. He read the famous Burns' poem while making dramatic gestures with his sword.

He then left with his mates to repeat his Ode to the Haggis in the other restaurant.

The menu was very Burns-based and most of us had a go at the haggis starter: very nice indeed!

While dinner was being digested, we sat in the cabin for an hour before going to Carmen's for the show from The Base Tones. It was as good as their first act and the audience lapped them up. From Carmen's we struggled through the crowds to the Curzon Theatre to watch Mark Shortland. He was absolutely terrific. There were only a few magic tricks, but the build up to each one was filled with comedy, and usually involved a member of the audience giving us even more laughs. Deb had an easy bit of participation whilst sitting in her seat for a supposed mind reading trick. She was given a book, and Mark Shortland guessed random words that Deb had chosen from the book.

The act ended with him involving the Royal Navy liaison officer, who was on-board Aurora for her passage through the piracy waters. His task was to fire sponge discs from a plastic toy gun into Mark Shortland's mouth. It was a good trick, and made hilarious by the sight of an officer who worked with an international fleet of naval vessels, shooting a tiny plastic gun.

Both The Base Tones and Mark Shortland were getting off in Salalah the next day, so there would be some fresh acts for the final two nights towards Dubai.

After a lovely evening it was bedtime, and in the morning we would be in the Omani city of Salalah. We had an early tour booked, so this was the first time on the cruise when we needed to set the alarm clock, to be sure of getting up on time.

Thursday 26th January – Salalah, Oman

Temperature on the balcony today reached 30°C.

The alarm woke us at 7:20 am and when I looked out through the curtains it was a bright sunny morning but just a little windy. The garden had gained several cranes and hundreds of containers, plus a ship bringing in yet more colourful metal boxes. Through a light mist I could see a ghostly range of hills, or mountains, just like the desert scene we had in Jordan.

The captain parked with the starboard side towards the dock, but when we looked at this view, it wasn't much better than from our balcony. Aurora was docked in the middle of a commercial port with a concrete car park for the coaches, and certainly no terminal building with free WIFI here.

Our tour was called an *'Introduction to Salalah'*, and soon after our breakfast had ended we made our way to the mustering point, and set off.

Salalah is on the southern coast of Oman. It is the third most populated city in the country, and capital of the Dhofar Province. Although probably not the best known of the Arab States' tourist destinations, Salalah is definitely pushing itself forward to gain more visitors.

When our coach left Aurora, we realised just how large the dock was. It took 20 minutes before we passed through the gates and began our journey through the sandy countryside of Oman. As usual our enthusiastic guide talked all about his country, telling us that it was a very safe place to visit, and doing very well economically. Then he got to the more interesting stuff about how the indigenous people are looked after. Everyone, male and female, is given a free plot of land at the age of 23, and there is free schooling, a free health service, and no taxes.

It seems that camels are a valuable and treasured asset. What I didn't know until then was that there are normal camels, and then what our guide described as "beautiful" camels.

Umm, how can you tell?

The country was a place of no consequence at all until Sultan Qaboos Bin Said Al Said took over in 1970, by overthrowing his father. He was educated abroad, including at the Royal Military Academy at Sandhurst. The beginning of his reign coincided with oil being discovered in Oman, and he has used the revenue to build up the status of his country, and is very popular with his people.

The only obstacle appears to be that he has not got a natural heir, and has not agreed and nominated a successor.

As I said earlier, Oman is trying to attract more tourists, especially those from Northern Europe. The climate is perfect for winter breaks with temperatures into the high 20s, and is ideal to top up the tans on the miles of almost white sandy beaches.

On with the tour, and our first stop was the Mughsail Beach. This is on a huge bay that stretches over a mile, offering gorgeous soft sand. One of the attractions at this beach are the Manreef Caves that have been created by the action of the sea wearing away the sandstone.

As well as caves and overhanging rocks, there are weird shapes that might be mistaken for animals or witches. Where the sea is still smashing into the rocks, there are blowholes that spray water up and over tourists standing too close. Unfortunately the wave action was quite minimal when we were there, and just produced the occasional gentle hiss of mist to excite us.

From the beach we drove back into the city of Salalah for a photo shoot opportunity at the Al Husn Palace. This is just one of the Sultan's palaces, and we were only able to photograph the impressive external walls, but it was obviously very beautiful, and definitely vast. Some of the girls from the Headliners were there at the same time as us, and one of the very outspoken local guides was going mad, offering 1,000 camels for one of the girls. She turned down the offer, remarking that when they were at the Wadi Rum a few days ago, the offer was 10,000 camels.

Next stop was the Al Balid Museum that deals with the production and growth of Oman's frankincense trade, and a little about the country's maritime history. Oh, and there were some clean toilets there that actually had paper to dry our hands.

Our tour was almost over but there was an hour set aside to visit the Frankincense Souk. Many of the passengers were tempted to buy some of the frankincense in either the actual incense form, or like us, as the perfume.

And yes, we bought a fridge magnet as well.

An hour for shopping was far too long, so we wandered off to the nearby Al Bahri Beach. The sand was so soft that our feet sank into it, and it was lovely to see the remains of sea shells in the sand. Deb went for a paddle in the calm and clean waters of the Indian Ocean: well, technically it was the Arabian Sea, part of the Indian Ocean.

That was the end of a simple, but very pleasant tour. It had lasted about 4½ hours, and we were back on Aurora before 1:30. It was time for a quick lunch before relaxing back in the cabin. It was very hot, in the high 20s, and it was tempting to go and soak up the sun's rays, but we had already overheated today, so our cool balcony was just right.

The heat was too much to do anything energetic, and as the afternoon moved towards evening, we decided not to eat in the dining room, but to have room service instead. Once the plan was made, Deb took the opportunity of doing some washing. Well, that was the plan but it took her three attempts to find an empty washing machine. Twice she carried the holdall loaded with clothes and checked out laundry rooms on A and C decks - totally full up. Twice she carried the holdall back.

After another failure at the individual quiz, Deb's third attempt at the laundry was successful.

With the washing doing its thing, we ordered our meal and were soon tucking into spaghetti Bolognese, with apple pie to follow. We drank a bottle from our quiz red wine stash, and watched the Salalah views from our balcony as dusk arrived. As we sailed away we watched the lights coming on around the shoreline. It's always a beautiful sight when leaving a port at dusk, but sadly we couldn't enjoy it for long as it was time to go into piracy mode. The curtains were drawn and all over the ship Aurora was becoming cloaked against unwanted visitors.

The washing was moved to the dryer and we went to Masquerades for the early evening quiz. Richard and Angie turned up just before it started and we failed yet again to restock our wine stocks.

Perhaps the passenger change-over at the weekend would mean a little less competition.

The clothes were eventually dry and those needing ironing made ready for the wardrobe.

After a long hot day, we relaxed and read our books for an hour. Then after 9:30 we went up onto the deck for the Tropical Party. It was windy by now and although many people were dancing, most were confined to a sheltered corner. The party atmosphere was certainly there, and soon we were wearing our flower lei garlands and jigging along to the music.

After about 20 minutes my lei finally gave up trying to cling to my neck and flew away behind me. I turned to try and see where it went, but it had gone. All I could see was a group of the Headliners looking at me with questioning faces wondering why I was flinging flowers at them.

We gave up and returned indoors and went back to the cabin. We enjoyed a late-night cup of tea, and caught up on the news at home in chilly Britain, via our very expensive internet.

Aurora was now jiggling her way eastwards across the Arabian Sea. We had a further day at sea until we reached our second Omani port, Muscat, on Saturday morning. Tomorrow we would return to our routine with a port talk, Salsa, and maybe cricket.

Friday 27th January – Sea Day

The temperature in the garden at 8:00 was 23°C, and it rose to 26° during the afternoon.

There were some bumpy moments during the night, but it became much quieter by the time we got up.

Looking out from the balcony, the sea looked crumpled with lots of wave action, but Aurora wasn't being affected much by the grumpy sea. In the distance we could just see the coast of Oman with mountains and cliffs that were being bathed by the glorious sunshine, making them appear almost white like those at Dover.

For breakfast I fancied a change, and tried a boiled egg: personally, I didn't find the extremely hardboiled egg the nicest way to start the day.

After breakfast Deb went for a swim and I went to the office.

As usual, after a few minutes of catching up with my blog, the shop team arrived and set up their tables with *"sensational offers - back by popular demand"* to tempt any gullible passengers, or those getting off in Dubai with unspent on-board credit to waste.

It was time to move, and I didn't even bother looking at what was on offer.

Just before 10:00 we relaxed into the Curzon theatre seats to listen to another port talk from Crystal about Colombo in Sri Lanka. We already had a special P&O Heritage tour booked there and Crystal's description suggested it ought to be very interesting.

As we left the theatre we went out onto the Promenade deck for a mile's walk. There seemed to be some confusion about which way to walk today. It was almost the same number walking clockwise as those going the other way. One young lady was actually aggressively running around the deck at quite a pace, and she was managing two circuits to our one. If she was so engrossed in running this much, I think she would have benefited more from the gym's running machines.

And it would have avoided annoying a lot of people who just enjoyed walking!

Anyway, having exercised it was time to ruin all the good work and we gave in to coffee and chocolate doughnuts...yummy!

Next we did a bit of housekeeping and checked our cabin statement. We still had a lot of on-board credit left, and were not running up any bills yet.

Meanwhile Michael Buerk was giving a talk in the theatre again, and today it he was talking about the city of Dubai. I lost interest after his first talk because of his attitude, and hadn't returned to hear any more. He seemed to blame the uneducated public for the world's troubles. Mr Buerk, and many other commentators, journalists, politicians, and supposed educated people seem to believe themselves to be superior to the masses. They cannot understand why so many British and Americans democratically voted overwhelmingly in what these "experts" believe to be *'The Wrong Way'*.

So many of the intelligent, but blinkered experts think we were all wrong by wanting to upset the 'status quo'. Our rebellion was a wakeup call to worldwide politicians, business leaders, and yes, journalists. We are fed up with *"let's have more of the same old thing"*.

We want a change.

Sorry, but Michael Buerk brought out the worst in me!

Lunchtime came and went, and Aurora was making gentle progress towards Muscat at a serene 16.5 knots. Deb and I went in search of a place in the sunshine. The wind was quite strong at that moment, and after spending a few minutes in one less than pleasant spot on the high decks, we settled out on the stern deck again. It was still windy but not as bad as many other places around the ship.

...***Bing, Bong***!

The officer of the watch interrupted my snooze to advise passengers on the open decks that dolphins were having fun and games around the ship. A noisy scraping of sun loungers was followed by a stampede to the sides of the ship.

One of tonight's cabaret artists sitting near to us said, *"I have never seen these people move that fast before"*.

Yes, there were a lot of dolphins very close to the ship, and they were magically showing off their swimming and gymnastics routines to bring smiles to hundreds of Aurora's passengers.

The sunshine session was over and Deb went to the final Salsa class for this sector, and I went to the final cricket match...normality had returned.

An hour or so later we met up in the theatre for a talk and song show from Bruce Morrison about the life of Queen Victoria. This was a part of the 180 Years Heritage celebrations for P&O. We have seen and heard the show before but it still made us chuckle. With culture over, it was time for a cuppa...and a couple of sandwiches.

The entertainment tonight had the Headliners performing a Queen Tribute show in Carmen's, and Belle Noir, (the trio of girls who were out in the sun near us) was singing in the theatre. We quickly decided to give both of these a miss. We can watch 'Killer Queen' again later in the cruise.

As I was dressing for dinner (casual tonight) I noticed a rather obvious red wine stain on my very light-coloured trousers. It meant a quick change, but more worryingly we had no stain remover. After dinner the trousers were put into a bath of cold water to see if that would soak out the stain. If not then it will be another item going to the laundry on a rescue mission.

The evening ended with Deb and I having a drink in Anderson's with Richard and Angie. Much of our talk centred on our experiences since the 9th January, but families and friends were also topics, and yes, we had a few laughs as well.

Time for bed.

Saturday 28th January – Muscat, Oman

The balcony temperature was over 20°C when we got up, and rose to 30° during the afternoon.

We had a peaceful and calm night, and by the time we got out of bed at 7:15 we were already joined up with the dockside at the Port of Sultan Qaboos.

I looked outside and someone had parked a ship at the end of the garden!

It was the Thomson Celebration, and a little way off on our right was an Australian warship (number 151) with a picture of a kangaroo on its funnel.

In the distance were the very familiar mountains that we had grown used to in this area of the world, but they were much darker than those around Salalah. We also spotted the huge beehive-shaped incense burner on the hill at the edge of the port that had amazed us when we visited here five years ago. There are also a couple of forts nearby in the hills that once guarded the city.

The first job of the day was taking my stained trousers out of the bath, and inspecting the damage. It looked as if the stain had gone, but we would have to wait until it was fully dry again to really know.

We didn't have an official tour today. We looked around the highlights on our first visit, and this time decided not to venture very far. Today's plan was to simply go on the free shuttle bus to the souk for a bit of shopping, so there wasn't any real rush. We went to the buffet as usual and were quite shocked that it was very busy. I felt out of place as nearly everyone else was in their conservative clothing required for Arabian visits, while we were in shorts and tee shirts.

Deb had developed a sore throat, so when back in the cabin she took a dose of paracetamol. In reality most of Aurora's passengers were either suffering from a bad throat, a horrible cough, or both, and the doctor had been very busy with this problem. Just as a personal comment here, we hadn't had more than a few isolated cases of norovirus on the cruise, which was very good, but if you contract norovirus, you are very ill for a few days and then you are well again. If you caught this cough and sore throat there appeared to be no quick fix, and the illness lasted for weeks.

As I said, just a personal comment to ponder upon.

While I was on the sunny balcony I heard the Thomson ship announce the same welcome message as we had earlier. The only difference was that the gangway was from deck 2 rather than our deck 4, and the Thomson officer added the dress code for the day ashore. Today the reminder for the recommended dress code was *'conservative'*. P&O assume we read this sort of information in the daily paperwork, and don't bother to make this perhaps useful final reminder.

At 9:00 we set off for the souk. The local taxi companies don't like cruise ships using free shuttle buses, so our transport this morning was labelled as *'Muscat On Your Own'*. I suspect the taxi drivers are suspicious about this, but haven't found a way of stopping it – yet.

Taxi drivers at ports around the world always try hard to get your custom, but the taxi drivers here in Muscat were overly demanding of our attention, and extremely persistent with their offers of trips to the special sights, or tours of the area. This had been the first time on the cruise that they were being really *"in your face"*.

The traffic was busy, but after about 15 minutes we were getting off the bus at the souk. Another swarm of taxi drivers descended immediately offering us tours. It was really difficult to make them understand our refusals, and they even followed us right up to the entrance of the souk. Inside we wandered around exploring the alleyways as well as the main shopping lane. We had no real list of things to get, but we always keep an eye out for interesting fridge magnets and Christmas tree decorations. Well we found some suitable ones and also splashed out on some frankincense for burning, costing us a grand total of 15 US dollars.

We might have stayed longer, but the market traders were hassling and demanding we went in and looked around their shops, and it was becoming very uncomfortable. Worse still Deb (and me) were continually being offered pashminas. All sorts of colours and material were thrust under our noses for inspection, and just like the taxi drivers these traders were almost impossible to put off. I suspect we were offered perhaps 50 various pashminas during the 20 minutes we were in the market.

We had nothing else to do, so we jumped back on the first *'Muscat On Your Own'*. bus back to the ship to cool down after a slightly stressful shopping trip. Back on the balcony the temperature had crept up to 27°C and was still rising. In the harbour between Aurora and the Thomson ship were several of the lifeboats from the two ships carrying out crew exercises. It was like a game, with the little orange boats circling around as though performing some strange mysterious mating ritual. The Thomson Celebration completed their exercise first, and their boats returned to be hauled up. That just left four or five of Aurora's craft in the harbour, plus the smaller high-speed inflatable boat. They were gently going round and round the sun-drenched harbour. It was rather mesmerising yet soothing, and gave me plenty of time to see the ship's call sign from above.

For the enthusiasts, Aurora call sign is ZCDW9.

After having lunch we found ourselves a spot on the upper deck to enjoy the sunshine. Most of the passengers stayed ashore so there were plenty of available loungers to choose from. It was very, very hot with little breeze to keep us cool. Deb lasted about 40 minutes and I stayed about 10 minutes more. The air-conditioned cabin was a relief, and now we could relax properly, and fall asleep without fear of becoming a lobster.

My only practical activity was starting a mass battery charging session, to ensure we were ready for Dubai tomorrow.

Across the harbour the Thomson Celebration passengers were being entertained by either a singer or band playing music while they lazed in the delicious and extremely hot sunshine. I suspected a few of them would be sorry this evening for not following our example and going back to their cabin.

Deb was still suffering with her throat, and spent the afternoon resting. I alternated between relaxing on the bed, and spending a few minutes on the balcony enjoying the sunshine. The temperature got up to 30°: it was really quite sapping to sit out in it for long.

At 5:30 the Thomson ship sailed away, although it needed serious assistance from a tug. Then it was our turn and Captain Hall's final sail-away duty on this cruise was a simple push away from the dock with the thrusters, and then away we went. We were going to have a quite fast overnight trip at more than 20 knots to get us into Dubai for a late morning arrival.

The evening entertainment was a second show from the New Zealand singer in the theatre, plus the passenger talent show in Carmen's. Our dinner table friend, Robin, was in the choir who were performing a couple of songs for the talent show, so we planned to go and watch him.

Deb managed to get up sufficient enthusiasm to go to dinner, but after picking at her main course she made her apologies and went back to the cabin. I joined her 15 minutes later, and by 8:30 she was in bed and reading her book.

There were just two days remaining of this first sector of the world cruise.

Tomorrow some 900 passengers would be packing and their suitcases would be left in the corridors. At least they would have the afternoon and evening in Dubai before getting off the ship on Monday morning. It would be strange to see people leaving and new people boarding, but we were sure we would all become friends before too long.

I didn't bother going to the talent show, and joined Deb in bed for an early night to allow her a chance to recover.

Night, night!

Sunday 29th January – Dubai, UAE

Balcony temperature rose to 27°C during the day, and it was sunny, although a little misty.

Deb didn't have a very comfortable night, but at least she slept. I must have also been very tired as I stayed comfortably sleeping or dozing throughout the night as well.

Anyway, we were still at sea as I looked out on the world at 7:30. The sky had a few clouds, but not enough to stop the dazzling sunshine banging on my eyeballs, and its delightful warmth tingling my skin.

Aurora was now into the final 60 or so miles to the port of Dubai in the United Arab Emirates. We had completed sailing through the Straits of Oman and were now in the Straits of Hormuz before entering what our map called the Persian Gulf. To the starboard side is the massive country of Iran.

Deb and I had a light breakfast in a rather quiet Horizon Buffet. This was going to be a busy morning however, as the arrival into Dubai meant getting our passports back, in readiness for a face to face inspection onshore with the country's officials. I queued up at Anderson's with our passport receipts and left with our little burgundy booklets quite quickly.

Back in the cabin we had our weekly chemist appointment with the suitcase under the bed. As the first sector was coming to an end, I was hoping to see the contents of that suitcase reducing, but the case still appeared as full as when we started.

There was a gentle tap on the door and Tamil (our steward) sheepishly handed over the satisfaction questionnaire for the first sector. He needn't have worried. He received the full *"excellent"* rating for anything concerning him or his work, but some other aspects of the cruise were not so impressive in our eyes. The entertainment had been less than exciting with far too many singers. The cover charges for the select dining venues were far too high, and certainly the quality of the menu in Sindhu did not justify the price. Of course, we also said that the internet was too expensive, the photographers and tours too expensive, and the shops a waste of time. Our other negative comment was a request that the cocktail waiters were stopped from hunting in packs in Carmen's – they really had been just too keen, and almost putting us off having a drink.

We took the completed questionnaire down to the reception post box, and then went for a word with the Loyalty/Future Cruises team.

Almost as soon as we boarded Aurora we had asked if there was any chance of a cabin upgrade. We weren't trying to get something for free, and were quite happy to pay for a more spacious cabin. Initially there had been nothing available, but they promised to keep looking as each sector came to an end, when occasionally cancellations left cabins free. With the second sector about to begin, they had told us that a mini-suite was free for the final sector, but the price to change was ridiculous, and we declined their offer. I think they were a little shocked to be thanked for their efforts, but at least they had tried and were still looking for anything that became available, so maybe there was still a chance.

While we passed the time before arriving in Dubai, I spent a few minutes simply staring at the sea, and it really was beautiful today. Although a keen wind blew into my face, the sea was like a silk sheet waving in the breeze just as I described it a few days ago. The sun also gave us one of its magical moments as it reflected off tiny crests of any small waves, and created a starburst like a million diamonds.

Deb was still trying any known treatment for sore throats and coughs, and was now on a hot drink made with honey and fresh lemon taken from the buffet. We had a serious tour booked for that evening and she wanted to be well enough. Tonight a group of us would be having a sundown buffet at the Burj Al Arab hotel, which is the one that looks like a sail. From there we would go to the Burj Khalifa (the world's tallest tower) to watch a display of fountains and lighting effects.

To be ready, we had to catch our coach at 5:30 this evening, and had been advised that the dress code was to be a very tidy casual. Our return to Aurora would be at 8:30, so room-service was being considered for our evening a meal, and maybe even a drink on the balcony.

At 11:00 Captain Hall made one of his last announcements as master of the ship. He would be leaving while we were in Dubai. It was the usual overview of where we were in the world, when we would be arriving in Dubai, where we would be parking, plus the important news about the weather. The new master of the ship was to be Captain Wesley Dunlop, just one of several changes to the ship's crew in Dubai.

Anyway, the Captain expected to have the pilot on board at 11:30 with a docking time of 12:30: the pilot was 15 minutes late but we did touch the quayside at around 12:30 as predicted. On our sail-in to the port we spotted the wonderful QE2 at rest in the harbour. She hadn't changed since we were here five years ago, although her paintwork perhaps looked a little shabbier. This was a sad end to the life of an amazing lady of the sea.

Virtually as soon as Aurora had touched the quayside the stevedores were grabbing ropes and making our floating home secure for the next day and a half. It wasn't long before the safety officer declared that it was clear to go ashore, and that was followed by the instructions for the immigration process to begin.

Sadly, an ambulance arrived to take a lady away before any of the main immigration procedure commenced. A gentleman left in the same way about an hour later. What a horrible way to have to leave the ship.

It was a little misty as we looked out across the city from our balcony. Our side of the ship was facing the dock and we had a glorious view once you ignored the fact that we were in the middle of a commercial port. The mist took away the visual sharpness in the distance, but there was no mistaking the phenomenal Burj Khalifa tower which seriously pokes out above the other skyscrapers.

The first people to have the immigration inspection were a batch of the crew, and they were followed by those passengers going on the early afternoon tours. At around 2:00 the announcements started to ask for the remainder of the passengers in batches of 100. Just after 2:30 we were called and we grabbed our bits and trotted down the stairs and out onto the dockside of Dubai. It was a sunny and hot afternoon with very little breeze.

As we were going through the immigration process, we noticed there was free WIFI in the cruise terminal, so we made plans to use it later.

Within little more than ten minutes we were back on board (minus our passports again) with time to spare before afternoon tea. By 3:30 the immigration process was over except for stragglers, and a small number of awkward passengers who were rebelling and deciding not to bother - prats!

Deb decided to have a soak in the bath, and I had a shower when she got out. We had to be ready to leave the ship before 4:50 for our visit to one of the most fantastic hotels in the world, where we would be indulging in canapes at sunset.

After a coach journey that took almost an hour, we arrived at the Burj Al Arab Hotel. It was magnificent. Our visit started with a gob-smacking walk through the lobby, with a sensational water feature trickling down over what appeared to be a small mountain. As we slowly gazed around us, we noticed aquariums built into the wall with delightful tropical fish watching us. Then we were ushered by smartly dressed and smiling staff onto an escalator climbing up the water feature. At the top yet more smiling people directed us to a shimmering golden lift.

Our quite exclusive cocktail party was on the 27th floor of the hotel, and the luxurious gold lift whisked us up to the dizzy heights where we were met by a host who welcomed and directed us into the reception room. This room was truly sumptuous, and was regularly used to host wedding receptions for 300 guests in comfort. It was on two levels, with a main lower area where our three coaches of passengers hardly made any impact. This delightful room was surrounded by a 360° gallery floor above. There was thick-piled carpet everywhere making it very soft to walk around while we stared in awe at the giant candelabras hanging from the ceiling far above us.

We were welcomed with a glass of wine or beer, and then offered canapes to enhance the spiced almonds, salted cashew nuts and delicious olives. As we chatted with our dinner table friends Robin and Rosemary, the waiters politely refilled our glasses and brought even more canapes. We were supposedly there to watch the sunset, but I don't think anyone bothered much, although there were some wonderful photographic opportunities from the huge glass windows on the gallery level.

An hour later we returned down in the lift, down the escalator, and had a few minutes to look around once more at this truly amazing place. Outside there were Rolls Royce cars, Bentleys, Mercedes, and a Lamborghini. The elegant army of concierges greet guests or direct traffic, and unlike many places we go, they treated us the same way as the obvious millionaires around us.

The coach now whipped us away to the Dubai Mall, biggest in the Arab world, where the parking for coaches was horrendous. We then walked for over 10 minutes to a man-made lake at the base of the Burj Khalifa Tower in time to watch a light and water spectacular. Just like the hotel, this was another sensational experience. OK, it was packed with hundreds and hundreds of other spectators but it was worth the crush. At the appointed time the five-minute show began with a fountain and colourful light ballet accompanied by music. The water display became more and more spectacular with sound effects to enhance the show.

It was superb.

At the end of the display, a good deal of the crowd slowly left the lake, but hundreds stayed for the next performance that repeats every half an hour. The people coming towards us for the next show made it very difficult to squeeze our way through the congestion until we found our meeting point. Then it was another walk to the manic coach park, and a 30-minute drive back to the ship.

The last time we were here, we had an amazing meal accompanied by entertainment in the Jumeirah Beach Hotel. That was truly unbelievable, but this had trumped that experience.

What a truly beautiful and amazing place Dubai is.

We got back to the ship a little after 9:00 and immediately grabbed some cheese and biscuits from the buffet: there was nothing else available. Then we had a cup of tea in the cabin on the balcony watching the almost deserted scene below on the quayside.

It had been a wonderful evening.

Tomorrow we would be doing our own thing, and probably going back to that Mall on the shuttle. It should be a little quieter in the daytime...hopefully.

Monday 30th January – Dubai Day 2

It was sunny and humid on the balcony and the thermometer showed a peak temperature of 25°C during the day – but it felt so much hotter.

Today was the end of the first sector of the cruise, and the beginning of the second.

We didn't have a good night as poor Deb was really suffering from her cold, and was restless again. As always seemed to happen, we were both fast asleep when woken by the sound of people getting up and moving around. Today was disembarkation day for a lot of the passengers, and that always meant a rush to get breakfast.

Deb and I lay in bed for a while with a cup of tea and our daily pills, rather than interfering with the urgency of those going home.

When I eventually looked outside at the scene below us, the suitcases were already on their way to the arrival/departure hall, although it would be an hour or more before the passengers could go and search for them.

By the time we got to the buffet (8:00) it was beginning to get quiet as passengers went off to their waiting areas, but a few were blundering around with cases and looking rather overdressed as they demolished their last breakfast on the ship. A mid-cruise changeover day can be rather strange. A lot of people were in unfamiliar trousers or skirts with shirts and often jackets, plus handbags which were much larger than those seen around the ship for the previous three weeks. The rest of us were in shorts and tee shirts, and we appeared much calmer than those whose holiday on Aurora had ended.

After a wash, and checking our cabin statement for the sector, we made our way down to the terminal building where we had seen signs advertising free WIFI. Well it was quite true, there was free WIFI, but it had no internet connected to it. Slightly miffed we packed up our kit and returned to the ship and put on some suitably respectful clothes for our trip into the city. I always struggle wearing trousers when it is hot, but I feel obliged to respect the cultures of the countries we visit.

The shuttle bus took us to the huge Dubai Mall where we had been last night. The journey was horrendous, with Dubai's traffic as bad as I have seen anywhere. When the driver was asked if this was normal, he replied *"yes every day except Fridays"*. Of course, that is the religious day.

After leaving the ship at 9:30 we got to the Mall at about 10:15. We were gone again by 11:00 having decided that the Mall was absolutely beautiful and glitzy to extreme, but not a place to go shopping unless you have a seriously bigger bank balance than we have. My suggestion to anyone coming to Dubai is to definitely visit the Mall, but think of it as a tourist site, and simply enjoy the gold, enjoy the glitz and enjoy the décor. If you have a yearning for designer clothes or jewellery then you will have no problem spending more than you probably intended. Oh, and apparently there is a huge waterfall and aquarium in the Mall somewhere, but we never stumbled upon it.

Before we came away, we attempted to get an internet connection again. This time we were successful...except it was barred for sites like my blog, and emails. Our spending was limited to a few things in Waitrose.

Yes, I did say Waitrose.

Here we bought some snack items and a new notebook for my diary records. We also wanted some chocolate but it was ridiculously expensive, and amazingly it was cheaper on the ship.

Back on the ship we had lunch, and Deb decided to do some washing, while I deserted her and had an hour in the sunshine. As I lay with sweat running down my sunglasses I looked at the blurred images of new passengers (trousers and jackets again) as they investigated Aurora clutching their little maps of the ship. I was sure that as soon as their suitcases had appeared they would join the shorts and tee shirt club, and the ladies could use their much smaller handbags.

After I had achieved my quota of sun, I virtually bumped into Deb on her way to look at the progress of the washing. I tagged along and came back to the cabin with the first load of dry bits to be hung or squeezed into the drawers.

All our clean clothes were tucked away by 2:30 and I suggested we have an ice-cream. So we sat on Riviera deck on the bar stools licking and eating our

Magnums as we watched the passing people, deciding if they were new or existing passengers. We then treated ourselves with a cup of tea for Deb and coffee for me in the buffet. And I would like to point out that we didn't have anything to eat!

Back in the cabin it was now time for me to relax a while on the balcony, and after Deb had been to the library to find a new book, she dozed as well. A little before 4:00, the number of new arrivals down below on the quayside had dwindled to a few stragglers, and the last shuttle was about to leave from the city.

A few minutes later we heard announcements about Muster Drill. We didn't stir as we had been told to ignore it this time.

'Bing Bong'

Change of plans. We were now told that **EVERYONE** had to attend the Muster Drill on each sector. So we stretched ourselves awake and made our way to the theatre. The interruption was only 30 minutes out of our *'busy'* schedule so wasn't really anything to get upset about.

This was the first time we heard from our new Captain (Wesley Dunlop) who let us know about our departure that evening, and the two sea days before we would reach Mumbai.

The evening entertainment on offer was a female Sitar player from India called Roopa Panesar who was in the theatre, and in Carmen's was the superb resident band Caravan.

We were nearly two hours late leaving Dubai, and Captain Dunlop was rather keen to explain that this delay was solely down to *'red tape'* issues with the port administration, which also held up the Royal Caribbean ship (Vision of the Seas) that has been parked behind us over the last two days.

Richard and Angie from our dinner table were feasting in Sindhu tonight, and although Robin joined us for dinner, Rosemary sent her apologies as she was also suffering from this horrible cold. Two ladies have joined us to fill our table again.

We would get to know all about them over the coming weeks as we made our way to Singapore.

The sea became a little rocky as we retraced our passage down the various Straits and Gulfs towards the Arabian Sea, and set a course to India. I didn't think the movement was going to cause any problems for such salty sea dogs as ourselves.

Fingers crossed.

With Deb's cold as bad as ever, we abandoned any plans to investigate the entertainment.

The cabin lights were turned off, and we were heading for sleepy-land before 9:00.

The first sector was over, and hopefully Deb's cold would soon clear up as we made our way east across the Indian Ocean.

Sector 2 - Dubai to Singapore

The countries we visited:

- India
- Sri Lanka
- Malaysia
- Singapore

Tuesday 31st January – Sea Day

I was up to make the tea at 7:30. The sea was calm, there was a clear blue sky, and the temperature was around 22°C on the balcony. Later in the day it managed to rise to 26°.

The Officer of the Watch made his 8:00 announcement, and said the closest land was Karachi in Pakistan which was several hundreds of miles east of Aurora. He ignored the fact that we were considerably closer to a seriously large country called Iran: was this a political decision?

Deb was still not well, and after breakfast she decided to go and see the doctor.

While wasting a little time until Deb returned, I went for a walk around the ship, and feeling a little lazy I used the lift. Inside was an unusual sight of a man with a guitar. I bade him good morning, wished him the best with his busking, and hoped he managed to find a good spot.

Oops! It was the classical guitarist on his way to a sound check before the day's concert in the Playhouse cinema!

I hadn't noticed this on previous cruises, but there were a lot of whistlers on board! Many decades ago I remember enjoying Roger Whittaker whistling along with his songs, and I have been known to quietly whistle to myself when working in the garden, but these passengers were just unconsciously tweeting random notes. The annoying sounds they made were quite loud, and it was difficult not to listen and try and work out what tune they were attempting. I vowed to avoid ever whistling myself again.

I went for my walk and completed mile number eight. I also did a further lap of the ship to make up a little for the days off. I was now walking in the Indian Ocean, and had spread my marathon over two oceans so far.

Deb reappeared soon after I returned to the cabin. The doctor had prescribed her some antibiotics: apparently there were a lot of people waiting for our friend the doctor from Helston. Her name was Susan Dring, which was a very familiar name to me. After some thought I realised that her father had worked at Goonhilly Satellite Earth Station while I was there.

While poorly Deb relaxed in the cabin I spent 45 minutes up on the deck dozing in the sun with my music. It was hot, but a cooling breeze made it very pleasant. When I went back, Deb and I went for a cup of tea in the buffet, and had a cake to keep us going. The ship's shop had set up an obstacle course of tables around the Riviera pool this morning, trying to coax people to spend money. The unmissable offer today was a 'Price Match' on designer shorts and shoes. It was very difficult to check if they were cheaper than buying ashore unless you had bought an internet package, but of course the price of any internet time would have wiped out any benefit from finding a cheaper source.

At midday the clocks advanced an hour making us at GMT+5.

I decided to join the choir and had a wonderful hour. I'd not sung for many years and thoroughly enjoyed allowing my vocal chords a moment to express themselves. I began the hour not really knowing where my voice would be, and sat with the Bass section, but after growling for the first song I moved over a row of chairs and joined dinner table Robin in the Tenor section. That felt and sounded much better.

When the singing ended it was time to go to the cricket session. This 45 minutes of exercise was rather good as well. I scored quite a few runs, and caught several people out. I just wish I could master the bowling again. Afterwards, on the way back to the cabin I noticed a greeny-yellow slime floating on the sea. I remembered seeing it in roughly the same place five years ago. Apparently it's some form of algae.

By now it was after 3:00, and I was seriously hungry. So, after peeling off my rather sticky tee shirt and cooling down a little, it was away to the buffet for a sandwich and a cup of coffee.

During the afternoon, Bruce Morrison gave another performance in the theatre called Port Out Starboard Home: this was another part of his themed presentation on P&O history. We missed it completely with our busy schedule.

It was a strange evening with Deb staying on her own in the cabin while I enjoyed a formal night. The action began with a 'Welcome on Board' cocktail party, and my first sight of Captain Wesley Dunlop. He appeared to be a jovial character, and certainly looked as if he enjoys his food, judging by the tightness of his uniform shirt. I stood with Angie and Richard and we had a generous supply of alcohol before going to dinner.

The table was two people short with Deb and Rosemary both recovering in the cabins. The two new ladies were very chatty, but Robin and I were on the other side of the table and found it difficult to hear them. Aurora was travelling quite quickly at over 21 knots, and the noise from the propellers was a little loud today.

Tonight, along with busking from the classical guitarist, there should have been a singer from New Zealand, who was once a part of the Strictly Come Dancing chorus. Sadly, she had the wrong visa for India and had to stay in Dubai, so a comedian had been rescheduled to entertain us.

So after dinner I went to the theatre for the comedian's show. His fame is that he managed to get to a final of "Britain's Got Talent". I can't remember his name because he was a last-minute stand-in and so not listed in the Horizon Guide.

Anyway, he was good, but as usual the jokes were rather familiar. He also did impersonations and they again were good, but a little predictable. Fortunately, he added his own twist to many of the voices so there were plenty of moments to chuckle.

From the show, the remainder of our dinner table team went to Masquerades for a quiz about film theme tunes. We were doing quite well, and managed to think of several correct answers, but unfortunately, we gave them for the wrong questions. But it was a good laugh.

It was bedtime, and I remembered to take back a can of orange juice for Deb, who was all but asleep when I got there.

Tomorrow would be another sea day, and hopefully Deb would begin to get over the cold and get her strength back before we arrive in Mumbai on Thursday.

Wednesday 1st February – Sea Day

Temperature on the balcony at 9:00 was 23°C, and the maximum temperature recorded was 25°.

With quite a friendly sea, Aurora ploughed across the Indian Ocean towards Mumbai. The sky was a bit hazy, but the sun made it quite warm. Unfortunately we were on the side of the ship in shadow. As the day went on the humidity noticeably increased, and it became uncomfortably sticky.

Deb looked and felt a little better this morning, and we hoped that another 24 hours would see her ready to face Mumbai tomorrow. She began to eat again and actively went searching for food.

The talk in the theatre this morning was by Robin Knox-Johnston, the first person to sail single handed and non-stop around the globe some 50 years ago. He was sitting on the table behind us at breakfast, and a couple of people said hello to him. He is most definitely seen as a very British hero.

His talk would certainly be interesting, but I was keen to enjoy the fresh air. Hence, I went for a walk and marched quite aggressively for a mile, plus another lap. That clocked up nine miles plus a couple of spare laps towards my Trans-Oceanic marathon.

One noticeable thing out on deck was that the anti-piracy precautions had ended. The detection equipment had been packed away, and the hoses put out of sight in their boxes.

The clocks went forwards again at midday, but only by 30 minutes (GMT+ 5.5), to match Indian time. By the time the announcement of the change was made I was in Carmen's ready to begin the choir practice. Today we reviewed the songs from yesterday and added two more. At our next session we would be attempting "Bring him home" from "Les Misérables" and I felt really happy with the singing. Strangely one of my eyes kept watering throughout the session.

Once singing was over, I rushed back to the cabin to get a cold drink and put on some scruffier clothes to go and play cricket. Being the beginning of a new sector, we had some new players today, which meant it was a bit of a lottery balancing the teams to make it fair – that's my excuse anyway, as I was on the losing side.

I was getting a bit of a reputation for stopping and catching the ball quite well, and as yet I hadn't been '*out*' while batting.

It was 3:00 by the time we finished and I grabbed Deb and we went for a cup of tea and something to eat. That was my lunch.

My eye had stopped watering by now, but I was suspicious that I had the beginnings of a cold. My nose continuously ran. It looked like Deb had passed her cold on to me.

With all the activity over for the afternoon I decided to have a soak in the bath for a while, and hopefully wash away my germs.

It was casual dress code tonight, and we had a full dining table for the first time in several days. The six of us that had been together since Southampton were very relaxed with each other, but the two new ladies struggled to get into our conversations very much.

We had a shock when one of our friends announced that they had been caught out by a photographer when they visited the Burj Khalifa Tower in Dubai. They had their photograph taken as a memento of being at the top of the tallest tower in the world. They happily paid what was quoted but didn't take much notice of the figure in the local currency. They had now looked at their credit card account and discovered that the photo cost them £65!

There was no suggestion that anything dodgy happened, but for those of you visiting this tower, be aware of what you might be paying for a souvenir.

During dinner it was becoming very obvious that my cold was getting worse, and the continual need to blow or wipe my nose was embarrassing me. Deb was still sneezing occasionally and coughing a little, but she was definitely getting better – my turn now!

After dinner we completed all the paperwork for immigration in Mumbai tomorrow morning. We were on an early tour so needed to be up in plenty of time for the face-to-face interview.

Deb and I met up with Angie and Richard in Masquerades a little later to play Trivial Pursuits. We had a good laugh as we sipped a drink before the evening quiz started. Tonight it was supposed to be all about things we should remember from school. Well, all I can say is that I don't remember covering more than two of the questions while I was in school, and they were both about mathematics. There were a lot of well-educated people on this cruise and most of them were just as astounded by the questions as we were. The winning score was just 14 out of 20.

It was bedtime but I was feeling terrible. I searched through the medicine box and dosed myself up with anything that might help, but we already had concerns that I might not be well enough to go on tour in Mumbai in the morning.

Thursday 2nd February – Mumbai, India

The balcony temperature at 6:30 was 22°C, and rose to an astonishing high of 37° during the afternoon.

Our alarm went off at 6:00am, but it hadn't actually been necessary to set it as I had been awake all night feeling hot, then cold, and constantly holding my handkerchief against my nose throughout the seven hours in bed.

I felt awful, and sadly there was no way we were going on the tour today.

We had a cup of tea as Aurora was completing the docking procedure in this busy port. It was still dark but we could make out the buildings and an abundance of naval vessels. I managed to struggle to breakfast with Deb, but only had a croissant and yoghurt. The yoghurt turned out to be really tasty, so I took another back to go in the cabin fridge for later.

Even knowing we almost certainly wouldn't be going on the planned tour, we still went for our face-to-face immigration check at the planned time for those passengers on tours, rather than waiting for our manifest number to come up. That gave me time to get to the doctor at 8:00 when the medical centre opened, and get his professional opinion.

I felt absolutely terrible! I was the only walking wounded for the morning, but still had quite a long wait while the doctors and nurses looked after the patients temporarily staying overnight in the centre. Eventually the doctor checked me over, and told me I had flu. It seemed I had probably been suffering from it for a couple of days already, hence I was no longer a threat to others, but I still had to avoid mixing with people too closely, and to be careful to wash my hands regularly to minimise the chances of me spreading it further around the ship.

I didn't need any medication, but I was warned this virus had been rampant around the ship and had produced a secondary bacterial infection in some of the passengers. So, I had to watch out for any worsening.

As expected, the doctor said I needed rest and shouldn't be going on a tour today. My tour ticket was stamped and I took it straight to the tours desk to have it cancelled, and my money was refunded.

My little trip to the medical centre cost me £52, which was less than the tour refund, but sadly Deb's ticket wasn't cancelled and she didn't fancy walking around the backstreets of Mumbai without me.

I went back to the cabin, broke the bad news to Deb, and promptly lay down and fell asleep.

When I woke about an hour later Deb and I went for coffee. The ship was deserted so I didn't think I would infect anyone at the moment.

Then I went to sleep again.

Deb went out onto the deck to enjoy the sunshine, and about 30 minutes later I surfaced and joined her. Goodness it was hot!

Deb became my nurse for a while. At lunchtime she ate by herself, and then brought a cheese and pickle sandwich from the Grab and Go food counter for my lunch, along with a fruit salad. Then I sat on the balcony for more than an hour watching the scene below on the quayside.

By now some of the morning tours were coming back, so there was a steady trickle of passengers arriving, while others were setting off for their afternoon trips. To our right the dockside was a storage area for hundreds of giant rolls of steel. These were being loaded onto a fleet of lorries, and I realised after a while that each roll of steel was selected by its new owners before being loaded for transporting. I presume a price was agreed based on how good the quality of the steel looked. This steel market went on all afternoon.

For warship enthusiasts this dock could be a real treat. There was an aircraft carrier, lots of different-sized vessels bristling with radar dishes and guns, and a small flotilla of little boats that could have been for training. A helicopter regularly buzzed around, and at one point it was hovering just a few feet above the sea.

Wildlife was a little sparse. I saw two thin dogs, and there were various birds flying around. Quite unusually, there weren't any gulls. There were pigeons, and what looked like crows, then bigger versions of crows that had a louder cry, and finally much bigger birds of prey that I think might have been kites.

Just below our balcony was a soldier with a rifle stopping any unwanted visitors getting onto Aurora's berth. Like the workers from the steel market, to stay cool our guard was using any shade created by the grey drab dockside buildings.

By the middle of the afternoon the thermometer was showing 37°C. It was too hot to stay on the balcony for long, so I slept on the bed with the wonderful air-conditioning.

I began to feel a little better as the afternoon went on, but I had no plans to go public tonight. At least Deb could pass on my apologies at dinner, and I hoped I hadn't given them this awful virus as well.

Just before 5:00 the sounds of gangway de-construction could be heard below, and the last straggling crew members were rushing back to begin work again. I assumed the tours were all back, and we soon had the '*bing bong*' to herald the regular evening announcement from the captain.

Tomorrow would be a sea day as Aurora continued down the west coast of India to Cochin, the second of our stops in this country. We had another tour booked there, and I hoped to be ready to gambol around India like a young spring lamb by then.

...time for some more cough medicine and paracetamol

While Deb went to dinner, I sat out on the Promenade Deck looking at the last of Mumbai's buildings in the setting sun. India is a country that has taken the opportunity to throw off the shackles of colonial rule, and has developed so much. I was a little sad however to see how dirty it was. The water in the harbour was a filthy brown colour and full of plastic rubbish. As we headed back out to sea, there were numerous objects floating by, and several vast patches of man-made garbage. The so-called developed countries have begun heeding the warnings about how we treat the planet, and a country like India also needs to actively make an effort.

As it became completely dark, I crawled back to the cabin to suffer again. Deb brought me back a couple of bread rolls and a hunk of cheese. Our assistant waiter, Cyrus, had put the little package together with a covered plate. These guys really do so much to make a holiday special.

Our steward, Tamil, had had a visit from his family today while we were in Mumbai, and he is now both happy and sad. His mother, wife, and son came to see him. His son was only six months old, and just three months old when Tamil began his contract. It must be so hard to do this job, but presumably it means the crew have more money than they could have earned at home.

Later in the evening Deb and I went to the Crow's Nest for a drink, but I quickly began to get cold and it wasn't long before we were back in the cabin. After the usual little read, I was tucked up in bed and struggling to stay warm.

Friday 3rd February – Sea Day

The temperature today went up to a very warm 26° in the back garden.

I was no longer cold. In fact, I woke up oozing sweat from every part of my body. I had an awful night, regularly waking up to cough. My knees were aching so badly that when I got out of bed I struggled to walk. This was really an awful bout of flu.

Although it took me a long time to dress, we did go to breakfast together. I had a glass of orange juice, plus some yoghurt. I tried a cup of tea but it felt too hot to drink. My poor body just refused to function correctly.

When we got back to the cabin I curled up on the bed and dozed off. By late morning I was cold again and had to put on my dressing gown as I slept.

To be honest this was all I did until 3:00 in the afternoon, except for a half-awake period when we both had to go for a face-to-face immigration interview ready for Cochin tomorrow.

On the other hand, Deb had a productive day.

We had been offered a cabin upgrade for Singapore onwards, and Deb sorted it out with the people at Future Cruises. It cost us a fair bit of money, but was what we had been trying, unsuccessfully, to get from almost the moment we booked the cruise.

Anyway, the outcome was that on our second day in Singapore we would be moving our belongings (with the help of the housekeeping group) to a Superior Balcony Cabin up on B Deck.

Deb also finally gave in and bought the world cruise tee shirt from the shop. She'd wanted once since almost the beginning of the cruise, but had been reluctant to buy it because of the price, together with the fact that it showed some destinations that we didn't visit.

During the afternoon I began to feel slightly more human, and went for tea in the buffet for my first solid food of the day. Although slightly better, I was still not well enough to go to dinner tonight. To improve how I felt about myself, I had a shower and a shave. I wasn't in the mood to do either yesterday or this morning, but by now the bristles were making me feel uncomfortable.

We actually ate in the buffet in the evening as I was still feeling a little unsociable. It was a chicken themed menu, but sadly most things were a little spicier than I prefer. At least eating in the buffet gave us a chance of getting to the first show by Caravan in Carmen's. Their show was a tribute to the Philadelphia Sound and their normal line-up was enhanced by the orchestra's wind section.

From Carmen's we dashed the length of the ship to the theatre for a show by the Headliners that we hadn't seen before: it was called Fantasy and was all about disco music. This was also the first time the show had been performed on Aurora.

All in all, it turned out to be a very good evening's entertainment.

Deb and I then climbed up to the Crow's Nest for a late-night drink. This is where things began to go wrong again. The air-conditioning up there was very effective and I began to shiver, so it was time for paracetamol and bed.

Tomorrow we would be in Cochin where we'd be on a walking tour of the city. Even after the late-night setback I was sure I will be ready for it, and hopefully a good night's sleep would recharge my batteries.

Saturday 4th February – Cochin, India

Balcony temperature was over 20°C when we got up, and rose to 29° later in the day. It was also very humid, and making us feel sticky with even the slightest exertion or movement.

I hadn't fully recovered from my flu, but I felt well enough to resume normal activities.

Cochin (also known as Kochi) is on the western side of India, and less than 500km from the southern tip of the country. It was a port we missed out on five years ago, due I believe to a double booking of our berth, but it was too long ago to remember clearly.

Our arrival time was supposed to be 8:00, and we were up early to be ready for our tour. We needn't have bothered as the pilot was late getting to Aurora and then insisted on going very slowly.

He must have had a late night!

It was a hot and sticky morning with hazy sunshine pushing the temperature up very quickly. We were scheduled to be in the theatre at 9:15 for a 9:45 getaway, but we were told to go away and relax for a while as tours were running seriously late. Eventually we got on to our coach at 10:15 for the *'Cochin Heritage Trail'*.

The clue was very much in the name.

During the three and a half hours that we drove around the older area of the city we visited Fort Cochin (which is no longer a fort), a church and a cathedral. We missed out on the planned visit to the synagogue, as Saturday is the Jewish religious day. The guide went to great lengths, repeatedly, to ensure we knew that there were now only five Jews left in Cochin, so the synagogue couldn't have been very busy.

Between the two religious visits that did go ahead, we had a slightly more interesting walk along the waterside, past some rather pungent fish salesmen. There were also huge numbers of market traders trying to sell us wooden boxes created to look like cats (not really) and wind chimes made up of elephants.

Oh, and yet more pashminas, postcards, bangles and toys.

The real purpose of the walk was to see and watch the Chinese fishing nets in operation. These vast nets are held upon wooden poles that are counter-balanced with stones to allow the net to be dropped into the water and then hauled back up teeming with fish.

Several of the tour passengers (Deb included) had a go at pulling the net up whilst we all chanted the fishermen's' good luck song. Sadly, the reward for their effort was the grand total of two small fish which were the size of fairground goldfish.

It was time to move on and we boarded the coach again.

Two passengers were missing!

After more than 30 minutes while the guide and the tour escort searched the area for them, they ambled back along the road without a care in the world, and took their seats. They made no apology, and I think they were rather confused by the looks they were getting from the rest of the passengers.

On the return journey to the port, we visited the local open-air laundry. We should have stopped there earlier, but there had been nowhere to park the coach. So it was the end of the morning by the time we got there, and most of the laundry process was complete. Hence all we saw was the clothes drying in a huge field of white and coloured materials. Inside the ramshackle building several hot-looking people were already putting the finishing touches to the ironing, before packing and making them ready for collection. This is an amazing industry without a single computer, or even a paper label in evidence, and it rarely goes wrong.

One or two of the passengers were desperate to shop for spices, and the guide organised a stop at a souvenir/spice shop. This also allowed passengers who were a little desperate for a toilet to relieve themselves.

Finally, the guide offered us all the chance to walk across the 1km-long British Bridge. Please note this was in the open with no shade, and the temperature was in the 30s by now. Amazingly most of the passengers agreed. Boringly, Deb and I and a few other sensible people stayed on the coach as it drove to the other end of the bridge to retrieve the red-faced walkers.

In hindsight the tour wasn't the best we have ever been on, but some people seemed thrilled by it. I will leave you to make up your own minds in case you ever get here one day.

By the time we got back to the ship I was regretting the decision to go on the tour. I was feeling pretty ill again and spent most of the afternoon sleeping, while watching for the clock for the next time I could have more paracetamol.

It was quite obvious from our balcony view that Cochin has a modern skyscraper district as well as what we had seen. There was also a vast waterway with ferries and tourist boats buzzing around. A number of the ferries resembled the Vaporetti-style boats of Venice.

We did go to dinner in the restaurant again, and it was a reasonably nice meal, but I had no appetite, my taste buds weren't functioning, and I was sweating from the exertion of eating.

We ignored the evening entertainment. In Carmen's there was a three-piece boyband called the Undertones who sounded quite good. Meanwhile in the theatre was Jon Clegg, the comedian I had seen a few days earlier. Our dinner mates said they wished they had heeded our warning about him as he was pretty bad. How could his act have made it to the grand final of "Britain's got Talent"?

Richard and Angie met up with us at 9:30 for the Masquerade's challenge which was themed tonight on company logos.

We were first equal......hurrah!

We lost the tie break…. ahh!

The winners didn't drink, so they let us have the wine…. hurrah!

So how was I feeling as I went to bed?

Not good to be honest. My chest hurt and I had a clicking, wheezy sound when I breathed. I think I might be going back to the doctor in the morning.

Sunday 5th February – Sea Day
Still hot and sticky with a maximum temperature on the balcony of 27°C.

This was a day when I planned to return to the choir, and have a game of cricket again. Instead I woke temporarily around 6:00 with a horribly painful chest and the clicking continued when I breathed. My fear was that the flu-like virus I had started with had now evolved into the bacterial infection the doctor had warned me about.

We got up just before 7:30 having been rather rudely woken by next door banging their drawers inconsiderately. I wasn't well but I had decided I must try and reverse my body's decline by having something to eat. My breakfast treat was a slice of bacon, some baked beans, and a few bits of fried potato. It was very nice, but having eaten it my body decided to sweat once again from the exertion. To be honest, that food was the first thing that had tasted pleasant for some time.

Back in the cabin it was our 'chemist' day, and we sorted out our pills for the week to come. We had both come on the cruise with four months-worth of prescription medicines and today I broke open the second month's packet of pills.

It was just 8:30 and outside the sun was creating one of its magical displays. As it shone down, it created a pathway of shimmering silver from the horizon to the ship. It was such a beautiful sight, and had an added twist, that it reversed perspective. There was a wide band at the horizon that narrowed to almost a point at the ship.

Just before 9:00 Deb went off to the theatre for a port talk on our stop in Malaysia. I waited a while longer before wandering down to the dreaded deck 4, and the Medical Centre.

Because it was a repeat visit I was quickly ushered in and given the preliminary checks by a nurse. Almost immediately I then had a consultation with a doctor.

Although feeling rotten, outwardly I appeared quite healthy. There was no sign of an infection and I didn't need any antibiotics. We had a chat and the friendly doctor from Helston suggested I give myself a rest from my blood pressure pills for a few days, as they might be causing my coughing. We also had a moment reflecting on growing up in Cornwall, and I told her that her father worked at Goonhilly while I was there. It really is a small world.

Anyway, rather than completely ruling out antibiotics, she created a prescription for me if my symptoms changed in the next few days. In the meantime, I was told to relax as much as possible and get my strength back.

Deb and I met up again and went for coffee, before I went to listen to a P&O Heritage talk from the Captain. It was very interesting, but I embarrassed myself by having a five-minute coughing fit.

Then it was lunchtime, followed by doze time.

Aurora had reached the southern end of India. Sadly, the seas of the west and east basin of the Indian Ocean were fighting to see who was the more dominant. The wind got up and the seas were officially reported as 'moderate' state.

That means quite rough.

I was uncomfortable and took to a little white pill.

After a less-than-active afternoon it was time for dinner, and tonight was formal dress. At the table the eight of us talked constantly about what we had done, and what we were going to do. We were all on tours tomorrow, with some having to muster at 7:00 while the lazy ones, like us, would go out in the afternoon.

We avoided the entertainment.

Deb and I did venture out of the cabin for the 9:30 gameshow in Masquerade's. It was called "Less Means More" and was a version of BBC's "Pointless". In the previous sector, there had been loads of volunteers to take part, but this time Danny and Coral had to coax enough people to fill the eight seats. Hence, we took part and even managed to be paired up.

Cutting a long story short, we won. It wasn't easy with rather a lot of film topics but fortunately my mate from the cricket came up with a suggestion for a pointless answer in the final round, and we won two memory sticks and two bottles of wine.

Rather pleased with ourselves, if a little confused, we walked back towards the cabin. In the Atrium area we saw preparations for a champagne fountain, so we found a spot to watch this spectacle. It was a bit of fun and we ended up with free glasses of the champagne. Actually, it was Spumanti, but it was still free. We could have had a lot more but we thought better of it and went to bed.

Aurora was no longer rolling around. The wind had dropped and the sea no longer fighting our ship as she sailed up the western coastline of Sri Lanka to Colombo where we would be visiting tomorrow.

Monday 6th February – Colombo, Sri Lanka
Maximum temperature on the balcony today topped 33°C.

I had a sleepless night. It was possible that I had actually caught up on what I needed with my daytime dozing, hence the restless six hours. Quite a while before I eventually got up, I heard the sound of a boat alongside the ship as Aurora picked up the pilot and began the approach to the port of Colombo.

The island nation of Sri Lanka lies at the south-eastern edge of India, and it is a teardrop shape. Colombo is the capital city of the island, and as well as having a long history associated with British Colonial Rule, it is now a huge commercial port. We stopped here briefly five years ago but our tour had been cancelled, so we only explored the dockside market. It has changed since then, and been vastly expanded over the years making the harbour side look far more inviting.

But the market stalls were still here!

We were up a little after 7:00 and the sun was blinding as I opened the curtains to peek out. Our garden is a dockside today and there were a number of those market stalls to visit later.

On the way to breakfast, Deb put a load of washing on. We weren't leaving for our tour until 1:15 so our morning was a lazy one. At breakfast we discovered that Maurice Grumbleweed and the MacDonald Brothers had joined us as entertainers. We'd definitely seen Maurice Grumbleweed before, as I remember playing cricket with him five years ago, and our friends also recommended the Scottish pair of singers.

By 9:00 the temperature was approaching 30°, and just like the last week, it was sticky.

While the washing began its drying cycle, we went down onto the quay to watch the local dance troupe, and to buy a few bits from the market. This was a much cheaper place to buy things than India.

With washing done and put away, I spent almost an hour on the stern deck getting some sunshine on my body. I was alone for most of that time, and it was very pleasant as a cool breeze began to blow across the deck. Obviously, I dozed off.

I was rudely awoken by the emergency signal for the crew exercises. That was the time to go back to the cabin, threading my way through groups of crew in their life jackets. The garden was now up to 32°.

Our tour this afternoon was called *'Colombo Heritage'* and was part of the P&O 180-year celebratory tours. This was a long tour for us, and we wouldn't be back until 6:30, but afternoon tea was included at one of the stops.

We made sure we had a reasonable lunch before we went, and we considered the possibility of room service for the evening when we got back. Aurora wasn't sailing until 7:30 at the earliest, and there was also a planned 60s/70s party on the deck tonight, and a chance for us to wear our fancy dress costumes.

We left Aurora at 1:00 pm to find our coach. Our guide was a happy and outgoing local with a couple of helpers to assist with the logistics.

Now, this tour obviously suited some of our group, and would no doubt appeal to many others who would come here, but we were almost as disappointed with this "heritage - themed exploration" as we had been in Cochin.

The coach initially took us through the chaotic streets of the city, before arriving at our first stop at what was called The Dutch Church, where some P&O crew or passengers of the past **might** have attended a service.

All I can really say about it was that it was old, and falling down. After looking around we had to wait at least 10 minutes in the hot sun before our coach returned.

After a few more minutes' drive through the chaos of Colombo we got off the coach and began a 90-minute walk. We were shown a few Colonial-style buildings that our guide suggested P&O passengers and crew **might** have visited since they began coming to the island.

We then visited another religious building with a fair degree of Dutch influence once again.

Back out on the very hot streets we criss-crossed the traffic lanes to get a look at more of the historical colonial buildings where P&O passengers *may* have visited. Most of these buildings are now owned by banks from around the world. Others have been adopted as Government buildings, but many were simply crumbling away. The need to cross roads was becoming a major obstacle at times, and someone described the scene as being like "Wacky Races". Our tour group was regularly split up with people stranded on one side of the road waiting for the tuk-tuks to allow people to cross to where the rest of us were.

Our last stop was another old building complex that has now been converted into retail outlets. Surprise, surprise, it was once the Dutch hospital.

Deb and I had actually enjoyed seeing some of the buildings, but the tenuous link to this being a P&O designated heritage walk around Colombo wasn't impressing us.

At least the tour ended on a very big high. We visited the Galle Face Hotel for afternoon tea. This is a huge hotel on the waterfront that has retained a wealth of tradition. Our guide was sure that P&O passengers **"would have come here many times"**, and this time he might well have been right.

The afternoon tea was superb. There was local tea that tasted delicious, and the sandwiches and cakes were better than on the ship. We had 90 minutes to relax and soak up the atmosphere of this delightful hotel, but there was an even more spectacular end to our visit.

Our evening ended watching a fantastic custom that the hotel performs daily. As the sun was just about to set, a piper marched out from the hotel playing a lament, before the hotel's Sri Lankan flag was lowered, and carried away for the night.

Absolutely wonderful!

We were soon on the way back to Aurora. The food and exhaustion left us with no appetite to rush to dinner so we just chilled out on the balcony after a refreshing shower. Some of the tour buses were late so our departure was delayed (again). Down below, the market was being dismantled, and the stevedores relaxed until their assistance was finally required.

Just after 8:00 the last coaches returned, and almost instantly the noisy ship's engines powered up and Aurora was under way again.

We went to the theatre to watch a pickpocket, who was really more of a magician, but he was good to watch and gave us all a good laugh. He struggled because there were only three or four people in the room with jackets, making it difficult to find someone to work with.

From the theatre we went to the buffet to get a cup of tea, and our tiredness meant we didn't spend any time at the deck party, let alone dress up for it.

Aurora was now beginning three days at sea, sailing east across the Indian Ocean. On Friday we would be in Malaysia at the port of Penang. After that there would be a further sea day, before the second sector came to an end at Singapore.

Three sea days to Malaysia

Tuesday 7th February

Our balcony temperature today was a little cooler with a maximum reading of 28°C.

It had been another less-than-comfortable and sleep filled night.

Aurora was just five degrees north of the equator and the early morning temperature was a sticky 27°. We were most definitely in the Tropics.

After breakfast we decided to have an hour in the sunshine. There was a breeze making the towels flap around a little, but it also took the edge of the heat making things a little less oppressive.

I was slightly disappointed to realise that I had missed a talk by Captain Martin Reed (retired) who had been a well-known master of various P&O ships. Famously he commanded the Canberra on her Falklands adventures. While on board he was giving four talks in total before Singapore, so I still had a chance to listen to him.

At lunchtime the clocks went forward again by 30 minutes to GMT + 6 hours.

I spent a lot of time during the late morning simply sitting on the balcony looking out over our garden. Today it was an almost smooth sea with just a few dimples and the occasional mole hill. The sun wasn't directly on the water but its rays were creating beautiful mystical patterns in the sea, and refracting off any little edge of a dimple it found. This created tiny pin spots of light sparkling like tiny pieces of a mirror ball.

Then my dreaminess was disturbed by a splash of light.

This was the second time this cruise that I had seen flying fish. I called Deb out to look and we began to see more and more of what appeared to be little birds the size of sparrows, but from this distance it was difficult to work out size. As the big white hull of Aurora disturbed these creatures, they leaped out of the sea and fluttered their side fins to skim just on or above the surface of the water. They flew for certainly in excess of ten seconds, attaining distances of 20-30 metres.

When they achieved a perfect launch, they glided with hardly any fin action following the contours of the little waves. Sometimes they gently touched the water as they glided and left little splashes to mark their trail across the ocean.

We had been fascinated by these delightful fish in the Atlantic Ocean five years ago, but then it was even more exciting as the shoals were followed by flocks of birds that watched for them to fly, and then dived down on them as they glided. The shoals of fish were so large then, that it was like a starburst from the hull of the ship as tens of them scattered together after their relaxed swimming was disturbed.

Anyway, lunchtime called us away from the aquatic delights, and when we returned to the cabin we had a decision to make.

Deb and I were in a critical moment with our coughs. Our planned tour in Penang was to an orangutan sanctuary. If we were to show any sign of a cold or cough we wouldn't be able to go to the island sanctuary, to avoid us passing any of our Northern European bugs to the animals. We were certainly almost better, but were still both coughing badly occasionally.

After one of us coughed again we had made up our minds. When the afternoon Salsa and cricket sessions were over, we would go to the Explorer's desk and change our tour to something different.

So, at 2:00 we went our separate ways for the afternoon exercise sessions. I returned hot and glowing after a really energetic game. Deb hadn't been as successful because the Headliners had a matinee show during the afternoon, and her class was cancelled.

At the Tours desk we cancelled the orangutan trip and swapped to one looking at butterflies and flowers, so it was still a little bit cultural. We also swapped an all-day trip on the second day in Singapore for a shorter one. We needed time to sort out our room move that day, and felt it would be better to be around to help it go smoothly.

Finally, we had a little moan about the heritage tour we had in Colombo. It really wasn't up to the standard required, and at least this gave Aurora's tour's team a chance to pass on the complaint to the team on Arcadia, before they arrived in Sri Lanka in a few weeks' time.

Time for coffee.

Well, actually we had an iced lemon drink in Costa that was delicious, and extremely cold. Oh, and we had a slice of cake each as well – whoops!

We were getting back into our evening routine slowly, and went to the individual quiz for the first time in several days. A well-needed shower came next, but we avoided canapes and prosecco in Anderson's, and just sat on the deck until dinner time.

There was a full house at dinner. Sadly, I still had a very limited appetite and really just wanted to pick at my food. It seemed that as soon as I had a few decent mouthfuls of food I broke out into a sweat. My body hadn't recovered from the virus yet.

As we walked away from the dinner table, Richard dragged the rest of us to Masquerade's for the early evening quiz. Having turned up late, and getting the first five questions repeated, we won another bottle of wine.

Deb and I then strolled to the theatre to watch Maurice Grumbleweed.

Absolutely hilarious, and three quarters of an hour of chuckle-muscle flexing. It was so good that we bought a copy of his very expensive book about comedy routines on cruise ships.

Now it was back to Masquerade's for another game show called "Majority Rules". We were pretty hopeless here and proved we don't think the same way as the majority.

It was bedtime, and after a little read we turned off the lights. Less than ten minutes later there was an announcement for the stretcher team to go to a cabin on deck 5. It wasn't going to be a good night for someone on the ship.

……………………………………………

Wednesday 8th February

This was our second sea day of three and at 7:30 on the balcony it was already 26°C, rising to 29° during the day.

We continued with the tropical theme and it was sticky again, during the afternoon we even had a bit of a shower.

Deb and I went to the morning port talk on Semarang in Indonesia to see if there was a tour suitable for us. In the end we went for a short four-hour *'Glimpse of Semarang'* trip to get a little flavour of the city.

After a cup of coffee, we set off for a walk around the Promenade Deck. Today we did four laps (plus the usual bit) which brought my total so far to 10 miles. To round off the morning I stared at the sea in the back garden and watched the flying fish again.

At midday the clocks magically shot forward another hour, and we were now at GMT + 7.

By the time we had enjoyed a bit of lunch there was hardly time to catch our breath before Salsa and cricket increased our pulse rates a little. Of course, once they were over we had an excuse for a cup of tea and a scone.

It had been too hot and humid to spend long in the sunshine today, so I resorted to snoozing on the shaded balcony.

We were showered in time to go to the individual quiz in Champions where Deb succeeded in winning our first gold sticker for the cruise. She managed 19/20 and beat me by just a single point. Yes, it was an easy quiz today.

The early evening report from Captain Dunlop confirmed that our progress was on schedule, and then it was dinner time. I still didn't feel very hungry. Although I was over my virus, the constant high temperature and high humidity was sapping my energy and killing my appetite. I did enjoy a chicken with a Chinese salad as a starter, but then disinterestedly picked my way through a gammon steak for my main course. I rounded off the meal with a couple of scoops of ice-cream. You might think it sounds like my appetite was quite good, but in reality, I never finished any of the courses.

The evening entertainment featured a concert pianist in the theatre called Tian Jiang, but we had decided to go to Carmen's at 9:30 to watch the Headliners perform their Abba tribute show called 'Thank-You for the Music'. But our plan wasn't to be as Carmen's had a technical problem. The Abba tribute show was cancelled, and the girl singer from the Headliners performed her personal portfolio of songs as an alternative show. All four of the primary Headliner singers helped with the choir, and did a magnificent job at it, but neither of us fancied watching a solo performance.

Instead Deb and I had a rest in the cabin before going up to the Crow's Nest, thinking we would be watching Caravan perform. We didn't find Caravan, but we did find the rest of our dinner table gang playing Trivial Pursuits, so joined in as they struggled to get the final cheeses. It was the usual "girls verses boys" challenge, but neither team won as the pink cheeses proved totally illusive.

The clock ticked towards 9:30, so we abandoned the game, and dashed to Masquerade's. It was time for another quiz hosted by DJ Martin. This evening the challenge was all about TV quiz shows, and our team was sensational beating our nearest rivals by seven points.

Another bottle of wine for our virtual cellar!

This was the end of the second sea day as we crossed the Bay of Bengal towards the eastern rim of the Indian Ocean. The Captain promised more of the same weather tomorrow with a warm breeze and sunshine from dawn till dusk.

"Gad Carruthers, it's hot!"

....

Thursday 9th February

Out on the balcony the temperature began at 27°C and peaked a degree higher through the day.

As I got out of bed and peered out at the world, the sea had a few small hills and white horses running around, but nothing very serious. The weather was as predicted by the Captain, with clear skies and a breeze coming from the north-east, taking the edge off the heat and easing the humidity a little.

Our cabin was on the shaded side of the ship, and with clear skies I imagined the other side of the ship was basking in wall-to-wall sunshine.

Today we had been at sea for a calendar month. If by any chance I have inferred that we were not having a good time, then that was purely accidental. It was different from our world cruise five years ago, but was still a sensational way of spending the winter.

I felt sorry for friends and family at home as they struggled with the cold and damp British climate, but that wasn't going to stop us making the best of our holiday.

Anyway, I had a good night's sleep after experimenting by changing the pillows around. Better still, I didn't wake with a stiff neck and a headache.

After breakfast we spent an hour in the sunshine. It was a little less restful than usual as we struggled to hang on to our towels in the breeze, but Deb and I persisted in our attempts to give our pale skin some colour. From sun-worship we went for a walk and my total has now reached 11 miles.

I think that I should clarify that we had walked considerably more than 11 miles on the cruise while on our tours, but my personal marathon challenge was only about the Prom deck laps. And unlike a lot of the passengers, we also increase our heart rates by avoiding the lifts for most of our climbs and descents through the decks.

It was time for mid-morning coffee, and today we went to the buffet for a change, and yes, we avoided the cakes this morning.

We were heading towards midday, and the clocks bumped forward another hour to make us GMT +8. That will set our time to that of Malaysia for our visit to Penang tomorrow. Sadly, it meant the post-lunch activities were squeezed once more.

Today at 2:15 the Aurora Choir performed in the theatre and we went along to listen. It was really a good 30 minutes, but I was a little sad knowing that I could have been singing with them.

Hopefully things would go better in the next sector.

We spent the rest of the afternoon avoiding the worst of the heat and enjoying the air-conditioning in our cabin. Deb and I did crawl out to take part in the individual quiz, but that was our total expenditure of energy for the afternoon.

It was the final Formal evening of the sector with a special Marco Pierre White Gala Menu dinner. We have always enjoyed these meals in the past, but sadly it inspired the six of us so little that none of us actually chose his dishes.

After eating we went to the theatre to listen to the MacDonald Brothers, and were rather glad we did. Between them, the two young men played the piano, accordion, guitar and violin, as well as giving us some really good harmony singing.

From the theatre we made our way to Carmen's for the Ball. We took to the floor for five or six dances, and by the end I was overheating and out of energy.

It was time for bed. Aurora was moving quite smoothly now across the Straits of Malacca for our early morning arrival at the penultimate port of this sector.

We had a tour in the morning when we arrive in Penang, so the alarm was set, although I doubted it will be necessary.

Friday 10th February – Penang, Malaysia

Our back garden today managed to top 29°C, and it was very sticky.

I was right about not needing the alarm. As Aurora made her final approaches to the busy port of Penang, the noise of the thrusters woke me.

It was hot again, but only around 25° on the balcony when we finally got out of bed.

We were 'parked' with a view out over the water towards mainland Malaysia.

Our tour was called *'Butterflies, Fruit and Spices'* and was due to leave at 8:45, so we had to be in the theatre by 8:30. There was plenty of time for a relaxing breakfast.

One of the regular events at ports is the appearance of the local authorities. Once they have boarded, checked paperwork, and checked for any unsavoury characters, the officials are let loose on the buffet for breakfast. Many are prepared for this and make the most of the delights on offer, but sometimes you wonder if they have been given some bad advice about the food on offer.

Today for instance I noticed one of the men with a croissant. He initially folded it over and then spooned a little pot of Marmite over one side. This was followed by a dollop of butter and rounded off with a pot of marmalade. I couldn't look away as he squeezed the croissant together and took a bite. Initially there was a slight glint of surprise in his eyes and a concerned stare at what he was eating. It may have been a pleasant surprise, but I think it was more a shock at the taste explosion in his mouth. He continued eating this newly-discovered delicacy, but the look on his face suggested he just wanted to get it swallowed and forgotten.

I wonder who suggested he tried this unusual breakfast treat?

We returned to our cabin and got ourselves ready for the morning out in Penang.

The tour was superb, if a little tiring from standing and walking for around three hours. Firstly, the spice trail in a rain forest tested our climbing skills as the enthusiastic guide described the different plants to us. We were thrilled by the colours and appearance of the different flowers, we sniffed many different perfumes, and tasted various edible plants. By the time we got back on the coach we were already 15 minutes behind schedule.

Our next stop was a fruit farm where we had another excited farmer filling our heads with the names of fruits. His descriptions and obvious passion for the sweet and juicy fruit showed that this was more than a job to him. Our visit was rounded off with a tasting session of freshly prepared fruit drinks, plus a buffet of pineapple, mango, melon, as well as sweet treats that I didn't recognise, but which I thoroughly enjoyed.

Back on the coach again and we were almost an hour late now.

The final stop was a butterfly centre. Oh, this was absolutely sensational.

There were butterflies of all colours and sizes ranging from what we see in Britain through to some the size of a tea-plate. Alongside the beautiful insects flying freely around the flowers, there were lizards, snakes, birds, fish, and various creepy-crawlies to keep my camera busy. We were told we only had thirty minutes here, but by the time we had bought a souvenir we were a further ten minutes late.

The return journey to the ship was a chance to snooze (if wives allowed) while our guide, Ronny, described and explained more about his homeland. He also told jokes, most of which were new to us, although I did miss the last one while I got away with shutting my eyes...just for a moment.

Back on Aurora we dashed up to the buffet to get something to eat. It was 2:30 and our trip had been longer than we anticipated, but it really had been very good.

After eating, we went to reception to find out when we would be moving from our current cabin to the new one. No-one seemed to know or care, but after standing our ground at the desk for long enough, we discovered we are moving on the first day in Singapore. Of course, this meant we have to make an effort at packing tomorrow as we make our way south towards our next stop.

We also found our cabin steward, and made sure he knew we were leaving on Sunday morning. He wasn't aware of how many of his cabins will be changing occupants, so our little bit of warning was welcomed. He suggested that we might be lucky and find our new cabin will be ready during the morning on Sunday. He will have ours ready by 10:00 for new passengers, and other stewards will be trying to keep to similar time-scales.

Maurice Grumbleweed was performing his final show in the theatre that evening, and if we were enthusiastic enough after his show, there was a tropical deck party out on the decks later. Aurora wouldn't be leaving port until after 10:00 tonight, so it might not be as breezy as it often got for these parties.

Well at the dinner table we were alone with just the two ladies who had joined us in Dubai. By now they were far chattier than when we first met, but it was almost time to say goodbye to them as they disembark in Singapore. Our late return with a mid-afternoon snack in the buffet meant neither of us had much of an appetite. We both decided on a bowl of soup, followed by a starter for our dinner…. plus, some ice-cream of course.

As we wandered back towards our cabin there was a tap on my shoulder from Richard. He was tempting us into Masquerade's for the early evening quiz. We were actually very successful with 18/20 but another team beat us by one point. The four of us agreed to meet up later for the deck party.

The theatre show from Maurice Grumbleweed was a lovely, and amusing, 45 minutes. From there we went up to the Riviera deck and our dinner table six camped at a table for an evening together. It was really fun as we all danced and laughed the evening away.

The Captain interrupted the music for a moment to announce we were leaving Penang, and that Aurora would be arriving in Singapore at midnight tomorrow rather than the following morning as originally planned. It meant we would have two nights in port, allowing an early getaway for some passengers on the Sunday morning.

Aurora gracefully turned around in the harbour area before setting off down the Malacca Straits again for a gentle 26-hour journey to the island of Singapore. On Sunday and Monday some 800 or so of the ship's passengers would be going home, to be replaced by a similar number for the third sector.

Our deck dancing resumed and DJ Martin was delighted to actually have a really happy group of people dancing to his music for a change.

Then it began to rain.

We discovered the suddenness and heaviness of tropical rain for the first time. It persisted for half an hour, which was enough to convince our little gang, and many others, to call it a night.

It reminded me that the first truly delightful tropical deck party we had in 2012 ended in a similar fashion. On that evening as we neared the Caribbean, the DJ played a series of songs about rain, and many people attempted to stay in the mood until their clothes were eventually soaked through.

Memories!

Good night.

Saturday 11th February – Sea Day

We woke to a cloudy morning, and within a few minutes while we drank our morning cuppa, it was raining but it was still the usual hot and sticky tropical morning. The maximum balcony temperature today was 29°C.

Breakfast was a quiet affair with very few people up and around at 8:00 in the morning. There was another reminder of five years ago, as there were plastic buckets strategically positioned around the buffet area to catch the rain water that was collecting in the roof space.

As well as having our usual sea-day fun, plans included packing away our clothes and belongings before our cabin move tomorrow. We didn't have to put everything in suitcases, as they would move our hanging clothes as they were. One thing we did have to do was to put the original hangers back into the wardrobe: they had been inside a suitcase under the bed since we boarded the ship. To make life as simple as possible for ourselves we always pack our clothes with their own hangers and just transfer them straight into the cabin's wardrobe.

At 9:00 we were up in the Crow's Nest from where a great number of ships were in view. We had been warned that the Straits of Malacca is one of the world's busiest waterways.

And it hadn't stopped raining yet.

At one point during the morning, while enjoying the breeze on the balcony I spotted 35 ships (just on port side of the ship). Among them was one tiny fishing boat that was smaller than one of Aurora's lifeboats. It was working in the middle of this maritime M25, oblivious of the mayhem all around it with vast ships going in both directions carrying oil, cars, liquid gas, dry goods, as well as the thousands of metal containers containing vast amounts of something to fuel the lust of mankind for MORE!

Late in the morning it was apparent that out cabin air-conditioning had failed. I reported it to Reception, but was told to wait for 30 minutes for it to stabilise after having the balcony door open. After lunch I reported it again and they promised to send the 'ventilation' man. During the afternoon the temperature actually rose to 28° **inside** the cabin. This was only one degree lower than outside on the balcony. It took until almost 5:00 before the engineer came to tell us it was working again. Whatever the problem was, it had actually affected all of the forward end of C Deck.

I had a chance to play cricket again. This was a match between those who were leaving and those who were staying on Aurora beyond Singapore. The 'remainers' were victorious, but tempers got a little heated as the banter went further than usual.

At dinner we had a chance to say goodbye to our temporary lady visitors, and also to Cyrus our assistant waiter who was going home tomorrow. We warned Adison that there was a chance that no-one would be going to dinner tomorrow because of our various tours.

After dinner we packed away the bulk of our bits and pieces in the cabin ready for our move tomorrow. We hoped to move between 9:00 and 10:00, and hopefully would be in our new cabin by mid-morning.

We didn't bother with the entertainment on offer during the evening. Instead we played Trivial Pursuits with Angie and Richard before Rosemary and Robin joined us for a quiz at 9:30. Tonight was themed on the Best of British: we were pretty successful...and beaten by just one point.

It was time for bed.

Aurora was already making her final approaches to Singapore, at 11:00 and although we went to sleep almost straight away, we were woken by the docking procedures at midnight. Slightly annoying to us was the very well-placed floodlight shining into our window, so we had to pull the curtains properly tonight.

Of course, by now I was wide awake and sleep became elusive again.

Sunday 12th February – Singapore

The balcony temperature was just 26°C today, but very humid.

We were awake by just after 7:00. Tea was made and pills taken. The bulk of our bits and pieces were ready to go as we made our way to breakfast at 7:30.

It is a strange morning, with a lot of people wearing tidy clothes in readiness to leave the ship, while others were in their usual scruffs, and staying aboard.

By a little after 8:00 we had camped in the Crow's Nest and listened to the announcements for disembarkation and immigration processes.

By 10:00 we had moved to our new cabin on B deck...

... and by 11:00 we had key cards that actually worked.

It then took until midday to pack away our clothes and bits, but at least we now had extra space to store our things away.

We had our lunch quite early and then prepared ourselves for our afternoon tour. We were off to Raffles Hotel for afternoon tea followed by a bit of an historical trip around the city of Singapore.

OK, so the Raffles Hotel is a special place, and the afternoon tea was quite outstanding, but the service left a lot to be desired. It took three attempts to get some milk, and we waited nearly twenty minutes for the Singapore Slings to arrive. These cost about £25 a glass, and I expected faster service at that sort of price.

We looked around the hotel as well, and even checked out the souvenir shop to find something as a memory. Unfortunately, the prices were worse for souvenirs than the drinks. At about £14 for a fridge magnet we decided to save our money.

We didn't have much of a chance to enjoy the hotel grounds as we had the second almighty tropical shower of the day that sent everyone under cover.

Eventually we re-joined our coach and had a tour of the city, and as the rain had stopped we walked to the area of the city where Mr Raffles actually landed on the island. The city has expanded greatly since then, and that original landing site is now a long, long way from the sea.

The city has certainly got a vast array of different styles of architecture. The majority of the older colonial buildings have been preserved and modernised, and other Dutch style buildings have also been kept, to maintain the history. Alongside all of the history there are the shiny skyscrapers, but many are imaginative, and few seem to have any straight lines. It was quite pleasant to see the way the city has been developed.

The coach took us back to Aurora: we were exhausted from the humidity. We decided to give dinner a miss, and simply had a snack in the buffet to keep us going.

As we anticipated, the ship was full of new people going the wrong way in search of their cabins and restaurants. We tried to help them, but many were just too confused, or stubborn, to listen.

Deb put a load of washing on while a machine was free. This will get our – much larger – wardrobe full of clean clothes to last us another couple of weeks. In the meantime, I had a shower to freshen up my body from the walk in the tropics. I wasn't sure if we would do anything else tonight: there was only the local Folk Laureate show in the theatre, and that means putting some tidy clothes on. Instead we stayed scruffy and relaxed in the cabin before an early night.

Tomorrow we were going on another tour: quite early in the morning we'd be off to the city's Botanical Gardens.

Monday 13th February – Singapore Day 2

The balcony thermometer recorded a maximum temperature of 29°C.

We had a very good night's sleep. It was motionless, quiet, cool, and somehow the bed and pillows in our new 'home' felt more comfortable.

We were awake just after 7:00 and set ourselves up for the day with a cup of tea.

The buffet was busy, with a lot of strangers trying to feel at home on Aurora. We were welcomed by our familiar cheerful tea-waiter who recognised us and brought the teapot to our table. It felt good to be a 'regular'.

Our tour was due to begin at 9:15, but with possible delays because of having to go through Singapore immigration again, we set of a little after 8:30. Of course we were in the departure lounge after less than 10 minutes with ages to wait for the coach.

Sadly, one couple were less successful getting through the immigration process, and we eventually set off 15 minutes late.

The first stage of our tour was at the Botanical Gardens to look at the orchid collection. Wow, it was spectacular. In Britain, or Hawaii where we have seen other collections, these amazing plants have to be grown in special greenhouses. But not here in Singapore, where they were growing and flowering outside in their natural tropical climate. It was a glorious display of colours, shapes and sizes.

From the beautiful gardens we had a narrated trip through the colonial area of the city before stopping to look at the waterside development area. Our guide (Peggy) was so knowledgeable about her home and the humour she was able to bring into the tour made it very special. Onwards again and our final stop was in China Town. This was supposed to be a chance to look at the city's oldest mosque and earliest Buddhist temple, but we went walkabout amongst the market stalls looking for souvenirs.

By the time we headed back to the coach our stash of Singapore dollars was spent – and yes, we bought one of those 'lucky' cats that wave their arm.

As we arrived back at the cruise terminal we were treated to another tropical rain storm. Fortunately, we just managed to get back onto Aurora and shelter before it started. It was 1:00 so we trotted quickly to get some lunch, before putting our new treasures away.

Across on the other side of the terminal there was a Royal Caribbean ship just beginning to let her new passengers come aboard. This was the 'Mariner of the Seas, very similar in size to Aurora. I suspected we would both be leaving at a similar time this evening.

I did try having a few minutes on the balcony in the warm sunshine, but the rain came again. It was no surprise really: we were just over one degree north of the equator, and this was the monsoon season. At least the rain was warm.

Our departure from Singapore was delayed for over an hour because a number of passengers didn't return their passports. I will be polite and say that they must have missed the repeated announcements, but I think it was more because several people were stubbornly ignorant. The Singapore authorities won't let a ship leave until they have seen with their own eyes that all passengers are back on the ship, and passports are safely locked away.

Many of us would have preferred the ship to name and shame the worst of the offenders, who refused to comply for over an hour.

The dress code was casual tonight, and it was time to check out the new people at our dinner table.

Well, the new people turned out to be a couple who had simply requested a change of dinner time. Hence it wasn't the surprise that we were expecting. As we sat and introduced ourselves, Aurora was finally leaving Singapore. It is a beautiful city with so many historical buildings hidden away below glass and glitzy skyscrapers. As I said earlier, the architects seem to have thrown away rulers and set-squares, and instead, slopes, wavy lines, and non-symmetry appears to be the normal. Of course, they have made mistakes. They copied two segments of the Sydney Opera house as stand-alone buildings, but the excess of glass created ovens that people couldn't survive in. The engineers overcame the problem by fitting metal segments that cover the outside of the glass buildings making them look like shells of an armadillo. They look nothing like the Sydney Opera House, but are iconic buildings in their own right.

With dinner over, and after getting to know the new people a little, we went our separate ways. First an early evening quiz which we won, and then onwards to the theatre for the Headliner's 'Modern Romantics' show. This was excellent, and only the second time we have seen it.

The Captain promised a change in the sea conditions and he wasn't fibbing. Aurora began to bump and thump around in seas described as "moderate" and a wind that he suggested would be a Force 4. We would be sailing along the southern edge of a nearby low-pressure system. This weather would be with us for a while.

After our trip to the theatre, five of the dinner six met up in Masquerade's for the late evening quiz. Rosemary wasn't feeling well again. This flu virus was proving to be a persistent little devil. The quiz was hosted by DJ Martin and was quite a good test for everyone. We failed to win this time, but we were very close.

It was bedtime, and our first in our new bedroom while actually sailing. It was going to be a bumpy night, but I had taken a little white pill and felt quite confident of a good night's sleep.

So that was the second sector of the world cruise over.

Our various illnesses, plus the less-than-special tours, meant it hadn't been the most amazing couple of weeks. It had however still been special, and we had a wonderful time. The third sector would be taking us towards Australia, culminating in a second visit to Sydney, a city that is my favourite port in the world….so far.

Sector 3 – Singapore to Sydney

The countries we visited:

- Indonesia
- Australia

Tuesday 14th February – Sea Day

The temperature peaked at 27°C today on our new balcony.

I had a very comfortable (if a little noisy at times) night, and slept very well. There was nowhere near the same level of noise as we had from the balcony door in our previous cabin.

During the night we crossed the equator and were now sailing south-east towards our next stop at Semarang in Indonesia tomorrow.

It was raining. The wind walloped into Aurora at a Force 6 or 7 and the sea appeared distinctly angry with our ship for daring to cross the magic line without permission from the Gods.

When I said it was raining, I need to add that it was truly tropical precipitation. The huge drops bounced off the open decks, and to get to breakfast we had to paddle. But at least the rain was warm.

Today was Valentine's Day. And no, I hadn't bought a card or any very expensive roses for Deb. She is the love of my life but we have never sunk to the commercial depths of this celebration.

However, Deb did have a present, as the Captain sent every cabin a single red rose.

After breakfast we went to our 'office' to catch up on diaries and journals. By the time we had finished our paperwork for the morning I noticed the rain had subsided a little. Aurora was travelling very fast to presumably avoid the worst of the promised bad weather.

At 10:00 we went to a port talk on Bali where we had such a strange and disappointing day five years ago. We had booked a tour for this island before leaving home, but after the talk we cancelled it: it just wasn't right for us. Worse still, we couldn't see anything on offer that interested us enough to put up with a 45-minute tender ride each way. Our day in Bali would be a simple *'stay at home'* day.

By the time we left the theatre the weather had really brightened up and the sunshine was becoming hot again. This was good news, as Aurora would be honouring Neptune with the traditional 'Crossing the Line' ceremony around the pool during the afternoon.

After a quick lunch I joined the choir again and thoroughly enjoyed myself, even if a few of the notes in the new songs stretched my voice a little.

Deb and I ignored the 'Crossing the Line' ceremony, and while Deb enjoyed a Salsa session, I had a game of cricket. Goodness it became hot, but today it wasn't the oppressive humid heat that we had been suffering recently.

We noticed a change in the passengers, with a large number of people talking with that so-recognisable Australian accent. They are such lovely people, and a joy to meet, but they really do speak very loudly when having a private chat with their country-mates.

With our exercise and afternoon tea over, we returned to the cabin and found a letter warning us that tomorrow's trip in Semarang had been extended by over an hour to include new places to visit, and some refreshments – and all at no extra cost. With that piece of good news to cheer us up, we lazed on the cool balcony before having our showers. The rest prepared us for the formal dress code evening that would begin with the third 'Welcome on Board' cocktail party.

The cocktail party was a real hoot. We met up with Angie and Richard, and in 30 minutes succeeded in drinking far too many glasses of 'fizz', and even left with full glasses of red wine each for the dinner table. I was slightly inebriated.

No, I was very inebriated!

After dinner we had a delightful show in the theatre from a group of young men called Ukebox, who play various ukuleles and sing a wide range of songs from pop to heavy rock. We had seen them on our last cruise and knew what to expect, and they were brilliant. Yes, it was the same act as we saw in September, but wonderfully different to so many of the turns we see on the ships. Fortunately after our recommendation, our dinner table mates also agreed that it was a really good show.

From the theatre Deb and I headed towards Carmen's for a dance, but on the way we said "good evening" to Mike Mullane, the Entertainment Manager. We had a candid chat with him in the corridor, and we expressed our concerns about the lack of entertainment hosts, and the abundance of vocalists. We also told him of our disappointment that Café Bordeaux had been changed to the Glass House, and stood virtually empty all day. He listened and agreed with many of our moans, but we know the decisions are made far away from his influence.

We did eventually get to Carmen's but decided to give dancing a miss and went for a late night drink in Anderson's instead.

Other entertainment tonight came from a young couple who are classical musicians, with the man playing the trumpet alongside his wife on the piano: interesting mix!

Also during this sector there were some new people on board giving talks. A lady historian (Jane Robinson) was going to talk about successful women, another person (Clive Catchpole) would talk about the wildlife of this area of the world. Finally Martin Roberts from BBC's "Homes under the Hammer" had something in store for us about his life in house buying, as well as his television programme and an appearance on "I'm a Celebrity…"

And there were rumours that another comic had boarded Aurora to cheer us up.

It was late, and time for bed. Aurora was only a few hours away from an early morning rendezvous with the pilot, to assist us into the Indonesian port of Semarang for a 7:00 arrival.

Wednesday 15th February – Semarang, Indonesia

Today it was a little warmer at 28°C in our back garden. Actually, that is really very hot.

One quite strange thing was that although we had sailed further to the east than Singapore, the clocks went back an hour during the night. So today we are at GMT +7 hours. The variations in time zones can be a little confusing sometimes.

I woke during the night with a hangover to remind me that we had a very pleasant evening. I also had a seriously sore little finger where I caught a ball very awkwardly playing cricket yesterday.

Just before 7:00 I switched off the alarm clock and put the kettle on. A quick glance through the curtains told me we were nowhere near our port, and Aurora was going extremely slowly. The Captain had warned us yesterday evening that conditions needed to be just right to get us safely into this port, because the approach channel is shallow and narrow. Any wind would make it hazardous, and it looked like we were struggling.

So we were very late arriving, meaning all the tours were set back by an hour.

Eventually we were allowed to get off and hundreds of us rushed along the dockside to find our coaches. We also rushed because of a horrible stench on the dockside that nobody managed to identify, but which we all suspected was probably a little hazardous.

Our tour was called '*Semarang at a Glance*' and it was quite a shock to have a police car at the front of the four coaches on this same tour. Even with the police escort the journey was sometimes a nightmare, with the vast numbers of motorbikes and cars whose drivers seemed to have no appreciation of what other road users were doing around them.

Anyway, our trip wound its way around the island of Java for five and a half hours. It began with several miles of less than attractive lanes with examples of how the local people struggle to live. As with some of our earlier visits, it wasn't the cleanest vista, with dusty roads and random rubbish tips as major features.

Eventually our convoy reached our first stop at a Roman Catholic Church that was built by the Dutch and is now used by Protestants as well. Not overly interesting, and there was a major battle between the different guides as to who was going to describe it, which turned into multiple descriptions being shouted out at the same time. This wasn't a good omen for the rest of the day.

Having found our coach again in the nightmare called an Indonesian street, we went to a massive shopping mall to look around for 45 minutes. It was very modern with lots of high-end outlets, though every shop assistant appeared to be more interested in their mobile phones rather than the influx of British tourists.

We didn't buy anything, and the lack of bags coming back to the coach suggested we were not the only ones to keep hold of our money.

Then our police escort threaded its way through the busy roads and up into the nearby hillside to a Buddhist temple complex, which was stunning. Our guide took us around the brightly-coloured temples and described the differences between the shapes and figures that adorned the buildings. Deb and I saw many examples of these temples five years ago, and they still remain a delight to look at.

We were rounded up again and sat back in the coach to move on to a small village where we would be eating. The journey began with the police car closing off a dual carriageway to allow our convoy of coaches to make a U-turn across the four lanes of the road, and go back down the hill. That showed us just how important tourism is to this region. We now started to leave the relatively built-up area we had been in, and the coaches took us into the depths of a rain forest along narrow and dusty lanes.

Our lunch venue was a complex of open wooden buildings covered with some form of leaves as the roof, and partly walled with reeds and more leaves. As we arrived it began to rain, and we all dashed into the dining area where we were offered a drink and various plates of local food. The food was interesting, if a little bit of a mystery as to what it was. Sadly our welcoming rain turned into a full-on tropical storm that dumped thousands of gallons of rain on us for the next hour. The village was also a small factory for local crafts, so we managed to stay dry by rushing between the huts in plastic ponchos given to us by our guide. A look around the factory was less than inspirational, and it preceded a mad dash to the coaches which left everyone wet, and many soaked to the skin.

Off we went again, to another temple complex that was even more spectacular than the first one.

Semarang is a beautiful place to visit with lots of older colonial-style buildings. It also has a high number of churches and temples to reflect a very religious nation. Sadly, like our experiences in India, it is not one of the cleanest places we have visited around the world, and there are a very high number of poorer people who simply exist, while others nearby are living a very good lifestyle.

The island of Java really suffers from its tropical climate. The monsoon rains in the higher parts of the island cause floods and landslides that regularly damage the road infrastructure. More importantly the floods wash away the soil at the lower coastal areas, and the port of Semarang is getting significantly lower every year. The only solution is to plant teak trees with root structures that will stabilise the soil, but they grow very slowly. There doesn't appear to be any quick fix available to the people of this island.

As we left the final temple (called Sam Poo Kong) we thought we had finished for the day, but our guide said we were going to a museum now. Several of us questioned this, and eventually our coach broke away from the convoy and headed back to the dockside and Aurora. We were exhausted, and a lot of wet clothes needed to be dried.

For the first time on this trip our mobile phone was used, as today was the Golden Wedding Anniversary of my brother Ernest and his wife Joyce. It was only a short call to wish them the best, and to let them know that we were both thinking of them on this very special day.

There was another first this evening as we had invited our dinner table mates around for a pre-dinner drink as a sort of "cabin warming". It was also a chance to get through some of the wine we had won over the last couple of weeks. The plan had been to use our balcony, but we had another tropical shower making it a soggy out-of-bounds area.

Better luck next time!

Richard and Angie were eating in the Beach House tonight, and we planned to go there tomorrow. Hence our dinner table would be shorthanded for a couple of nights.

Aurora was late leaving the port because of a seriously delayed tour, but at around 6:30 she let go her ropes and set off for a day at sea before our arrival in Bali on Friday morning.

There was nothing on in the theatre or in Carmen's to interest us this evening. A female singer (Helen Ward-Jackson) gave an Adele tribute show in Carmen's, and Monique Montez at the other end of the ship offered us yet more singing.

Instead we all met up at 9:30 for the late evening mind-boggling in Masquerade's, with a challenge from Coral that appeared to be loosely about literature. We lost by a couple of points, but kept up our proud record of doing very well.

Deb and I said goodnight to our friends and made our way to bed. One of the major things on my mind tonight was a very sore little finger. It won't affect my singing tomorrow lunchtime but it might mean having to give cricket a miss.

Thursday 16th February – Sea Day

It was a lovely 27°C at 7:30 in the morning, creeping up to a humid maximum of 28° during the day.

The warmth of the sun was obvious, but it was hiding behind clouds when I got up. The garden was smooth and a milky green colour.

I had another rather restful night but was woken early by our neighbours, who seem to think 6:00 is a perfect time to get up while on holiday. Those of you who know about cruising will know the problem of bedside drawers that are very difficult to close without slamming them. Our neighbours didn't appear to even try to close them carefully.

Never mind, perhaps we wake them up when we come to bed late.

After breakfast Deb decided to have a swim and I lay nearby on a lounger in the early warmth of the day. Once dried and changed, Deb joined me for 30 minutes. There were spits and spots of light rain in the air, but it wasn't affecting our enjoyment of just relaxing as the ship came to life around us.

There was time for a cup of coffee before an hour in the theatre listening to Crystal talk about our first Australian stop in Freemantle and the nearby city of Perth. We had nothing booked for here.

When we came out after the talk, we decided to do our own thing and simply visit a few places in Fremantle, as well as taking the opportunity to do a bit of shopping. If we got really bored we could always take a river boat ride to nearby Perth to at least take a peek at the capital city of Western Australia.

Deb strapped up my poorly little finger against the next one with a plaster, to stop me moving the painful digit too much. The problem was that almost everything I did involved bending the offending finger. The plaster just about stopped me moving the knuckle, but it was still annoying.

At midday the clocks bounced forwards an hour (GMT +8) in readiness for Bali tomorrow. That meant it was time for choir practice and I had an enjoyable 50 minutes, except for a few painfully high notes in one of the songs called "Hallelujah".

As I came out of Carmen's, Deb arrived for her Salsa class. I trotted off to the Grab-and-Go counter for a sandwich for my lunch, and made my apologies to the cricket group.

Poorly finger stopped play.

When Deb came back from Salsa, it was almost 3:00, so time for a cup of tea. Tonight we were eating in the Beach House so we also indulged in an '*itzy teeny ween*y' snack to keep us going.

My finger continued to annoy me, so I gave in and went to see the medical team again. I didn't think I'd broken anything, but at least they would be able to strap the fingers together more securely than with strips of plaster.

It was an expensive 45 minutes.

The doctor's consultation plus X-rays cost a lot of money, and the only outcome was that my fingers were taped together slightly more efficiently than before. The x-ray wasn't totally clear and it was sent to Southampton for the experts to take a look, but I am sure the local thoughts were that I am just a wimp with a poorly ickle finger.

The evening was delightful and cheered me up.

Our meal in the Beach House was delicious, and we had learned our lesson from the past about trying to eat too much. We went straight to the main course and then had a pudding to finish off. I think this was the first time we had ever ordered and enjoyed a pudding in any of the select dining rooms.

We finished eating in time to get to the theatre to listen to Ukebox giving their final show. It was brilliant once again and there was a much deserved standing ovation at the end.

From the theatre we squeezed our way through the crowds to Masquerade's for the late night quiz. It should have been hosted by the new entertainment team member (Aaron) who came on in Singapore, but he arrived ill and was recuperating in his cabin. Meanwhile the existing short-handed team continued to work their socks off.

The quiz was actually run by DJ Martin and we did very well except for a round on flags that left us flummoxed.

We didn't need more wine anyway.

Aurora was slowly sailing across the Sea of Bali to the port of Benoa on the Indonesian island of Bali. We know that we will be woken early again with the sound of anchors being dropped, and tender boats being launched.

Goodnight.

Friday 17th February – Benoa, Indonesia

Just like the last few weeks, it is a hot and humid morning with temperatures rising to 29°C.

Last night while Deb was catching up on Facebook, she saw a photo of our grandson Oliver, dressed up in a winter jacket and a hat. It reminded us that we are living a dream of a warm winter while our family and friends were putting up with the usual damp and cold British climate.

As expected, the rumble of anchor chains was our alarm clock at 6:00, but the neighbours still managed to beat the ship noises by a few minutes.

Aurora was busy with passengers getting ready to go on tours as we went to breakfast. The buffet was full of tired people eating, while also sorting out picnics to take ashore. We were in no hurry as we had no plans to leave Aurora today.

With breakfast over, Deb put a load in a washing machine, then we both changed and went for a swim. This was my first venture into the water on this cruise, and I think it was probably also the first time for many months.

I might have been able to walk quite happily, and even play cricket contentedly for an hour, but the swimming left me breathless and panting after five minutes. As Deb and I learned when training to be swimming teachers, this is an exercise that really tests and works the body.

My next plan was to have a walk around Promenade Deck, but of course the tendering process meant the deck was closed off. I hadn't added to my marathon total now for several days, but tomorrow would be a sea day and no excuse not to get a couple of miles done.

Instead of walking, I sat in the Crow's Nest doing a bit of office work for a few minutes while I looked out over the beautiful bay that we were anchored in. The island looked green and lush, with very few buildings more than four or five stories high. There was a sensational view of hills or mountains in the distance, with fluffy layers of cloud part of the way up the tallest ones. I could also see a stretch of the coastline with the occasional golden sandy beach. In the water pleasure boats of all colours and sizes criss-crossed the bay, and there were a couple of parachutes being pulled by speed boats to give the tourists a thrill. Every few minutes an aeroplane disturbed the peace as it came in to land, bringing yet more tourists to this Indonesian holiday island.

At 09:30 a call for the second batch of tender passengers was announced. It was quite a distance to shore and our little orange bumper boats took 20 to 30 minutes to make the journey. There had been one load taken by a much larger local pleasure craft earlier, but it hadn't been back for more.

In the small port I could see a rather exclusive white Regent Cruise Line ship that was small enough to dock, but I think Aurora at anchor probably looked equally spectacular from the shore.

Then with hardly any warning a tropical squall started. I hoped it wouldn't spoil the day for Aurora's passengers for more than a few minutes.

That was my cue to go and help Deb with the washing.

Well, once the washing was clean, dry, and ironed, our day in Benoa was a lazy one.

We had an hour in the sunshine but gave in when another tropical shower crept up on us. We retired to the cabin although the rain soon stopped. I watched tender boats coming and going, and the local craft was again being used. The water state became a bit choppy and our fleet of little ferries were bouncing rather seriously for a while.

Aurora slowly turned on her anchors giving us different views every hour or so. This can be quite confusing when (like me) you doze off. One moment there's a view of the shore, then all that can be seen is the sea.

As the afternoon moved towards dinner time, the Regent cruise ship gave some farewell '*toots*' to the island of Bali and slowly made her way out into the bay and turned for her next destination. I finally managed to see her name: she was the Seven Seas Voyager, with five decks of luxury cabins.

The final tenders brought our fellow passengers home, and it was time for Deb and I to have a shower to freshen our bodies from the humid stickiness. At 6:00

the Captain gave his normal evening update of life on Aurora, and announced that we would be leaving late. One of the tours was running late and wasn't due back for another 30 minutes.

I don't think we had left any port on-time so far.

At dinner it was just us plus Richard and Angie. Robin and Rosemary and our two other dinner mates were on that late tour. Richard and Angie had spent the day at a local hotel complex where they had a bit of relaxation on the beach and around the pools.

In the theatre we had a bit of a change with a mind reader called Anthony Laye. OK, so he was really a magician but he gave a very good show, and was impressive with his skills at making people do what he wanted them to do. Of course sometimes the person chosen from the audience can make the show a success, and he managed to pick two really amusing characters.

We rounded off the evening with a Masquerade's challenge where we caught up with Robin and Rosemary and heard about their really enjoyable tour, even if it was late getting home.

Aurora had now started its southerly trip towards Australia, and there would be several days at sea before we reached Fremantle.

Three Sea Days to Australia

Saturday 18th February

Early in the morning it was 31°C on the balcony but that dropped by two degrees before lunch.

Now that we were sailing south, our port side cabin enjoyed the morning sunshine streaming onto it. The humidity was still high and the mirrors steamed up when the balcony door was opened. When we read our books out there we had to wipe and wave our glasses for several minutes for them to acclimatise and stay clear.

Deb worked off her breakfast by going for a swim, and I lay nearby in the sunshine watching her. Eventually she joined me and we relaxed in the sunshine almost an hour before it was time for the port talk on Adelaide. Even with a tour booked, listening to the talks was always time well spent, to check we had made the right decision. Robin sat behind us and reminded me that choir practice was at 12:30 today.

There was plenty of time for a coffee and cake in Raffles, and a chance to freshen up in the cabin.

This was my third session of the choir, but the tickly cough always returned after the voice had had a work out. Our repertoire was coming on very well, with "Memories", "Hallelujah", "Over the Rainbow", "Cheek to Cheek", "Chiquitita", "One Moment in Time", and medleys from 'The King and I' and 'West Side Story'. A few days remained before we were to perform in public, but Robin agreed with me that the songs were getting more complex as the cruise progressed.

After a good old sing-song, it was time to rehydrate my throat before going to play cricket. Although my finger was still strapped, I was confident that I could play without doing it any further damage. As I suspected, it proved difficult not to instinctively use my right hand, but I came away undamaged.

The rest of the afternoon was spent resting before another formal night. We could have gone and watched the Headliners with a matinee performance of 'Killer Queen' in Carmen's, but the warm balcony and a comfortable bed was more appealing.

Dinner proved to be a good meal, except that I managed to drip a tomato-based sauce over my dress shirt, so after finishing the meal, I scuttled back to the cabin to change into a fresh one. The stain looked bad enough that it might mean saying goodbye to the shirt.

Deb and I didn't bother with the theatre cabaret, which was yet another vocalist, called Stevie B. Instead we decided to have a quiet read of our books in the Crow's Nest for a few minutes. The karaoke-style singer, Lyn Frederick, was there when we arrived, but we put up with her singing knowing she would soon be going for a break.

I may sound a little harsh on Lyn Frederick, and I am sure many people enjoyed her singing. We are happy with background music in the lounges, but Lyn was performing a full set of tunes at a volume that couldn't be ignored. Her followers applauded after each one, and she also talked between songs making this a show, rather than background music.

Later there was a Ball in Carmen's hosted by the dance instructors. We had plans to go along to see if we could spot a friend from the past. When we lived in Stone in Staffordshire a few years ago, Patrick used to teach us to dance. He had now qualified as a dance teacher and we met him in one of the lifts a couple of days ago. He was on board for a holiday, but perhaps there was an element of checking out the possibilities of a working holiday to come.

We didn't bother with the dancing, and instead met up with the rest of the table gang for the 9:30 quiz. Tonight it was all about identifying iconic video clips from Olympic Games. There was a lot of moaning from the newly arrived Australian passengers who questioned some of the answers, and complained that the quizzes were biased towards the British.

To reiterate, Aurora is a *British* ship and the majority of the passengers were *British*.

Anyway we thought we had done very well in the quiz, but as usual there was a team who upset our plans to increase the wine stocks.

Time for bed.

Sunday 19th February

It was a very warm 28C° on the balcony today, and the Officer of the Watch predicted 30° to come later, as he gave his early report.

The ship was pitching a bit and the swimming pools were a little rough, so Deb didn't bother with a swim. Instead we lay in the hot sunshine, and with no sign of the humidity dropping, we welcomed the cooling breeze on the upper deck giving us some relief.

Later we had to be ready to go through the obligatory face-to-face Australian Immigration interview, so we made time for a cup of coffee before being called to the queue. The snake of passengers started just outside of Masquerade's and stretched all the way to Carmen's where the three Australian officials were working. They turned out to be quite human, and smiled as they said hello to us. The process may have taken quite a while, but it was painless.

Very soon we would be having the American Immigration face-to-face interview, and we didn't expect it to be quite as pleasant, and would probably take a lot longer.

Anyway, with the cheery *"G'day mate"* over, Deb went to a port talk on Kangaroo Island, and I went for a Prom Deck walk. As I hadn't been out there for several days, I managed seven laps, bringing my Marathon around the World total to a little over 13 miles. This was rating as being one of the slowest ever marathons, and the ship was sailing further than I was walking in the same time.

After lunch we had a few minutes relaxation before Deb went to a talk by Martin Roberts about his time on "I'm a Celebrity...." and I went for a hot and sticky hour of cricket.

It was really hot today and I was soaked through with sweat. When I got back to the cabin I had to change my clothes....and I mean all of them.

Deb wasn't overly impressed by Martin Roberts's public speaking ability.

At 3:45 in the afternoon, I spotted a little bit of land on the port side. Having checked our navigation information and the map, it appeared to be the point where Australia is at its widest (west to east) at a place named the North West

Cape. It is latitude 21° 54' south and we were sailing almost due south at 17.7 knots.

The temperature was still 30°, and the sea had become a lot lumpier than we had experienced for some time. Aurora was pitching enough to make things rattle, and the movement was confusing my brain just a little.

We still had a long way to go around this vast country before we would reach Fremantle on Tuesday.

Oh, and there were lots of flying fish amusing us, and even the birds have turned up to make the most of these tempting snacks.

Tonight there was a second show in the theatre from vocalist Helen Ward Jackson, singing tributes to various divas.

No thanks.

In Carmen's there was the return of Anthony Laye with his mind reading act. Deb and I planned to go and watch him, but eventually we met up with our dinner mates for a spot of Trivial Pursuit in the Crow's Nest followed by a musical quiz in Masquerade's. It was all about records that should never have been released – novelty ones in the main - and we won!

Although we impressed most people with our musical knowledge, our musical tastes were seriously doubted.

As we eventually made our way to bed, we witnessed a very special moment. Just by accident I looked out of the balcony window and spotted some lightning. 'Nature' had decided to give us a welcome show to Australia.

Wow!

The flashes and forks of energy were visible all the way along the port side of the ship. It was sensational, with the sky lighting up on the coast of Western Australia. I think virtually everyone on the ship saw it, and the display went on for well over two hours to gasps of amazement.

We decided that this was the southern hemisphere's equivalent of the 'Northern Lights', and whilst less colourful it was a very good spectacle and compared quite favourably to Aurora Borealis. Perhaps it could have been called *'Aurora by-Australis'*.

Goodnight.

....

Monday 20th February
Just a cool (ish) 24°C today.

We woke and discovered Aurora was still bumping and pitching in officially "moderate" seas, due to quite a strong south-east wind. It was uncomfortable, as this was the third day of having to work our legs hard to maintain balance.

The TV navigation channel said we were 113° east, meaning we have travelled a third of the way around the globe from the London longitude.

It was too rough in the pools for Deb to swim so we began our day with a mile's walk around the Prom Deck, putting me over the 14 mile mark now.

From there it was a spot of office work, and a port talk on Melbourne. We didn't have a tour for this city yet, and Crystal said we didn't really need one, as Melbourne (her home city) is easy to get around while seeing the highlights.

After a quick lunch it was time for choir practice, and we had a good session with the 'King and I' medley (which I now recognise) and Abba's "Chiquitita". Meanwhile Deb went and took part in the Battle of the Sexes quiz.

With a short interval for a rest, it was time for Deb to go to Salsa, and I was off to cricket.

Although I was really enjoying the exercise and competition of the cricket sessions, it began to be rather predictable with the same people on the same teams winning the matches each day, and with the same people winning the batting 'golden sticker' rewards. My gripe was the way that the rules of this cruise-ship version of the game had been changed, which was taking away the element of chance. Sadly the art and technique of bowling was being ignored, and now almost everyone was simply throwing the ball very fast and hard, at the batsman as if it was a game of baseball.

This was hardly describable as cricket, and certainly not the game I had played on cruise ships for many years. I still wanted the exercise, but I wasn't sure I wanted the cricket anymore.

Late in the afternoon, the sea became even lumpier, and Aurora began to roll as well as pitching. My stomach maintained its dignity, but I was feeling uncomfortable.

There was just us, Angie and Richard at dinner, and after eating we rushed to Masquerade's for the early quiz. It was on general knowledge….and we won.

From our successful brain test, we went on to the theatre for the Headliners show, 'Stop in the Name of Love'. Deb really enjoys Motown music, and this show is a good one.

We finished the evening with a late drink in Anderson's and then it was bedtime.

Aurora was still moving in a quite angry sea as we continued overnight for our stop tomorrow morning in Fremantle.

Deb and I were really looking forward to landing in Australia again after some wonderful experiences five years before.

Tuesday 21st February – Fremantle, Australia

Temperature today was 18°C in the morning, rising to 22° during the afternoon. Hang on, this is late summer and I thought it was supposed to be hot and sunny in this country!

Aurora began her noisy docking process, waking me up at 7:00 with side thrusters roaring as the ship manoeuvred into her mooring spot.

Fremantle was our first of five stops in the wonderful country of Australia, culminating in the sector ending in Sydney on 2nd March.

This city is more often thought of as the maritime gateway to the larger city of Perth. But rather than travelling the short distance to Perth, we were spending our day in the smaller Fremantle area for a little bit of exploration, but more importantly to do a bit of shopping.

And we planned to get our hair cut.

The Deputy Captain made the official announcement about our arrival at 8:00, and as well as the usual security and safety issues, he reminded everyone not to take any food etc. ashore. For those of you unaware of Australian rules, you are not allowed to take in items of food or vegetation. The country is determined to reduce the chances of bugs and diseases being brought in accidently.

Deb and I left Aurora at about 8:45 and were soon on the free shuttle for the short ride to the central area of the city. After a 10-minute walk through the quiet streets we found a hairdresser just opening her shop. We gave her a few minutes to sort herself out, before sitting down and having our hair cut. She was quite thrilled to have early customers and was fascinated to have someone from a cruise ship. By the time we left an hour or so later she was even happier, with another couple from Aurora waiting and another passenger who had popped in to ask about a trim.

Feeling much fresher, and lighter, we walked around some shops, had a cup of coffee, and then made our way to the historical site of the Fremantle Prison.

This visit turned out to be a really lovely couple of hours. Fremantle Prison was built by British convicts in the 1850s who were rewarded for their labours by becoming the first inmates. It then housed later arrivals of convicts until Britain gave up sending our low-lifes overseas. The building then became the primary Western Australian prison for serious criminals, and although changes were made, it continued as the main prison for the State until 1991.

Our guide was really knowledgeable and showed a passion for his job, with lots of humour as he told the story of the prison through the decades. We really enjoyed seeing this example of an early Australian prison, especially as our intention was to get to Alcatraz in San Francisco later in the cruise, where we could compare the two historic high-security jails.

The tour ended in the punishment block of the prison. After looking at the grimness of the solitary confinement cells, we moved on to the nearby whipping frame for prisoners that confinement failed to subdue. Our little group of explorers then made a short walk to the ultimate punishment cell: the gallows for the most serious of criminals. I don't know if it was just the heat, but our guide took his cap off as he described the scene and explained how the hangings were performed. I like to think he was showing some respect for those who had passed through this room.

With our wonderful tour complete, we had a quick toasted sandwich lunch at the prison café before retracing our steps to the shuttle bus.

Back on Aurora we volunteered to have a photo taken. We had also had one when we left the ship earlier, and now had 'before and after' pictures of our haircuts. Deb and I were regular customers of the gangway photographers, as we had bought a package which included all pictures taken on the cruise.

With our latest souvenirs thrown onto the bed, we relaxed for a moment with a cup of tea, and then set off again into Fremantle. This time we had a relatively short walk from our floating home to a shopping centre called "Coles". Here we stocked up on soft drink, crisps, chocolate, and medicines, which included some new sea-sickness pills. The walk back to the ship in the warm sunshine was a little more difficult as we carried our heavy carrier bags.

We were back on board by 3:00 and this had been a delightful visit to this lovely city. Deb took advantage of a quiet pool to have a swim, while I just relaxed on the balcony until she returned and woke me up.

Aurora wasn't due to leave until 9:30 tonight, and we had considered going out for a meal. This could have been a pleasant change but we decided it had already been a good day, and we hadn't seen any restaurants on our walk to tempt us, so we stayed put.

There was just four of us for dinner. Robin and Rosemary, as well as the new couple, were eating elsewhere. So after refuelling we went for the early evening quiz, and we won for the first time in quite a while.

More wine for our quiz team's booze cellar!

In the theatre we had an amusing 45 minutes listening to William Caulfield with some new jokes and stories. Unfortunately his act contained several jokes we have already heard. But while we laughed at the new jokes, the sector's newer passengers were extremely amused by the ones we had already heard. Even this made us smile.

From the theatre we trotted back to Masquerade's for a late night gameshow that they called "Scatterbrain". The host nominated a series of topics that we had to find examples of, and then gave us the first letter of those objects. For example we had to find *'things that grow'* beginning with the letter *'P'*. The team who came up with the most answers that no one else had thought of, won a point for that round.

It was a slightly manic game. Teams thought up various growing objects, including some unusual answers, but mainly every conceivable plant beginning with 'P'. And believe me there were a lot!

In hindsight, this possibly wasn't the best game for this audience. There were moans, and outright objections about the validity of some answers, and it didn't flow very well. A lot of people left early in frustration or boredom. We struggled on and actually came second to team *"Densa"*, who had become our quizzing Nemesis. On balance this wasn't a very pleasant, amusing, or culturally rewarding 45 minutes.

What a surprise - Aurora was late leaving again.

This time it was because the evening shift of stevedores was sent to tie up a container ship that took priority over us leaving. We were away by about 10:30 and as we reached the open seas it was obvious that it wasn't going to be a smooth ride. Aurora was rocking and rolling again, and the Captain had warned us of a 3-4 metre swell, with the sea state officially classed as 'moderate'.

As we went to bed, it wasn't easy to walk in straight lines, and everything that could flex was creaking. It was not going to be a quiet or smooth night.

Three Sea Days to Adelaide

Wednesday 22nd February

The temperature was 18°C when we got up, and hardly went above 20° all day.

It was a horribly noisy night. Aurora fought her way valiantly through an angry and confused sea, with huge rolling lumps of water tossing us around. I didn't feel ill, but I did struggle to stay in the bed at times. The new sea-sickness pills from Fremantle were in use, and although I felt uncomfortable with the movement, the dignity of my stomach was maintained.

With breakfast over we had a quiet and relatively stable 30 minutes in Charlies. Then we went for a walk: my total is now over 15 miles.

A few minutes after our exercise we were off to the theatre for the port talk about Sydney. After some deliberation we decided to stick to our original plans and do our own thing when we get there in roughly a week's time.

At midday the clocks went on an hour again to GMT +9. I went off to the choir practice as Deb went to the Battle of the Sexes, and after our regular early afternoon sessions were over, we went for a late lunch.

I didn't bother with the cricket. I had really lost interest in trying to defend myself against someone throwing a ball at me without the slightest hint of a cricketing bowling action.

During the afternoon we did consider going to find some warm sunshine, but Aurora was still bouncing around. So we simply rested in the cabin, and I even had a bath to soak away the aches in my legs. The act of automatically trying to correct the movement of the ship can give leg muscles quite a hammering...well it does for this 'land-lubber' anyway.

Tonight, was the third formal evening of the sector, so a set of our posh clothes were hung ready to put on after our afternoon individual quiz.

... no stickers for us again

Dressed appropriately we strolled down to Anderson's for a glass of prosecco before dinner. This had become quite a regular thing, and gave us a chance to chat to each other about our day, and to watch the familiar faces that frequent this wonderful lounge. Although we enjoyed a drink, we quickly decided to decline the canapes, although we did like the glass of savoury nibbles that appeared each day.

It was a full house at dinner for the first time in a while.

There was an afternoon matinee of 'My Generation' from the Headliners in the theatre, with the evening entertainment coming from a female vocalist from New Zealand called Ali Harper. Her show was a tribute to "Legendary Divas". Whoever booked the acts should think a little more: this was the second act in a week to feature tributes to divas.

In Carmen's there was a chance for a dance at the formal night ball, but my aching legs preferred the idea of something less energetic. So with dinner over we dashed to Masquerade's for the quiz, and having lost again, the six of us decided to go to the Crow's Nest and spend some time playing Trivial Pursuit. We also drank a bottle of red wine from our winnings stock.

After an hour in the Crow's Nest, we gave up trying to win the final cheeses and returned to Masquerade's again for the late evening challenge. Tonight it was a version of the TV panel show "A Question of Sport", and we thought we had a good chance to do well here.

Oops, we were soundly beaten by several other teams.

It was time for bed again. The ship was still rocking around, and creaking as we continued on our way towards the Port of Adelaide. There was a further two sea days yet before we arrived in this city in the state of South Australia. I hoped the weather would brighten up a little and the sea would calm down.

Goodnight.

....

Thursday 23rd February
Sadly the weather had not improved overnight, and the temperature only managed 18°C.

It was another bumpy and creaky night, but perhaps not as bad as the previous one. Deb and I slept, and in fact we didn't wake at our usual time, it was 8:00 before we had an early morning cuppa.

It was cloudy as we made our way to breakfast, and the open deck was almost deserted apart from a couple who were becoming very familiar to the passengers. They always appeared settled on their loungers very early each day. The loungers were always in the same position on starboard side at the rear of the Riviera Pool on the first level of the raised tiers.

Let me stress that they did nothing wrong, but they did become a common topic of discussions. I named them as the Mayor and Mayoress of the Riviera Pool. They obviously loved the sunshine and spent all day in the same spot absorbing the golden rays. Only when it was overly cold, or raining heavily did they change their habit. Then they would move undercover and wrap themselves in Wimbledon Tennis towels. Early on cold mornings their towels would often be used while they sat on the loungers eating their breakfast from the buffet. But as soon as was possible, they were stretched out and changing their skin colour.

After breakfast we went to our "office" in Charlies and updated diaries while the ship woke up. All too soon the shop brought out the temporary tables to tempt the passengers to part with their money. Today the offer was cheap jewellery and watches...again!

With the clerical work done, we went for another mile walk around the Prom Deck. That brought me up to 16 miles.

This was a busy morning as we then went to the restaurant for an 'Around the World' coffee morning. The cakes on offer weren't special but it was a chance to seek out new people to talk to for half an hour.

At midday the clocks bounced forward again and it became GMT +10 hours on board Aurora. Of course that meant we missed our regular lunch time, with me going to the choir practice and Deb taking part in the 'Battle of the Sexes' lunchtime challenge.

As the choir practice ended in Carmen's, Deb came in for her Salsa session, and we next met up again in time to have our afternoon cuppa and a little cake.

With the temperature struggling to warm up, the option of sun worship was forgotten, so late in the afternoon we logged onto the internet. We did this every few days to catch up with any news from home, publish our diaries on the blog site, and occasionally to check on our bank activities. Storm 'Doris' was just beginning to bash Britain and the wind speeds near to where we live were forecast to be extremely high. It puts the situation into context when we are quietly moaning about a lack of sunshine.

Captain Dunlop came on the PA for his 6:00 update and all seemed set for Adelaide in a couple of days. He did warn us that the seas would be lumpier (4 metres) with a stronger wind, meaning the official sea state might change from 'medium', to 'rough'.

I would be having one of my pills later.

The evening was quite enjoyable. There was a full house again for dinner and after a quick Masquerade's quiz failure, we trooped off to the theatre for the second and final show from comedian William Caulfield. His jokes were less familiar to us this time, and it was a wonderful hour of laughter. Elsewhere the talented musicians of Caravan were in Carmen's playing songs with the brass section from the orchestra.

The determined six from dinner table 228 struggled out of the theatre after the show and returned to Masquerade's for a themed challenge about cartoon films. Now, we are of an age beyond watching many children's films, so this was a struggle. We didn't do **too** badly....enough said.

Our cabin was creaking and the ship was rolling when we went to bed. There had been an obvious increase in the movement of the ship for almost a week, and the nights were worse when you wanted a bit of peace and stillness for a sleep.

Tomorrow was to be the final sea day before our arrival in Adelaide on Saturday. The weather forecast from the BBC was suggesting sunshine for when we get there, with temperatures back into the 20's and even warmer as we continue to Kangaroo Island and Melbourne.

....

Friday 24th February
The temperature on the balcony struggled its way up to 19°C.

We were late getting up again, and I was still tired after a noisy and roly-poly night. It was cool and cloudy outside, and the back garden was in need of a serious rolling. The weather forecast suggested similar conditions for the rest of the day.

As we sat in Charlies updating our diaries, I realised that at home it was still yesterday. There was another 30 minutes to add to our clocks at lunchtime to set us up for Adelaide.

Deb and I went out onto a cool Promenade Deck for a walk and completed another mile of the teak track. That was 17 miles now, and I really felt the walking had done my new hip a lot of good.

In three days' time there was to be a charity event in aid of the Macmillan Nurses. The challenge was for passengers and crew to walk around the Promenade Deck 44 times to reach a half-marathon distance. Although a lot of people planned to complete the full distance, many people (like us) were working as a team to share the distance, and others would simply do as much, or as little as they wanted. Each walker paid an entrance fee, and the hope was for a good turnout, resulting in a very good sum being raised. We were up for the challenge, and registered ourselves for the event in Carmen's with the ever-smiling Coral.

At 10:00 I was looking at the navigation information screen. Aurora was about halfway along the southern coastline of Australia, in a patch of water known as the Australian Bight. This was after more than two days and nights sailing from the south-western tip of this huge country. All through today we continued heading due east, galloping along rather quickly at 20 knots.

Late in the morning as we returned to the cabin, both of our neighbours spoke to us, and asked about the noise during the nights in our cabins. Although not very pleasant, we had accepted that the sea conditions make the balcony doors and various other bits and pieces creak and groan, but I suspected they were not so familiar with long periods of sea days when it could be a continual bumpy ride.

With the noon clock change beckoning, I got ready and went to Carmen's for today's choir practice. It was getting really serious now as this was our penultimate session before we would perform in the theatre on 27th February. That would also be the same day as the Macmillan walk, it looked like being a very busy few hours.

As usual, while I was away singing, Deb had her lunchtime appointment with the Battle of the Sexes, though we met up briefly an hour later, before I went for some lunch and Deb set off to Carmen's for her Salsa session.

This evening the entertainment wasn't to our tastes. The female vocalist Ali Harper was back in the theatre to sing songs from the Gershwin Songbook, and there was a classical duo in Carmen's called The Jeffrey-Martin Duo: one of them played the piano while the other stroked a violin. In Champions the entertainment team were fronting a 'British Pub Night' evening of games.

Deb decided to do some washing.

We also elected to avoid the main dining room tonight and go to the buffet where there was a Mexican themed menu.

When Deb found a free washing machine she filled it with the latest load of dirty clothes, and 45 minutes later they were washed and moved to the tumble dryer. This gave us plenty of time to go up to the buffet for a taste of Mexico. Admittedly I had roast gammon, but also sampled several of the less spicy Mexican bits.

By the time we left the buffet, some of the clothes were dry and I took a bag of them back to the cabin, while Deb started the ironing. It wasn't long before everything was back in the drawers or hanging in the wardrobe again. That would see us through to Sydney now.

After a read and a doze we went out to meet up with Richard and Angie for another quiz from DJ Martin. Tonight it was a special 50 questions in 50 minutes. Sadly we had another bad session, but at least we marked the winning team's paper – "Densa" again.

The ship continued her rather predictable wobbling progress, and we were in for another noisy night. Tomorrow we would arrive in Adelaide in South Australia where we had a tour of a village that became a settlement for a group of Germans in the late 1800s. We weren't sure what to expect, but were definitely looking forward to the day – especially if the sun came out.

Saturday 25th February – Adelaide, South Australia
Today the balcony basked in temperatures that reached 22°C.

Yes it was another noisy night as Aurora fought valiantly through the lumpy sea. I wasn't too uncomfortable until I woke up with cramp in my calf. As I lay there trying to ease my leg, I began to listen to the weird creaking noises coming from our ceiling. It was if something was rolling around as the ship tilted one way to the other. Discounting the strange idea that it might be a couple of footballs, I decided it might be some form of insulation or pipework moving around. Thinking that was probably not possible, I had another idea that it could be water sloshing back and forth. I just couldn't get comfortable and it was being made worse by my thoughts about the noise. Eventually I had to resort to getting up for a trip to the toilet, and a couple of painkillers.

By this time it was about 1:00 am.

The painkiller, and walk around the cabin did the trick, and I finally got back off to sleep.

I next woke just before the alarm went off at 7:00 and Aurora was on her way into the Port of Adelaide with her thrusters working overtime. After the early morning cup of tea we washed and dressed for breakfast: we had to meet up in the theatre by 8:45 to be ready for our tour.

Hey, it was dry, the sun was shining and it was warm!

There was a three-piece band on the terminal building veranda playing a welcome to us, and they had the volunteer guides from the city there to wave at us.

What a lovely country this is!

Just before Deb and I made our way to the theatre, they even played "Waltzing Matilda". Wonderful!

Aurora was actually docked at a place called Outer Harbor alongside a car transporter, with the familiar cranes as a backdrop for the container ships. From there to the city centre of Adelaide there was a free shuttle that took upwards of an hour. Hence you can realise that our ship was docked some distance from any of the popular destinations for tours. Slightly closer was Port Adelaide, a suburb of the city that took about 20 minutes to get to by train which left from a station just across the road from the docks.

Anyway, this didn't worry us as we were on an official tour. This was to the little village of Hahndorf, some 20 km to the south-east of Adelaide. The British allowed this settlement to be created in 1839 as a safe haven for the German Lutheran migrants who were being persecuted by the Prussian State. We had a guide called Kurt, and a driver (or Captain) called Peter. As we set off, Kurt told us that he was a German who had emigrated to Australia in the 1970s after marrying a Japanese woman.

Adelaide is the capital city of the state of Southern Australia. For those of you whose knowledge of geography is similar to mine, the city is about two-thirds of the way across the southern coast of Australia, and about 250km from the southernmost edge of the country. Our tour took us through Port Adelaide, the small suburb I mentioned, and then we had a drive through Adelaide City.

This city is vast. It is laid out on a grid basis of roads and streets and is beautifully clean compared to some of our earlier stops. The openness of Adelaide is also enhanced with green parkland surrounding its centre giving the people of this city a place to escape the busy traffic.

We drove through the city and headed up into the Adelaide Hills for a stop at a place called Mount Lofty. The warm sunshine at sea level now disappeared and a chilly wind was a shock as we left the coach. From this (as the name suggests) lofty position above the city we had a panoramic view down over Adelaide and out to the sea. It was a fantastic view, and the number of coaches with us showed how popular this place is for tourists.

Once we had had sufficient "Wow, look at that" moments, used the toilets, and bought suitable souvenirs in the shop, we headed off to our main stop of the day – the little town of Hahndorf.

It is a quiet sleepy town with quite a long main street and a few side roads leading to car parks and hotels, as well as the residential areas. The main street has a mixture of shops, pubs and cafes, with the occasional small museums or exhibitions to look at. Hahndorf retains much of the German influence, with what I would describe as typical Bavarian chalet-styled frontages. Visitors have lots of opportunities to purchase souvenirs, as well as sampling traditional German cakes, meats and, of course, beer.

To be honest, it is simply a piece of history in this vast country where tourists come to look back a century – and spend money.

When we booked this tour neither of us knew what to expect, and it turned out to be very different from many of the places we have seen around the world.

Perhaps rather strangely, I likened it to visiting somewhere like the village of Clovelly on the north coast border of Cornwall and Devon. Clovelly is a quiet fishing village that has hundreds of daily tourists in the summer walking down, and then back up, the steep cliff that the village has been built into. Visitors enjoy themselves having cream teas, buying souvenirs, or just staring at the unusual tiny cottages.

Hahndorf doesn't have cliffs, but again hundreds of visitors take it over and look at someone's garden or through windows of houses, and more importantly to the residents, spend money.

Having walked along much of the main street, we bought a few memories and then had a cup of coffee and a cake. Our time was up in Hahndorf and we returned to our coach for the drive back to Aurora. Kurt continued giving us more information about Hahndorf and his home city of Adelaide. He was the perfect guide for this visit with his knowledge of Germany, plus the experience he has gained after 40 years in his adopted country.

We got back to Aurora just before 2:30 and had a cup of tea before going out again.

Our afternoon plan was to go to nearby Port Adelaide to explore and find somewhere to eat. Deb and I walked across the road to the deserted station to catch a local train for a 20-minute journey to get there. The only issue with this train service (which also went to the city of Adelaide) was buying tickets. It is an unmanned station, and the only option was to buy the tickets from a machine on the train itself. The machine only took coins. And of course few cruise ship passengers are well stocked with much currency in coins.

Let's just say, we did our best to pay the correct fare.

We got to Port Adelaide at about 4:00, and it was rather warm. This residential suburb was extremely quiet with hardly anybody else walking around, and virtually all the shops were closed. We did discover some delightful old sailing ships on the quayside, but nothing else to interest us enough to continue wandering around in the sun. Apart from MacDonald's and KFC we found nowhere to eat that was open, so we got back on the train and returned to Aurora.

Back in the comfortable air-conditioned ship we had enough time for a shower and a change of clothes before enjoying a pre-dinner drink in Anderson's.

At dinner it was just us, Richard and Angie at the table. We chattered about our adventures for the day, before losing another quiz in Masquerade's.

The evening entertainment consisted of a folkloric show in the theatre from the local Tanunda Town Band. This is a traditional German-style band featuring those wonderful huge 'Oompah' Instruments. Elsewhere Carmen's had the Headliners show 'Thank You for the Music' and Caravan were playing background music in Champions.

All four of us were tired, and the entertainment for the evening didn't interest us. So, we had a rest in our cabins before meeting up again later for another quiz, and after another honourable defeat, we drowned our frustrations with a drink in Champions while listening to Caravan.

Our visit to Adelaide had been a lovely day and my love for Australia continued.

At about 11:00 the announcement was made that Aurora was ready to set sail again for a short overnight crossing to our next stop at Kangaroo Island tomorrow morning.

The sea was much calmer and we were far more confident of a good night's sleep.

Sunday 26th February – Kangaroo Island, Australia
The maximum temperature recorded on our balcony was 21°C.

Success, we both had a good night with calm water and no unnecessary noises.

Today was a tender port, and I was woken at about 7:15 by the sounds of anchors dropping and tenders being launched. It was a lovely sunny morning, but sniffing the air in the back garden was a shock as it was rather cool with the temperature way below 20°. At the bottom of the garden the mainland of Australia was some distance away to the left, and to the right was the very pretty coastline of Kangaroo Island. We had another tour today called *'Cape Willoughby, Wines and Views'*, that was leaving after lunch, so we had a leisurely morning on the ship.

So be honest, how many of you have ever heard of Kangaroo Island, and how many of you know where it is?

Personally I was totally unaware there was such a place until the brochure mentioned it, and even up until that morning I only had a vague idea about it, but it turned out to be a really lovely place.

Kangaroo Island is just a short overnight sail of around 100km from the Port of Adelaide, and is little more than 10km from the nearest bit of Australian headland. The island is the third largest island off the coast of Australia after Tasmania in the south and Melville near Darwin in the north. Even being the third largest, it's not very big – about 100km from west to east, and less than 50km from north to south. It has a resident population of a little over 4,000, but swells with tourists from a daily ferry, and regular cruise ship visits.

The island is very much a farming community with sheep, cows and cereal crops, along with GM-free vegetables and grapes. A local pointed out that the island was self-sufficient in bread, milk and wine, so didn't need much contact with the mainland.

We were anchored in Hog Bay just north of the little town of Penneshaw on the north east of the island. My first impressions of the island were that it appeared similar to a Cornish cliff, the main difference being that the vegetation here comprises of fir trees rather than the gorse of Cornwall.

The tenders started their back-and-forth journeys just after 8:00, and it was obvious that the sea was a little choppy as they bounced and rocked around. The Deputy Captain suggested the temperatures on shore were a little warmer than out here in the Bay, but the wind wasn't mentioned.

We had a light brunch at 11:00, and then got ourselves ready to get a tender ashore to meet up for our tour. We decided to be early, so joined the queue for a tender in plenty of time. Of course we were quickly onto a tender, and the crossing went so smoothly that we had almost an hour to look around on shore before the tour began. At least it gave us a chance to explore a little and have an ice-cream.

The view of the bay was delightful and Deb and I took several photos, including some of Aurora at anchor, and another ship called Astor. Apparently this ship is based in Adelaide and regularly visits the island on party-style cruises. This weekend it had arrived on Saturday morning when the passengers spent the day ashore on the island. Today the passengers were on the ship and doing whatever Aussies do on a day afloat. Astor left the Bay late in the afternoon to return to Adelaide to disembark people on Monday morning.

Eventually our transport arrived: three minibuses taking our party around the island in convoy. The transport wasn't very new, and our aging minibus struggled with the hilly terrain, and its suspension lacked some of the finesse of the transport we were used to. But that didn't spoil the experience.

Our driver/guide described his family connections going back to Arbroath in Scotland. They came to the island as boat builders and turned to agriculture, but this was no longer viable as a way of earning sufficient money, so like most people on the island, tourism has become their most important source of income.

Initially our journey was on tarmacked roads, but as the houses of the village ended, so did the smooth surface, and the roads turned into limestone-covered dirt-tracks, which were full of potholes and far from smooth.

Our first stop was at the Dudley Wine Gardens, a restaurant which featured home-produced wine, and we stopped there primarily for a wine tasting experience. I have never known these popular sessions to be anything other than delightful, and today was no exception. They have their own vineyards elsewhere around the island, and although we didn't have a lot to drink, the owner gave us a lovely description of the wines they make. They were introduced by the rather quaint names they have been given, with examples such as a sparkling one called "Dudley Bubbly", a very pleasant "Grassy Flat Sauvignon", the "Pink Bay Rose", and a very drinkable "Sheep Shearing Red". These were just what we were offered, but there were several others with similarly unusual names.

They really named and marketed their wine for local consumption, but were quite willing to sell it to us as well. Of course it was quite expensive, but one or two passengers did buy a bottle or two.

After the wine tasting we re-boarded our buses, and bounced and rattled our way on a panoramic trip around some of the island. The other official stop was at Cape Willoughby where there are some gorgeous cliff views and one of the first lighthouses to be built in Australia. The coastline of this island is rugged and has had several ships making unwanted arrivals on its rocks. As I had mentioned earlier, the island is quite similar to Cornwall and felt a little like home, except for the grass growing on the soil of the cliffs rather than being the bare granite in Cornwall.

Oh, and there was one more treat at this stop – free-range kangaroos!

We had a chance to photograph them as they lazed in the shade or quietly bounced away as we upset their slumbers.

Soon it was time for a few more minutes crashing along the roads and leaving a dust trail in our wake. Our tour had gone on for quite a while longer than scheduled, and was a lovely afternoon on this beautiful island.

It was around 5:00 when we set off on the tender back to Aurora. The water was still choppy, allowing us to get more of a feel of the water rocking us around, plus the odd bit of salty spray in our faces. Back home on the ship, we had just enough time to have a shower and change of clothes before a glass of prosecco and nibbles in Anderson's. Then it was off to dinner, and the full table of eight caught up on our day, and chatted about our adventures.

While we were eating, Aurora pulled up her anchors, and for once we actually set off on time for the next bit of our global adventure.

In the evening the entertainment wasn't to our tastes with Roy Lake, a vocalist, in the theatre, casual music elsewhere, and a gameshow based on ITV's "The Chase" in Masquerade's. Our evening choice was to team up with Richard and Angela in the Crow's Nest for a game of trivial pursuit, but our concentration was interrupted by Lyn Frederick. Her less-than-amazing karaoke-style entertainment was a long way from our personal tastes, so our game came to a premature end, and the four of us gave up and went to bed relatively early.

Aurora was now on her way eastwards to our next stop at Melbourne in the state of Victoria, but there was a sea day to come that turned out to be quite a wonderful day.

Monday 27th February – Macmillan Walkathon Day

The temperature today crept up to a pleasant 22°C on the balcony.

It was a sea-day as Aurora sailed eastwards to Melbourne. I woke at 7:00 to the sound of the ship's fog horn, and looking outside, our garden had completely gone and replaced by a thick blanket of fog.

Hey, isn't this the summer in Australia?

Today we had to get up reasonably quickly, as we were taking part in the 'Walkathon' for Macmillan Cancer Nurses. Going to breakfast we discovered that it was cold and wet outside in the fog. Perhaps it was a good day for a long walk, but the weather on this cruise continued to be a surprise at times.

By 9:00 there were over 120 of us out on a cool Promenade Deck getting ready to do our best to walk, and raise money for this very special cause. Deb and I had teamed up with Robin and Rosemary to walk as a relay to get as close as we could to the 44-lap half-marathon distance. There was no pressure to complete the distance, and some people just wanted to do a couple of laps, while others were aiming to complete the full 44 lap distance.

The klaxon sounded and we were off, with Robin and me taking the first few laps. It was a wonderful atmosphere with spectators all around the deck cheering and clapping from the first lap to the last. It was smiles and laughter everywhere and it really was a lovely experience. As the walk started it was obvious that the fog was lifting, and the sun soon came out to cheer us on as well.

To show the difference in the standards of those walking, there was one man on a pair of crutches who struggled to just move, but he completed 10 laps. At the other extreme, around a dozen people ran the course and completed the distance by the time the majority were about half of the way round. Robin and I managed 16 laps (5 miles) each, Deb did 14 laps (4 miles), and Rosemary did almost the same as Deb.

This now brought my marathon total to 22 miles.

We stopped at about 11:15 because Robin and I now needed to have a drink and bit of relaxation before the choir's performance in the theatre that afternoon, and we also had a final rehearsal at lunchtime. Today the rehearsal was in the theatre so we could sort out where to stand for the show, and once lined up we began to sing through our programme.

The rehearsal was going very well until one lady collapsed.

It turned out that she was a diabetic, and had been walking with the rest of us earlier. This must have upset her routine and her insulin balance tipped over the edge. While she was being assessed and treated by the medical team, our choir leader said we knew what we were doing and told us to go, and to meet later for the real thing.

This gave me a chance to have a bite to eat and half an hour with my feet up on the now very sunny balcony. It was really rather warm, and memories of the fog were gone.

At 3:15 the 'Third Sector Aurora Choir' did their bit, and entertained quite a good crowd of people in the theatre. I really enjoyed singing in public after many years when my voice was only used for my work.

I would be very surprised if I didn't have another go when the choir started up again in the next sector.

By the time I climbed down from the stage I was aware that my knees were not really doing what they should anymore. The normal climb up the stairs to our cabin was approaching agony levels, so using the lift would be necessary for the rest of the day. Robin had cramp in his legs so was also suffering, but individually we had only completed about a third of the walkathon distance.

Just to put it in perspective, our other table mates, Richard and Angie, walked together and both completed the full 13 miles (plus a bit). All I can say to them is "Well done" and a deserved "Respect".

I rested my legs for the remainder of the afternoon before going to dinner. It was the full house once again and we discussed the walk, the choir, and the day in Melbourne to come tomorrow.

After eating, the six of us lost in a quiz again, before Deb and I went to the theatre to watch the show. Tonight it was one of our favourites called 'Destination Dance' from the Headliners.

At the end of the show Abby, the Assistant Cruise Manager, announced that the Walkathon had raised around £2,000, and thanked us all for a magnificent result. We were both so proud to have been a part of it.

When we came out of the theatre at 9:15 there was nothing on our minds except an early night. We would be doing a lot more walking in Melbourne tomorrow and my legs needed as much rest as possible to recover.

The Captain said that we should be tied up at the port of Melbourne by 8:00 for part five of our Australian adventure.

Goodnight everyone.

Tuesday 28th February – Melbourne, Australia
Summer returned with the balcony temperature reaching 32°C.

Today we were visiting Melbourne in the state of Victoria. When I woke the sun was shining, and in fact as I opened the curtains to peak outside it was dazzling. The temperature on the balcony was already at the top of the 20°s and it wasn't yet 8:00.

Deb and I had no organised plans for the day. We just wanted to explore this Australian city a little bit, spend some time at a market, and if possible to visit the Immigration Museum.

Yes I said Immigration Museum.

In the last six months I had discovered that contrary to the belief that our family was very much based in Cornwall, we have several generations of my mother's family living around the world, including Australia. So this was a chance to explore a museum that is highly respected when talking about the history of immigration to Australia.

First things first, and our breakfast was our current favourite of fruit and croissant. Then back in the cabin we checked how much Aussie currency we still had before packing away the usual bits into our backpacks for the day.

The Deputy Captain suggested the weather was set to be hot and sunny during our stay, with a likely high temperature of 34°. That brought a smile to our faces, and I added another bottle of sun screen to my backpack.

By 9:00 we were bouncing along yet another air-bridge to be welcomed by friendly Australians to what looked to be beautiful city. Before looking for the shuttle bus we picked up a detailed map of the city after a quick chat with the smiling person on the tourist information desk. Our shuttle bus was waiting outside and a couple of minutes later we were on our way into the city.

Our drop off point was near Federation Square, and having already spotted the Immigration Museum on the way, we confirmed our location on the map with the coach driver, and set off towards the museum. As the driver had suggested, it took us a little over 20 minutes to walk along the busy Flinders Street in the already hot sunshine. A massive railway station dominated the area to our left, and we spotted a couple of groups of school children on organised tours. They were dressed in their school uniforms that included bush hats to protect their heads from the sun.

Our museum was found, and we crossed over the busy road with early morning traffic and trams before climbing the steps of the imposing building. Deb asked what the time was as she spotted a sign saying opening time was 10:00. It was two minutes past by my watch and we were able to go straight in. At the reception desk we were asked our age, and unchallenged, given free concessionary entries.

What a superb country.

Inside, the museum is built on three floors and concentrates on the way of life of an immigrant. On one floor there are examples of the difficulties encountered by the immigrants, and especially those with different coloured skin, different religious beliefs, different cultures and different languages.

Another section discussed the history of immigration over decades, and the way that Australia first refused, and then encouraged people from different countries and cultures. Then my favourite section was a mock-up of a ship with exhibits showing the cabins from a number of periods starting with the sailing ships of the late 19th century, through to the 1950s cruise ships. There was a wonderful series of diary entries and associated photographs of one immigrant from Britain as he sailed to his new home in this country. His journey took him to several of the places we had visited on this cruise, as I made a similar journal of my adventures. Over an hour later we left the museum, without finding any way of exploring my ancestry, but fascinated by the exhibitions we had seen.

Now we were on our way to the Queen Victoria Market in the north of the city, and we caught one of the **FREE** trams that go round and round the city centre.

Yes this city provides free transport on trams covering several square miles of the main city centre.

The market was vast, and as we had been warned it had a lot of stalls selling tat, as well as a fruit and veg section. Never mind, we quite like tat, and found a few souvenirs to take home. We also had a snack of pizza and coffee.

By now it was about 1:00 and very hot, so we decided to make our way back towards the shuttle bus area. We got on a tram again, which was packed with standing room only for a few stops. Quite a few of the passengers were from our ship, as well as other tourists alongside the locals going about their daily business.

We still had to find a chemist for a few things, including more sea-sickness pills, and soon found one where helpful assistants sorted out our needs.

The wait for the shuttle was a little long, made worse by the heat on our slightly less pale, but still quite soft skin. After we had sheltered in the shade for about 20 minutes the coach arrived and we sank into the air-conditioned comfort. On the return journey we passed by the sports area of the city, and had a view of the magnificent Melbourne Cricket Ground to add yet another sporting landmark to my list of places I had seen on the television.

Melbourne is beautiful. It is clean, with a mix of older colonial-style buildings that have been (or are being) preserved, alongside the more expected skyscraper glass towers. The people rush everywhere, but are polite and appear to notice strangers and make way for them. There are parks and green areas to go to and relax from the hustle and bustle, and the shopping streets are narrow and designed to give shade. And of course transport is free!

Another wonderful place in this delightful country.

When we got back to the ship we simply relaxed in the cabin and rehydrated ourselves.

It was dinner for just six tonight, as our new companions had been out to see some relatives in Melbourne and were too late back to be ready to eat with us. Our table-mates were doing their own things tonight, with one pair off to see a film, and the others venturing to the evening cabaret in the theatre to watch a pair who call themselves Tight Fit who have a form of circus act.

We returned to the cabin and rested a bit more, as we had other plans. At 9:00 we dug out our fancy dress costumes and put them on. The costumes are 60s and 70s (ABBA and Hippy) which coincided with the evening's deck party theme.

For once, the weather was warm and there was no wind to upset the atmosphere around the Riviera pool. DJ Martin had started to get people in the partying mood and Caravan were the main entertainment to tempt the passengers to dance around, between sipping at their drinks. It was a good atmosphere, except that we were the only passengers who'd dressed up. No-one was recognising us from a distance, but many total strangers congratulated us for doing our bit and having fun.

Several of the conversations we had were similar to others over the last few weeks. The Aussies couldn't understand the difference between their typical holidays afloat and this world cruise. They openly suggest that the Brits are boring, and are just "fuddy-duddies" who don't know how to enjoy themselves.

I had long given up defending ourselves, except to a few people who politely ask, rather than instantly condemning us. A world cruise is not a standard 14-day cruise. In fact many of the Aussies were on board the ship for just two or three days, and saw it as a non-stop party. The global circumnavigation is a journey of exploration and a chance to discover new places and cultures, rather than going on a normal holiday and drinking in a pub for a couple of weeks. If we had adopted their attitude and attempted to party every night, our livers would have been destroyed already. Yes we had what they consider to be fun, but not every day. And yes, probably we don't go to the same excesses of partying as these wonderful outgoing people from one of my favourite countries in the world.

Anyway, the deck party was going well until about 10:30 when Aurora changed course and the wind blew across the decks making it chilly. Within half an hour many had left and the numbers were dwindling. We called time and returned to the cabin where our beds were beckoning.

It had been a good evening, and in fact a very good day.

Wednesday 1st March – Sea Day
St David's Day

The maximum temperature on the balcony was 22°C, and a chilly wind was making Aurora jiggle a bit.

We woke a little later than usual, but the kettle was boiling by about 7:40. I peeked out at the garden but couldn't see anything – it was foggy again. The early temperature was just 19°, so we are back to autumnal levels again.

The morning announcement from the bridge confirmed that it wasn't warm, but that the sun was actually shining above this thick layer of fog. The weather did improve later in the morning after we had been to a port talk for Dunedin in New Zealand.

Aurora was now sailing north-eastwards across the Tasman Sea, part way around the bottom right-hand lump of Australia. We were sailing at some 17 knots to get us to our next stop on time tomorrow morning.

Throughout this sea day towards Sydney, the sea grumbled at us with a small, but niggling lumpiness. I actually felt slightly queasy by mid-afternoon, and once again had to resort to a little white pill. The sun didn't make an appearance until late, and the wind blowing over the open decks made it too chilly to relax except in rare sheltered places. We went to the Crow's Nest to read our books and it was warm and comfortable up there.

I fell asleep of course.

It was a formal dress code evening and our table was up to full strength again with us in our finest. We discussed our plans for Sydney, and we discovered that we would all be eating elsewhere tomorrow evening. Our waiters would have yet another empty table.

Most of us were planning long days out, and we all needed a good night's sleep. So after dinner we met up with Richard and Angie for a drink before they disappeared to bed. Deb and I were very tired, but finished off our evening by joining in with the St David's Day themed quiz. We did very well, but our lack of deep knowledge about Wales let us down.

Early tomorrow we would be approaching the wonderful port of Sydney, anchoring in the harbour near enough to see the Opera House and the Bridge. The Queen Mary 2 was on her own world cruise and going to be in the city with us. She has the primary spot at Circular Quay tomorrow, before we take her position on our second day in this beautiful city.

The weather forecast for Sydney wasn't brilliant, with temperatures just creeping into the mid-20°s. Sadly there was also a good chance of showers to annoy us.

We had lots on our wish list for our two days in Sydney, and we hoped to be up to see the sail-in tomorrow morning, so it was time for bed.

Thursday 2nd March – Day 1 in Sydney, Australia

The day was warm and humid and our balcony crept up to a pleasant 26°C.

My alarm woke me at 6:00, supposedly in time to watch sail-in to the beautiful city of Sydney. As I peeked outside it was obvious that we had already arrived at our spot in the harbour area. Aurora was stationary, but the anchors had not yet been dropped. It was still dark, and the lights from the skyscrapers were showing that Sydney is a beautiful sight even at night.

The Queen Mary 2 had priority today and was parked majestically at the Circular Quay cruise terminal. She would be disembarking many of her passengers before refilling with new smiling adventurers, and resuming her way around the world.

Very soon our anchors rattled down, and as Aurora moved around on her chains we caught our first sight in the morning twilight of the iconic Opera House and then the wonderful Harbour Bridge.

Sensational!!

After an early breakfast we started getting ready to go ashore. By 9:00 we were boarding our tender, which was a local sight-seeing boat from a company called Fantasea Cruises. They supplied the primary vessels operating the ride to and from the shore all day. Aurora did have a couple of tenders helping with the early busy period, but they were stored away by the end of the morning.

The tenders were coming ashore by the Opera House steps, which was a wonderful landing spot. Our cameras were already busy as we walked around the Circular Quay to where the Queen Mary 2 was towering above us. Our plan for the morning was to walk around and explore The Rocks area behind the quayside, and it was just a few minutes before we left the bustling dockside area and disappeared into the quiet streets of Sydney.

We were so early that many places were still closed, so we wandered until we could get a map from the information centre. That gave us a clearer picture of where we were, and where we planned to go.

Our first target was to get to the Harbour Bridge, and walk out until we were over the water to get some views of the city from this lofty position. We didn't think about climbing over the top but we did see several groups of thrill-junkies who were going up towards the Australian flags flying at the highest point of the bridge.

We remained firmly on the tarmac.

Just getting as far along the bridge to be over the water took us quite a time, but the early cloud had melted away and it was scorching hot. The walk was worth it to get the views of the harbour area, and take a few very special photographs as well.

Back down to the Rocks area, and we went for a cup of coffee. The little café we chose looked very nice, and although expensive, the mixed fruit muffin appeared quickly and was delicious. Sadly, the coffee took another 25 minutes, and a few strong words, to appear. It wasn't good enough to justify the wait, and we gave the waiter/coffee maker, a bit of a true British complaint. This was the first time in five Australian ports that we had had bad service.

Slightly grumpy, we moved on to a much better place called the Rocks Discovery Museum. This little building houses an exhibition of the creation and development of the Rocks area, from Aborigine times through to years of British colonialism, right up to the present. It was fascinating and enlightening to see how the cove named Sydney has changed from the time the first convicts arrived and began to build a settlement. There were stories of the problems Aborigines faced when the settlers failed to accept they had rights to the land. Many were killed by the diseases inadvertently brought from Britain, but many more were killed violently

We stayed there for a couple of hours, and spent almost 40 minutes just watching a series of films about Sydney. They included stories about the local Aborigines, how the Rocks district was created and preserved, the use of wooden blocks to surface the roads, and how the bridge was built. There was also a temporary exhibition about soldiers who came from the Rocks area who were killed during various conflicts.

It was a real treat to spend time here – and it was totally free.

We had timed our visit perfectly. It had been hot and sunny when we entered, but within five minutes we noticed an increase in people coming in, and realised that it was raining outside. By the time we left it was dry again as we made our way towards the harbour. Deb and I were quite hungry by now and looked for somewhere to get a lunchtime snack. There was a lot of choice, but this time we were much luckier finding a little café serving delicious beef pies and cold drinks.

And the service was prompt, from the friendly waiters.

The rest of our time in the Rocks area was spent exploring the shops, and keeping an eye out for a place to eat that evening. We found lots of possible restaurants, but I have to say that Australia is not a cheap place to eat. The only things we bought were from a chemist and included some throwaway razors for me. I had dropped my electric razor a few days ago, and one of the three heads had been damaged. Hence it no longer worked very well.

We went back around Circular Quay and investigated how to get ferry tickets. We could have bought individual one-way tickets, but as we were planning a trip to Manley the next day we opted to buy an "Opal" card with enough credit for any trips we might make. After that we continued past the Opera House, for a few more photos.

While we waited for a tender back to Aurora, we noticed that the Botanical Gardens was no more than a minute's walk, and there was a little land train giving guided rides. It seemed a nice way of seeing the gardens, so we sat back on the rather hard wooden benches and enjoyed a 20-minute ride around this botanical highlight of Sydney.

After that we caught the Fantasea tender boat for the ten-minute trip back to Aurora.

It was nearly 3:00, so we had a cup of tea and then relaxed for a while in the cabin. Then it was time to have a shower and change into some clean clothes for our evening back in the city.

By 5:00 we were on the tender boat again. We had decided to go to Darling Harbour to eat, as nothing we had seen in the morning tempted us. We timed it perfectly and caught a ferry which left a minute after we boarded it. The ride was lovely, with such different views of the city than you can see from the streets.

Darling Harbour was busy and there were restaurants for as far as we could see. Most of them were already filling with both tourists and locals, and it appeared that eating out was a common thing, with all ages from children to pensioners sitting side by side. The culture of eating out seemed different to Britain, where there are restaurants that are more popular with either the young or more adult ages.

Well I think so anyway.

After several minutes of consulting menus, we chose a restaurant that didn't have loud music playing. We had another pizza, but this time it was a huge one each, and although I managed to eat mine, Deb had to give in and leave the last slice of hers. Once again the service was superb, fast, and with a smile.

Our meal was over by 6:45 and we set off again for the ferry. We had to wait a few minutes this time, allowing us a chance to look at the different pleasure craft taking groups of business people or other organisations out onto the water for a meal and a party. This waterway of Sydney plays an important part in the lives of the locals, and combining it with eating seems to be natural to them.

As we sat on our ferry returning to Circular Quay the sun had set and it was just beginning to get dark. The change of light gave yet more alternative views of the city to photograph.

And there were still people climbing up to the top of the Harbour Bridge, this time in the twilight.

It was fully dark by the time we arrived back on Aurora. Deb and I were tired after our long day and vast amounts of walking. We simply went back to our cabin, put on some scruffy clothes and sat out on the balcony with a bottle of fizz. We relaxed and chatted there for over an hour watching the ferries, water taxis, and private boats passing back and forth. We had a lovely view of the Opera House and the Bridge for most of the time, and the lights of the city and the stars above made this very special.

Slowly we noticed the stars were not so visible any more, and we realised that clouds were gathering above us. Then a rippling sound could be heard that heralded a downpour. Fortunately our bottle of prosecco was finished, and as we were getting wet we gave up looking at Sydney in the dark and went to bed.

At around midnight, the QM2 left her berth, and a few minutes later Aurora dragged up her anchors and slowly took her place at the dockside. I woke once and heard the sound of the thrusters as we moved, but I was shattered and went back to sleep almost instantly, with a smile on my face.

Goodnight Sydney, we'll see you again tomorrow.

Friday 3rd March – Day two in Sydney

Today it was cooler on the balcony at 22°C, and there were a lot of showers.

As I opened my eyes, daylight was coming through the gap in the curtains. It was 7:20 and time to get up for another day in Sydney. The kettle was switched on for a cuppa, and I peeked outside at our back garden. We were docked, and the view had been transformed overnight to Sydney's Circular Quay with the Opera House across the water to our left, and the six ferry wharfs below to our right. The water traffic was already busy bringing workers into the city on the multi-coloured ferries. They came and went to Darling Harbour, Manley, and the other districts of the city. As each boat left the wharf, they tooted their horns to warn others that they were moving away. Another day in Sydney had begun.

Oh, and it was raining!

Our plans were to go to Manley which is a 30-minute ferry ride away. We had been told it has a wonderful beach that puts Bondi to shame. But at this particular moment the rain was putting us off.

Deb initially thought about doing some washing, but so did many others, and the machines were all busy. This was quite a surprise as around 900 passengers were disembarking today, and others would be exploring the city, so we'd expected it to be quieter.

Eventually, after bravely gathering our bits and our waterproof jackets, we took a chance in a lull between showers and set off for the ferry terminal. Our ferry was one of the three green and yellow boats that are cleverly constructed with two front ends. They have two separate control rooms so rather than having to turn around when arriving at a wharf, the captain simply goes to the other control room when he leaves again.

As we set off we thought it would be ideal to sit outside at the front (well the end that was currently the front) but it started to rain again and there was no point getting wet unnecessarily. Sitting inside we watched a trail of people going to the outside deck and sitting there for a moment, before shaking their heads and coming back into the dry.

Manley is quite a way from the city centre, and our route took us out to the narrow channel leading back into the Pacific Ocean. The squally weather was making the water quite rough in the less sheltered water, and our ferry lumbered a little in the swell. Never mind, it was only for a few minutes and we were soon docking at Manley.

OK, Manley has a long and beautiful sandy beach. It was even hosting the National Surfing Championships and there were a lot of young surfers showing off their skills, but my personal view was that the town itself was nothing special.

It has a large Sea Life Centre, lots of cafes, restaurants, and shops, including several surfing supplies and a surprisingly high number of chemists. Obviously surfing is popular but maybe not very healthy. It was certainly quieter than anywhere we had experienced in Sydney so far, but there was nothing much that made us go *"Wow, look at that"*. Well actually that wasn't strictly true, as we spotted an Aldi store and exclaimed *"Wow look what's over there"*!

Our morning visit to Manley stayed dry, and we walked to the beach, looked at the surfers practicing, and then walked back again looking down some of the side streets. We had a coffee that was very nice, with very prompt service, and it was cheaper than in the city centre. We also found a souvenir (and tat) shop where we bought quite a few bits at very acceptable prices.

But with nothing else to tempt us (not even the no-doubt very nice Sea Life Centre) we caught a ferry back. It rained again so once more we sat inside and were quietly amused watching another trail of people going outside and coming back in again.

Back in Sydney it had gone midday, and was still raining. The weather had really turned very British, so we put on our waterproofs and strolled back to Aurora for lunch.

Deb did manage to do the washing after we had eaten. That took up almost two hours before we had a cup of tea and talked about what we should do. There was still dampness in the air, but we put on the waterproofs again and went for a last walk around Sydney, and one final experience of a city that I love. I couldn't see that we would ever come back here, and I was so thankful that I had seen it again.

While exploring the Rocks area of Sydney again, we set ourselves a challenge to spend the last of our Australian coins. Deb was really rather interested in buying a didgeridoo, so we looked out for a shop we had noticed yesterday that sold them, and bought a short version of the aborigine musical instrument. The shopkeeper even played a similar one to prove they were real. At the counter Deb tipped out all of our remaining coins plus a ten dollar note, smiled at the shopkeeper nicely, and asked if that would be enough. It was only a small victory, but we got it for a dollar less than ticketed, and walked off very happy.

We headed back to Aurora, and it was still raining. Sydney had been a little wetter than we would have liked, but we had seen a lot, and done a lot over the two days. Back in the cabin we spent the late afternoon and early evening on our balcony absorbing the final views of the Opera House.

Tonight, to round off sector three of our adventure, we would be eating in Sindhu restaurant at a later time than our normal dinner. This was to allow us to watch sail-away from a city that I have fallen in love with.

Goodbye Sydney, and thanks for some wonderful memories.

Sector 4 – Sydney to San Francisco

Countries we visited:

- New Zealand
- Fiji
- Samoa
- USA

Sea Days to New Zealand

Saturday 4th March

The temperature in the back garden managed to creep up to 22°C today, and it rained all day.

As we left Sydney, I suppose most of the 1,800 or so passengers on board were looking forward to a couple of days in the warm Southern Pacific sunshine as we sailed south and east towards New Zealand.

How wrong we were!

Captain Dunlop had announced that the weather wasn't looking to be very good, and as usual he was correct. As I woke up this morning (well actually I had hardly slept at all during the night) Aurora was creaking, rolling, and pitching around quite seriously. There was a force 7 wind, and the sea state was described as 'rough'. My little white pill had got me through the night, but I quickly took another, and hoped my stomach would survive the day.

I nibbled a bit of fruit for breakfast, but with no real enthusiasm, and soon Deb and I were in Charlie's just outside of Anderson's. Deb was working on her diary, but I just sat and watched the ship wake up. I've found Charlie's is a good place to be when the sea is showing her power, and this morning there were several other unhappy-looking people sharing the relative stillness of this lounge.

The outside decks were soaking wet and the wind was making it difficult to maintain balance, while inside the sick bags were left in prominent positions. The upper decks were roped off to stop foolhardy idiots going up there. Walkers were limited to Promenade Deck, and those braving the wind were struggling to maintain their dignity as the ship swung wildly from side to side.

Before too long I began to feel better and ready to move again. By 10:00 Deb and I went to a port talk in the theatre. This was another venue that I found suitable when my eyes, stomach and brain had different opinions on life. This morning we learnt a little about Akaroa, which would be the second port we visited in New Zealand. After listening to the description given by port lecturer Crystal, we decided not to book a tour and just do our own thing.

I was getting braver by now, and after the talk we went to Carmen's for a beginner's lesson on dancing the jive, or Rock and Roll. We learnt the basic steps plus a few turns and spins, and it felt as if we could possibly master this dance.

As the lesson ended at midday, the clocks went forward another hour to GMT + 12. I immediately dashed off to choir practice. This was the start of another sector, and there were many familiar faces, but several new ones as well. It was time to learn a new set of songs. During the earlier dance lesson, the movement of the ship had made us shuffle around quite wildly, and now it was creating quite coordinated swaying while we sang, but not necessarily in time with the music.

By the end of the session I was ready for something to eat. The sea was actually feeling a little less confused and angry, and the television navigation information had reduced the sea state to 'moderate', but it was still not a pleasant time.

While I had been singing, Deb continued with the Battle of the Sexes, and now at 2:00 we managed a few minutes catch up together before she dashed off again to the Salsa class. It was a busy day by our standards, and an hour later we were back in Carmen's for a continuation of the jive dance.

This is where it all went wrong.

Instead of reminding us of the steps we had learnt in the morning, the instructor simply told us to start dancing. We tried, but we had forgotten some of the moves. It was very apparent now that many of the dancers were already familiar with the jive, and certainly not beginners. The instructor was ignoring those of us floundering around the room. Deb and I struggled on for a few minutes but then gave up in frustration and anger. Rather embarrassed, we quickly dashed away.

It was time for a cup of tea together, and then a rest in the cabin until dinner time. With no enthusiasm to do anything else, I had a bath. My legs were still aching from the Walkathon and the days of walking in Sydney. It was a strange bath with waves in it, but they were a lot less dramatic than those outside.

Later Deb and I took part in the individual quiz: I had quite a surprise, as I actually got more questions right than Deb, for the first time on this cruise. I was still a point short of getting into the tie-break, but felt quite pleased with myself.

There were just six at the dinner table tonight. Peter and Helen had been at the table with us for the last sector, but they had had a cabin change, and also taken the opportunity to change their dinner arrangements to Freedom Dining.

Did we do something wrong?

The evening entertainment was a female singer, Alana Conway, in the theatre, and in Carmen's Coral Law from the entertainment team sang some songs, and shared the show with an illusionist called Danny McMaster. Up in the Crow's Nest, Lyn Frederick had her spot for the evening.

After much consideration, we had a rest in the cabin.

At 9:30 the dinner table six met up for a quiz in Masquerade's and did very well. We tied with another team and Martin decided to give both teams a bottle of wine. While we were still enthusiastic we decided to have a go at the Syndicate Quiz. Hey, we did very well again and finished just a couple of points behind the leaders.

All six of us enjoyed the Syndicate quiz, and we decided we'd almost certainly have another go at it in a few days' time.

By now it was late and we were all very tired, so it was bedtime. The sea was still tossing Aurora around as if she was a ping pong ball, so we expected another rough night to come.

....

Sunday 5th March

As we sailed further south it was just 18°C on the balcony today.

Yes it was another bad night. When I got up, it appeared to be slightly less of a roller coaster, but this wasn't what we expected in this part of the world. Officially the wind was Force 2, and the sea had calmed to 'slight', although I would beg to differ...but I'm not a sailor.

There was a surprise when we looked out of the balcony. We had company in the form of the Dawn Princess sailing alongside us. The Officer on the bridge announced that she would be with us for several days visiting the same places as ourselves.

After breakfast I needed to get out of the cabin, so while Deb did her diary I went for a walk. My Oceanic Marathon total has now gone up to 23 miles.

Just after 11:00 we both made our way to the theatre for a port talk about Tauranga. We had a tour booked here to visit a kiwi centre…the fruit, not the bird. The talk gave us a bit of background to Tauranga, with some ideas as to what else to look out for.

At midday the clocks went forward again to GMT +13 and I had to leave the port talk early so as to be at choir practice in time…what a busy life!

I came out of there at what was now 2:00 and went for some lunch while Deb had returned to the theatre for another port talk about Auckland. We hadn't got anything planned for there yet, and although the talk gave Deb a few ideas, we were still not totally sure what to do.

As the port talk ended I arrived at the theatre for a presentation by Christine Noble.

Christine was P&O's first full time female Cruise Director (a role now called Entertainment Manager) and we sailed with her on various ships during our cruise history. More importantly, she had been on the World Cruise in 2012 when we had such wonderful, and sometimes not so wonderful, experiences. Her talk was about the ships she sailed on, the captains she met, and a lot about the ships that she worked on as cruise director. And there was a little bit about 2012 when Aurora was the subject of drug smuggling.

Time for coffee, and then a rest in the cabin.

Tonight was formal dress code, and dinner was preceded by the 4th 'Welcome on Board' cocktail party.

So far I had survived the sea's annoyance through the day, but I was now getting a little uncomfortable, so I tried one of the new sea-sickness pills I bought in Melbourne. Hence I was careful about alcohol at the party, and just had a couple of glasses. Well the warning on the package about avoiding alcohol must have been serious, as by the time I began eating I was feeling really unwell.

I struggled through a very light dinner, and while the others went to a quiz I gave my apologies and returned to the cabin – and instantly fell asleep.

Half an hour later I was aware that Deb was back in the cabin, and holding a bottle of red wine. It would appear that I was the bad luck charm at the quizzes I fell asleep again.

A little later Deb gently stirred me, and asked if I wanted to go to the late quiz. I was feeling a lot better by then, so off we trotted to Masquerade's. It turned out to actually be a gameshow called "Landslide" and we did very well, but lost in a three-way tie-break.

That was enough excitement for all of us, as there was an early start tomorrow to watch a sail-by of the New Zealand fjords.

Monday 6th March – Fjords of New Zealand

Today we are very near to Antarctica, and it wasn't nice out on the balcony with temperatures didn't go above 14°C.... brrr!

At 7:00 am this morning the balcony door stopped creaking for the first time since we left Sydney. The wallowing sea had calmed, but I suspected this was only while we were in the magnificent fjords on the west coast of New Zealand's South Island. Aurora was just entering what is known as Milford Sound as I peeked out.

This should have been a beautiful view, but sadly today it was shrouded in fog.

Milford Sound was the first of three fjords that we would be sailing into today for a look around, so we hoped the weather would clear up as the morning progressed. A local guide gave a commentary through the fjords, and I heard him say that this was unusual weather for the time of year, and the first time he had ever experienced it while on a cruise ship.

This was becoming a common theme on this cruise.

We went to breakfast and discovered that the ship's decks were soaking wet from the persistent drizzle, making the fog even more miserable.

This first foggy fjord had been spectacular, but I think it would have been even better if we could have seen the sheer scale of the cliffs, and get an appreciation of the colours. The fog had left our view a little grey as well as obscuring much of the detail.

Never mind, there were more fjords to come later.

By 9:30 we were sailing at speed again down the western coastline of New Zealand's South Island. Our next area of interest would be another fjord called Thomson Sound.

We went for a walk.

As we pounded around the Prom Deck I remarked that on one side of Aurora there was New Zealand, while on the other side there was nothing until South

America. We had really come a long way. My total Prom Deck marathon now sat at 24 miles.

Dawn Princess had been behind us in the first fjord, but had left before us and was well ahead by now. I think the two Captains had mutually agreed to avoid being together in the fjords, and so would be visiting different ones to give the passengers uninterrupted views of the dramatic landscapes.

We had quite a surprise this morning, as while Deb was out on the forward observation deck, a passenger asked her if I wrote books as she thought she recognised me from the mug-shot on the back cover. She had read *'Around the World without Wings'* twice already and really enjoyed it. Eventually it turned out that she was in the cabin next to us, and later she praised me for my "very easy style" of writing.

Fame at last!

At midday we had another hour added to the time making it GMT + 13. This meant me getting a quick snack before going to choir practice, while Deb would grab some food between Battle of the Sexes and her Salsa class. I really didn't like the clocks changing in the daytime as it crammed up the activities around midday far too much.

While I was eating I saw another white cruise ship powering past us in the opposite direction. I asked an Officer which one it was, and he said it was the Pacific Pearl sailing under the P&O Australia flag. I thought it looked familiar at a distance, and when we were logged onto the internet I checked it out. She was once in the British P&O fleet sailing under the name of Arcadia. This was the second cruise ship we ever sailed on, back in 2001.

Since that fleeting glimpse in the Southern Fjordlands, the ship has moved fleets again, and is now called Columbus in the 'Cruise and Maritime Voyages' company.

Choir practice at 12:30 was quite a challenge. We began to learn a new song ("The Impossible Dream"), and the arrangement put together by Paul the pianist was rather testing. It wasn't made any easier by the distractions through the windows of Carmen's Lounge, where massive cliffs covered in vegetation were visible as we began our journey along Thompson Sound. There was no time to enjoy the scenery as we had to concentrate hard on this beautiful, but complicated song. Many of us came away with strange harmonics, and some not so harmonious sounds, ringing around our heads.

From Carmen's I returned to the cabin for a quick catch up with Deb as she stared at the magnificence of the fjord surrounding us. She had taken lots of photos already, and now I joined in.

At 2:00 Deb rushed off to her Salsa session, and I continued to enjoy a fog-free view of this scintillating landscape. The cliffs were amazing, and so high and steep that it was difficult to see the tops of them. They were virtually all covered in trees, but Aurora was a couple of hundred metres away from them and it was difficult to distinguish that the vegetation was actually trees, and appeared almost like grass. The scale was unbelievable: our guide at one point had suggested that one of the cliffs was over 7,000 feet high. I found this difficult to believe, as that meant the tops of the cliffs were more than a mile up from us.

Another piece of information was given about the occasional gap in the trees with patches of bare cliff exposed. It seems these were the result of landslides from the 2011 earth quakes.

And then there were such delightful rivers and waterfalls. These streams of water usually drained directly from the top of the cliffs, but sometimes they just appeared from the cliff-side as if coming out from a tap, and then flowed for a while before falling down the sheer sides of the cliff in a torrential waterfall. The rivers would also occasionally disappear into the trees, and then reappear several metres lower. They all eventually splashed into the water of the fjord with a mighty force gained from falling several hundred feet.

It was mesmerising to look at the sheer magnitude of the cliffs, and with the sunshine now adding vivid greens to the scene, it was almost hypnotic, and difficult to look away.

There was one magical moment during the afternoon when the Officer of the Watch informed us that a whale was coming down our side of the ship. We both leapt for cameras and burst out onto the balcony. Yes we caught a fleeting glimpse as it spouted, before diving back into its watery home, but our cameras never managed to capture the moment.

Our guide also suggested we would see seals on the rocks. This proved correct later in the afternoon, when we spotted a large number of them basking on the rocks on a small island. Other passengers saw dolphins, but I suspected the cold weather kept much of the aquatic life under the water.

Even though the sun did eventually burn away the fog, there were always layers of misty cloud drifting around. Sometimes the scene became quite eerie, with mountains in the distance having a fluffy layer of mist part way up.

It remained cold throughout the day, with temperatures never getting above 'wrap up warm' levels, and a cold wind blew across the decks keeping all but the hardiest passengers inside. I know we were a long way south, but it wasn't what we expected from late summer in New Zealand.

Since leaving the first fjord, the Dawn Princess had been far away in front of us, and visiting different fjords to Aurora, but late in the afternoon she appeared again. We had left the Dusky Sound (wonderful names!) and the two ships both returned to the open sea and gathered speed towards our next destination of Dunedin.

At some stage that evening, Aurora reached the most southerly point of our World Cruise. As the ship rounded the bottom right-hand lump of New Zealand, we were approximately 46.5° south of the equator. When we set off from Southampton, we were at about 50° north, meaning we had travelled south more than half the distance of the earth from north to south, as well as virtually half the distance around the globe.

The return journey towards home had started, but there were still lots of places to see yet.

Our evening entertainment was also a bit of a special one. It was a New Zealand Maori group called Te Oranga Kapahaka. They occupied the theatre stage for almost an hour with traditional Maori songs, dances and demonstrations of weapons. And of course they performed the Haka. There was also a chance for several of the passengers to have a go at the Haka and make fools of themselves to amuse us.

And no, I didn't volunteer for this one!

Caravan were playing in Champions, and the orchestra trio were entertaining the passengers up in the Crow's Nest.

The six of us from the dinner table went from the theatre to Masquerade's for the nightly challenge. Tonight all about classic films, we once again did very well, but one superb team were streets ahead of the rest. As Danny, the quizmaster, said to them, *"You need to get out more"*.

It was bedtime, and the six of us went back to our cabins. Tomorrow we were all going on tours of some sort, so a good night's rest was vital. Aurora was still rocking and rolling a little, but after turning northwards up the eastern side of New Zealand, it didn't seem as uncomfortable as it had been since leaving Sydney.

Tuesday 7th March – Dunedin, New Zealand
Just 12°C at best on the balcony today

It had been a much more comfortable night, and I had sufficient sleep to get up at 7:15 feeling rather refreshed. I looked out of the window and there were cliffs some distance away, but we were still quite a way out from port.

We made landfall in New Zealand today, and our first call was at Port Chalmers, which is the gateway for the city of Dunedin. The port is about 100 km from the southern tip of the country, and first impressions were that it appeared quite small. In reality, once we had time to take it all in, it was actually spread out and quite big. Aurora was parked with a view from our balcony of a vast area of pine tree trunks. The port here is the main base for shipping this timber to the Far East.

Our guide voiced quite a passionate view that it is so sad that all this wood is exported to China, where it is turned into cheap furniture and sold back to the people of New Zealand.

Just a little way along the quayside was the Dawn Princess. It looked like being a very busy day for the coaches and tour guides of Dunedin with upwards of 4,000 passengers and crew looking to be entertained.

As we went to breakfast we realised just how cold it was. The Officer on the bridge confirmed our first impressions, reporting a temperature of 11°, and this hardly increased throughout the day.

Our tour started at 10:30 so we had lots of time to stare down at the quayside, as a huge queue built up for the shuttle buses into the city of Dunedin, as well as hundreds of passengers heading to tour coaches. Of course the same thing was happening along the quay with the Princess ship offloading at the same time.

We could also see the railway station a few metres across the harbour from us. This has a scenic train that takes visitors to experience the countryside and even have a meal on board. Our friends Robin and Rosemary spent the day on the train and thoroughly enjoyed themselves. Robin is quite a fan of railways.

At least the short walk to the warmth of the train wasn't as uncomfortable as the experience for the hundreds of passengers queuing on the bitterly cold quayside waiting for their tour coaches. They were desperately trying to find shelter from the wind among the metal containers.

Having seen their pain, we changed our clothing plans and dug out jumpers from one of the suitcases under the bed.

Anyway, off we went. The tour was simple but very enjoyable. After travelling for about 15 minutes into the city of Dunedin, we made our first stop at the Old Railway Station. It had closed over 20 years ago but kept by the city as a wonderful heritage site. It is a beautiful colonial-style building featuring stained glass windows, Wedgewood ceramic tiles on the walls and floor, and has been kept as close as possible to how it looked when in use.

After that photo stop we moved on to the main attraction of our tour – Olveston House, which is a large house up in the hills above Dunedin built in 1906 for the Theomin family, who made their fortune from importing pianos from Britain. David Theomin and his wife lived a life of luxury with holidays all over the world, and they brought back paintings, ceramics, and souvenirs from everywhere they went, and these souvenirs were a little more expensive and exclusive compared to our fridge magnets.

Sadly the Theomin family story had a tragic ending. They had a son and daughter, but the son died young without any children. When the parents died it just left the daughter who never married and was childless. Her final wish was that the house was to be given to the city of Dunedin.

So the house was kept as a time capsule, with almost all the rooms preserved in the way that the family left them. It has many of the original carpets, and much of the furniture, dinner services, and artwork, all laid out as they would have been in the early 20th Century.

It was stunning, showing how the rich people of that era lived, and it is now a museum for the future. We both thoroughly enjoyed the hour we had there, and I believe virtually everyone else on the tour were similarly impressed.

Back on our coach we moved on to the city's Botanical Gardens for another rather special hour. We simply wandered through late summer flowers, a forest of local trees, and an aviary of wild birds. It was peaceful, beautiful, and a dream for botanical experts and amateurs alike.

Finally we had a scenic look around this largest city on South Island, with views of churches, schools, and even the "Steepest Street in the World", Baldwin Street, which is built up what appears to be a small mountain. Our guide continually gave us facts and stories about his home, and now mentioned the local Cadbury Chocolate factory which was in the process of being shut down by its owners, bringing to an end a fun annual custom. Each year the factory produced thousands of individually numbered Chocolate Oranges that were sold to the residents before being rolled down Baldwin Street. Whoever had the winning-numbered chocolate ball won themselves a year's supply of Cadbury chocolate. Now as the American owners are closing the factory with the loss of several hundred jobs, they are no longer on the Christmas card list from the people of Dunedin.

Our tour was over, and we considered staying in the city for a walk around before catching a shuttle back later. In the end we decided against the idea and went straight back to the ship.

The morning had been very special, but it was time to get rid of the woolly jumpers, and get some food and a drink again.

I mentioned earlier that Port Chalmers appeared to have cornered the market for exporting tree trunks from New Zealand. Well, while on the balcony late in the afternoon, I was listening to a local Scottish style pipe and drum band, enjoying the music (well some of it) and staring around at the amazing amount of wood on the quay. With nothing else to occupy my mind I made a rough estimate of how many trees of various lengths and thickness were in sight. It was most definitely in excess of 20,000. Assuming some of these different trunks came from the same tree, it meant more than 10,000 trees had been cut down and now lay here ready for shipping to the Far East.

I remembered our coach driver/guide this morning saying that these pine trees were fast-growing and only took 25 years to get to this stage. Apparently they cut down a forest and immediately replant new saplings. I found it quite amazing to imagine the years and years that these numerous small forests had been slowly growing, but were now just huge piles of timber.

OK, enough about trees.

Before we went to dinner, I gave my aching knees an application of a "Deep Heat" style cream that I had bought in Sydney, which stated it was good for arthritic pain. Well, I quickly realised it smelt quite strong, and within a couple of minutes Deb remarked that I stank.

It was a smell that reminded me of my youth in football changing rooms, when a similar smelling lotion was applied to prevent cramp. Today I began to think that I may have been a little enthusiastic with the amount used and yes, the cabin was full of a quite noxious smell.

At least my knees felt hot, so perhaps it was doing some good.

To my embarrassment at dinner, Deb mentioned my knee treatment, and some of the others joined in with... *"Ah so that's what the smell is"*. Richard and Angie even said they had smelt it in the cabin corridor...whoops!

After dinner I washed my knees thoroughly to avoid offending my friends anymore.

We were not leaving Port Chalmers until late in the evening: this might have been because of the tidal difference here. From this morning's high tide when we arrived, it dropped ten feet to the low tide later in the day. Perhaps we had to wait for it to become high again before we could safely leave.

The table team met up again at 9:30 for the evening challenge that was about ghosts, Halloween and so forth. Wow, this was a strange quiz, and we failed miserably.

Elsewhere on the ship, Caravan were playing a tribute show to the Eagles, and there was a late night 'Adult' comedy show in Carmen's from Danny McMaster.

We didn't bother.

Aurora set off again around 10:00 pm and had an overnight trip to our next stop at the port of Akaroa, which is about two-thirds of the way up the east coast of South Island and is the gateway to Christchurch. We had no plans and intended to simply go ashore for a walk.

Postscript

Deb's cousin had been on holiday in New Zealand at the same time as our visit. During the evening Deb logged on to Facebook and discovered he had actually been in Dunedin while we were there, and watched Aurora sail by as she left.

It is such a small world, and such a pity we hadn't checked Facebook earlier in the day.

Wednesday 8th March – Akaroa, New Zealand

Our balcony was a little warmer today with a high of 13°C.

At 7:15 I was woken by various sounds of people getting up in the neighbouring cabins. It's difficult to be quiet in cabins with 'gulping' toilet flushing systems, and drawers that insist on **banging**, no matter how hard you try to avoid slamming them.

There was also the grating sound of the anchors going down, and then the clanking of the first tenders being lowered into the water.

Today we were in the bay of Akaroa. This sleepy town is about 250 km down from the northern tip of New Zealand's South island. It is the access port for the city of Christchurch which is about 40 km (as the crow flies) to the north-west.

I gave up trying to sleep and went to grab and fill the kettle. At the same time I peeked out through the curtains to look at what was in our back garden today.

Aurora was anchored in a bay almost completely encircled by mountains. It is the caldera of a volcano with deep sheltered water. In the distance I could just make out the little coastal town of Akaroa, and the beautiful backdrop of hills that grew into undulating mountains as I gazed further. The hills were mainly the colour of late summer scorched grass, but there were also lots of lush green trees, and no obvious sign of any other buildings except for the town below.

The kettle was on, and I prepared the teapot and cups. Then drawing back the curtains a little more, my less blurred eyes saw the scene in more detail, but in the space of a minute, it had begun to rain.

A mist had appeared and the hills and mountains were greyed out. This sudden squall, and several others like it, came along and temporarily brought a drizzly rain to our vista. The temperature was a little higher than yesterday, but never climbed high enough to feel really warm on our balcony.

The water of the bay was calm with small ripples, and perfect for a smooth tendering operation. This would help to make the rather long (15-minute) journeys to and from the shore reasonably comfortable.

As we went to breakfast it felt quite cold, but without the chilly winds of yesterday. The light rain had made the open decks wet, so there was little chance of any sunbathing today.

The buffet was busy, with hundreds of passengers filling their tums for today's tours, some of whom were venturing as far as Christchurch. The tenders would be giving preference to those people on tours, so there was no rush for us to get ready to go anywhere. Our only plan was to go to the town and have a stroll, possibly have lunch ashore, and find some souvenirs.

It was almost 11:00 by the time our tender raffle ticket numbers were called, and we were soon setting off towards the shore. As we arrived near our pontoon we saw a busy scene, with the Dawn Princess also in the bay and tendering to the same little town. We had to wait and bob up and down while a pleasure boat crew ushered their passengers onto their craft. The pier was being shared by several boats as well as the cruise ship tenders, and quite possibly the pleasure boat was loading P&O passengers for a tour.

Once on dry land we were given a map by cheery local guides, and as we orientated ourselves we scanned the scene. It was obvious that Akaroa really was quite a small and sleepy seaside town. It has a normal population of less than 700, but through the summer this is multiplied several times by visitors, including from today's two cruise ships.

The town is predominantly a single road running along the edge of the sea with a few side streets. We walked from the quayside end of the road towards what appeared to be the main shopping area, and passed by some possible places for lunch. At the end of the street, maybe 250 metres away, it became mostly residential, so we turned back and investigated the shops in more detail.

Many of Akaroa's shops were slightly unusual. This is the town's shopping centre for all the inhabitants' needs, as well as attracting tourists. So they had a rather odd mix of stock, with souvenirs and local craftwork alongside their primary purpose. One of the first we looked around was selling knitting and sewing bits in one area, and typical imported visitor tat in another. Then there was a hardware shop that sold souvenirs, and another store had all the looks of a chemist shop but with glass kiwi-bird figures and fern-badged hats. It was obvious that the shops were making the most of the summer influx to milk our wallets, but at the same time they have to keep trade going with the locals all year around.

Well, it rained on and off, and when we came to the restaurants we had seen earlier, they were now packed with people deciding to have a meal while they sheltered. We gave up the idea of lunch ashore and window-shopped back to the quayside. I am sure there were a few other shops hidden away somewhere, but we had helped the economy of Akaroa with a fridge magnet and a few other bits and pieces, as well as an ice-cream. If we had wanted to, we could have booked a tour with the local taxi drivers, or a trip around the bay on a pleasure craft, but the less-than-pleasant weather steered us towards the tender boat.

By 1:30 we were back on Aurora and on our way up to the buffet for a quick lunch. Akaroa was a beautiful little town, but just as we had been warned by the port presenter, Crystal, there wasn't an awful lot to occupy visitors.

After eating I relaxed in the cabin while Deb went and had a swim. During the recent lumpy seas, the pools had been emptied, but today there was fresh water in the Crystal pool again. There were a few passengers sitting around under the shade of the glass roof, but Deb was the only one daring to use the pool.

When she came back she had an early shower, and I then had a soak in the bath.

...and I promptly fell asleep

As the gang chatted over our dinner, Aurora hauled up her anchors and set off on her overnight sailing to our next port – Wellington.

There was a little Australian delicacy on the menu tonight: crocodile sausages. A lot of people were tempted, including Deb, but they turned out to be ridiculously spicy, and several of the people who tried them left a lot on their plates. They rated similarly as unenjoyable as the "carpetbag" steaks offered a few nights previously (Robin said they were tasteless, and as tough and chewy as a carpet).

After dinner the six of us finally won another bottle of wine, at a quiz based on the subject of musicals, which apparently no-one else knew much about.

Deb and I had a rest for a while and then went to Carmen's, to watch the second show from the Maori troupe, Te Oranga Kapahaka. It was quite similar to the first, but this time it was a workshop-style show with a lot of audience participation. Deb had a go at twirling the Poi, and I took my turn making a total hash of the Haka. They are a lovely group of people, and brought a smile to many of the passengers' faces.

Elsewhere around the ship Alana Conway played her harp in the theatre. This was her second show and although I never heard any comments about her performances, I am sure many people enjoyed them. There should have been a tropical party out on deck, but with cold weather predicted it ended up in Masquerade's instead. Lyn Frederick was singing in Champions, and Kool Blue were up in the Crow's Nest.

After we left the Maori fun and games, we were pretty exhausted, but rounded off the evening with a nightcap in the Crow's Nest listening to the gentle sounds from Kool Blue.

The sea was calm as Aurora sailed northwards towards tomorrow's visit to the capital of New Zealand. It was time to retire to our very welcome bed.

Thursday 9th March – Wellington, New Zealand

There was a suspicion that the weather was improving as we sailed a little further north, and the temperature on the balcony reached 16°C.

The sea had been calm and we both enjoyed a good night's sleep.

By the time I got up, Aurora was at her berth in the capital of New Zealand, at the port of Wellington. This city is on the North Island, although less than 50 km from South Island. The city was damaged in November 2016 by a serious earthquake centred about 250 km to the south. This was only three months before our visit, and the damage and disruption around the city was still very obvious.

Our side of the ship faced the water today and there was a vast bay in view, along with the more residential suburbs of the city. On the other side of the ship the view was a typical cityscape, dominated by the imposing – and very nearby – Westpac Sports Stadium. This stadium is an amazing sight, and hosts national events for rugby and cricket. For rugby union fans, this was where the British Lions beat the All Blacks by 24 points to 21 in July 2017.

The dockside was a bit of a mess, as the cruise terminal building was a casualty of the earthquake. It was damaged enough that it couldn't be used. The result was that passengers had to be escorted straight to a shuttle bus, or onto a tour bus. Hence everyone not on a tour had to collect raffle tickets, as used for the tenders, and wait their turn to leave the ship in shuttle bus-capacity numbers. This caused a bit of an early morning delay to passengers getting off, but world cruisers are far more tolerant of issues like this, compared perhaps to some of the more vociferous Mediterranean holiday makers.

Our tour today was going to a wildlife sanctuary where there are a number of endangered species of animals.

Our driver also gave us a commentary during the short drive and he was quite clear about the New Zealanders' hatred of possums. When they were brought into the country they thrived, and took a delight in attempting to kill off all the other small animals as food. One of the most threatened creatures is the kiwi. This national symbol of the country is flightless, and has no way of defending itself against the possum. When attacked it simply lies on its back and kicks. Even if it doesn't kill the kiwi immediately, the possum will almost certainly break off its long beak. This leaves the bird unable to eat, and so dies slowly of starvation.

The reason they introduced the possum was to kill of the rats that also attacked the kiwis. Sadly someone didn't realise that they might enjoy a tasty kiwi as well.

Hence the need for wildlife sanctuaries.

We were at the beautiful wooded sanctuary for over two and half hours, and walked up and down the sides of a valley. It was very quiet except for the calls of birds, and the clacking of beetles. We saw several types of birds in the trees or on the ground, and also had a glimpse of a lizard. We certainly walked several miles along the woodland paths, and across the dam of a reservoir that forms one end of the site. OK, we never saw a kiwi, and much of the wildlife was sheltering from the early morning cold, but it was still a wonderful morning.

While we were there the weather improved from a cool start, and the sun became warm on our backs. Perhaps the tide had turned and we would start to have some better weather from now on….please!

We took the opportunity of staying in the centre of Wellington rather than going straight back to the ship. Sadly, this wasn't overly exciting for us, as it was what it says on the tin…. a city centre. There were lots of upmarket shops, and the restaurants were busy with the lunch time rush. It was actually getting hot by now, and the shops weren't interesting us much. Eventually we stumbled on the waterfront area and the Museum of Wellington. Thinking it might have a café for a drink and a snack, we went in. It didn't have a café, but we did pass 20 minutes getting a bit of the history of the city before deciding we had been out long enough and were tired.

It was well after 2:00 by the time we got back to Aurora, and our first priority was some food and a drink. Deb was hoping to tackle the laundry but many other passengers clearly had the same idea. Instead we both relaxed in the cabin, Deb updated her journal, and as usual I fell asleep.

By 4:30 there were still no washing machines available so Deb hoped to have better luck during dinner time, and we planned to have a room service meal.

Well, all the machines remained busy, and with a queue of people standing around waiting for them. Deb changed her mind and decided to wait until later. So we had dinner as normal. As we strolled down towards the restaurant, Captain Dunlop came on the PA system and gave his little evening chat. He said we were about to cast off and make our way out of the Wellington Bay towards the open sea. We just had enough time to watch the final activities going on below us on the quayside, before it was time for dinner.

While the six of us chatted, Aurora was set free from the quay and we gently manoeuvred away from the dockside. We were off again. We watched a beautiful sail-away from our table by the stern window that we had occupied for over two months now. As Wellington gradually became smaller, there was even a display from a pod of dolphins that we watched from our grandstand seats. Soon several passengers came and crowded around the stern windows to get a view of the show. It was absolutely delightful.

Unfortunately Deb missed the dolphins as she had left early in another attempt at getting a washing machine. When I went to find her, we obviously crossed paths on the stairs, or the lift, and she was nowhere to be seen. I knew she had been successful, as I could see our clothing sploshing away in a washing machine. I quickly realised where she was, and went down to Masquerade's and found her with the others for the early evening challenge.

Another bottle of house red wine was added to the collection.

Deb then began the serious part of the laundry with the drying stage and ironing. I felt I ought to be around, but she sent me back to join the others while they played trivial pursuits. She returned a little while later, and was in time to ensure the ladies won the battle. That was followed by a weird quiz all about people involved with the ITV "Dancing on Ice" show. This wasn't our finest hour as none of us had ever watched the show, or the soap operas that the majority of the skating celebrities seem to have come from. Not to be put off, our team decided to have a go at the Syndicate Quiz to round the evening off.

We didn't win, but we were much better at that quiz than we were at recognising soap opera stars.

It was a late bedtime and I was quickly tucked up in bed as Aurora began the next phase of our journey going up the eastern side of New Zealand's North Island. We had a day at sea to come before our next adventure at Tauranga.

Friday 10th March – Sea Day

At last the weather was improving, and the balcony warmed up to a delightful 21°C.

Today was our daughter Lynsey's birthday.

Well that isn't strictly accurate, as we were 13 hours ahead of Britain and as I was writing this entry for the blog, it was early evening yesterday at home. We planned to call her tomorrow morning and catch her at home.

I was later than usual putting the kettle on for our tea. The day looked grey, and the sea a little bumpy, but the temperature on the balcony was showing a pleasant 18°.

As we lay in bed with our cuppas, the Officer of the Watch reported that we had travelled over 17,000 miles since we left home a couple of months ago. Wow!

Although a bit warmer, there was little sign of the sun after breakfast, and a cold wind blew across the open decks, so today looked like another "let's do things inside" sort of day. Of course there was another port talk, featuring Fiji, at 10:00, before the busy lunchtime period started with the Battle of the Sexes, choir practice, and Salsa.

And there was lunch to fit in as well.

My usual office spot was busy so I had to find a settee in Andersons to update my blog. While trying to remember some of the important aspects from yesterday, I stared out of the window onto Prom Deck where a lot of people were walking by. It reminded me that I only had two more miles to fit in to complete my personal marathon challenge.

It was nearly 10:00, so time to go back to the cabin and drop off the laptop, before getting to the theatre for an overview of Fiji. I did my best to stay awake for the 45 minutes, and afterwards Deb and I agreed that we already had an acceptable tour booked for this island paradise. We will be having the usual panoramic tour of the highlights of Fiji, before going to a village to watch a traditional Fijian song and dance performance.

Then it was time to put on our trainers and attack the boards of Promenade Deck. It was the full mile plus a bit more, and that brought my total to 25 miles plus a lap or so.

Having exercised, we went for a cup of tea in the buffet, and then returned to the cabin to get ready for the manic midday activity period. Deb went to the Battle of the Sexes at 12:00, and an hour later it was time for my choir practice. While I was singing, Deb got some lunch, and after I finished singing it was a chance for me to grab something to eat while Deb was away at her Salsa class.

As she was stretching her body to the Salsa rhythm I returned to the Promenade Deck and walked another mile.

That completed my oceanic marathon walk. I started in the Atlantic Ocean, continued in the Indian, and now completed it in the Pacific Ocean. Forgetting the numerous miles we have walked while ashore, I have walked 26 miles, plus enough extra laps to make up the odd distance. Meanwhile, the ship had travelled 17,000 nautical miles.

This must be a contender for a combined record for the slowest marathon, whilst moving over the furthest distance.

During the afternoon, Aurora was ploughing through some rougher water and the wind continued to blow a horrid chill across the open decks. It wasn't a time for sunbathing, and only the hardiest passengers were relaxing by the Riviera Pool.

And of course this included the Mayor and Mayoress of the pool, who had been lying on their thrones in the same place all day, although for much of the time they had wrapped themselves in their Wimbledon tennis towels to avoid hypothermia. By now they had quite a band of committee members who joined them, but today many had offered their apologies and missed the meeting.

At 3:00 Deb and I got together again, and went for a cup of tea, plus a sausage roll....oops.

Back in the cabin I took the opportunity to stare out to sea to spot wildlife. We had been very far south for a few days now, and the only real visitors were birds. The gull-like birds that were regularly flying alongside Aurora had all the looks of being albatross, but my limited knowledge of birds wasn't sufficient to distinguish between the common Cornish seagull and this rather more majestic bird.

After checking online for clues I concluded that they did indeed look like albatross, but I had always thought they were solitary creatures, and today we were being entertained by several birds. Also it is extremely difficult to judge size and lengths of wings when there is no other reference. It was a lonely sea, and these birds were flying quite a way from the ship and I had no idea how high they were up either.

Eventually it was confirmed by the crew and other far more knowledgeable people than me that they were indeed albatross.

They were quite magical at time, and flew alongside Aurora for hours, seemingly with hardly a flap of their wings. I assumed they were using the drag of Aurora to pull themselves along, and maybe even using the heat from her funnel to create a rising thermal. However their effortless flight was achieved, I couldn't help but be thrilled by them.

Now these birds created a bit of a question around the ship. Being as there were several of them, should they be referred to as albatrosses, or albatri perhaps, or are they one of a few animals who have no specific plural term, meaning albatross is the only word used?

Back to reality, the afternoon was coming to an end, and it was a formal night. Our posh clothes were chosen for the evening and we both had showers. I was struggling with a traditional scraping razor since my accident with the electric one. I just don't like blades of any sort, and was finding it an awkward skill to achieve a smooth shave, but at least I hadn't drawn any blood...so far.

Anyway, before going to dinner we had time to fit in the individual quiz, where I scored more than Deb again, but failed to get a winning figure. Defeated once more, we got dressed and went for a pre-dinner glass of prosecco in Andersons with Richard and Angie.

The usual six of us sat at dining room table 228 where we laughed about, and discussed our day while we filled our stomachs. The view from the window this evening was of a confused sea that moved around in all directions, and certainly nothing like the beautiful vista we had last night sailing out of Wellington.

The entertainment for the evening consisted of a Ball in Carmen's, while yet another female vocalist took to the stage in the theatre. Her name was Elisha Hulton, and although I heard no reports of her show, I doubt she got a large audience because of the excess of singers we've had during our cruise.

The new Entertainment Manager (Leon de St Croix) had quite a job convincing us that we had had a fair deal with the entertainment. As well as the unimaginative acts, the entertainment team had been short-handed from the start of the cruise, and yet another left in Australia without being replaced.

This was supposed to have been a prestigious cruise celebrating the history and heritage of P&O. But the entertainment really didn't come up to the standard necessary to make it such a special celebration. The Carnival Corporation influence has really dumbed down, and reduced the standards, that were such a distinguishing part of the magnificent cruise line that P&O once was.

After dinner, the Table 228 quiz team won another bottle of wine at the early evening quiz, and then we played trivial pursuit until the late evening challenge. That was where our success ended, with a humiliating failure trying to identify audio clips from movies. Still keen, we went to the Syndicate Quiz, and although we actually did alright, we didn't get near the winning score.

There was now a distinct desire to win the Syndicate Quiz. We had just six weeks to succeed.

That was enough for the night. We all had tours tomorrow in the port of Tauranga. Some involved early starts, and all would require getting up promptly for breakfast.

Saturday 11th March – Tauranga, New Zealand

This was the warmest day for some time, with 21°C out on the balcony.

The alarm woke us at 7:00, and we had an early start to the day.

As well as having a tour booked, we wanted to ring our daughter to wish her a happy birthday. The 13-hour time difference meant it was early evening in Britain. It was only a short call, and much of it was dominated by our grandson Oliver saying hello to *"Ganny and Ganpa"*.

We were in Tauranga. This is a city at the top end of North Island. It lies within the area known as the Bay of Plenty and has a wonderful temperate climate. It was certainly warm, but sadly to mark our arrival, it was also misty and it was drizzling.

The Deputy Captain made his usual "Welcome to…." speech and failed to cheer us up by announcing that the weather was going to be misty and drizzly all day.

Ah well, this is the sort of thing to expect when cruising in the tropical season.

Our tour was called *'Highlights of Tauranga'* and aimed to tell us about the kiwifruit industry, as well as taking us on a visit to a house called "The Elms" that was built by a missionary.

There was a late start to the tour operation. Dawn Princess had arrived just before us, and the dockside was already busy. The New Zealand officials were ensuring everything went smoothly, but their safety rules, and their laid-back pace of life meant it took a lot longer than we anticipated. We were due to be on our way at 9:30, but our departure was delayed by about 15 minutes.

Now, let me point out that Deb and I were not worried about being a little late, we were not angry with the tour team, we were not angry with the New Zealand officials… but a few, just a few, of the other people on the tour decided that their treatment was worse than Armageddon.

Because of the slight delay, and because it was still raining, our guide made a decision to change the order of the tour. So while she told us all about the region, we made our way to a village community hall where we were going to have a cup of tea and a scone.

And of course we soon had the predictable message that..."*This weather is really unusual for this time of the year*".

Well, the scones were delicious, and made better by having kiwifruit jam and local cream on them. Around the walls of the hall were stands with tasting opportunities for the kiwifruit, drinks, jams, and liqueurs. This was the first time I had knowingly tasted the golden kiwi, which is a sweeter version of the more common green ones.

45 minutes later we paddled across the soggy car park back to the coach, and yes there were a number of carrier bags of kiwi products. We bought some of the jam we had enjoyed on the scones, plus a bar of kiwifruit chocolate.

The next part of the tour was a visit to a kiwifruit orchard where a guide would be telling us all about the fruit, the orchards, and the process behind getting the furry little fruit to our supermarkets. This guide's name was Graeme Crossman, who was once an All Black Rugby player in the 1970s. His career record showed he played 19 matches for them as a hooker, but strangely wasn't awarded a cap, so presumably he was just a substitute player. In retirement he had joined the huge number of people involved in the kiwifruit industry.

I won't bore you with too much detail, but the orchard we saw was just one of many in the area of the Bay of Plenty. The soil and growing climate is perfect, and they produce two billion dollars-worth of the fruit each year. They have to employ migrant workers from the rest of New Zealand, and even from neighbouring islands such as Samoa, Togo etc.

Now we were supposed to have had an opportunity to get up close with the fruit and stand under the vines that they grow on, but it was really far too wet for that. So, we had a drive through the orchard area while we listened to the knowledgeable giant of a guide, before moving on towards our next visit.

Because of the weather restrictions, we were now a little ahead of time, so the coach guide asked the driver to make a detour so that we could see vast piles of wood on the harbour quayside. I don't think she was aware that although

Tauranga might be a major port where the timber is brought and exported, we had seen just as much at Dunedin.

Of course we smiled and made suitable sounds of amazement, as she described the wood, and then we continued with the planned visit.

This was our final stop, and it was at a house and garden called "The Elms". Originally this was a mission station established in 1835 and overseen by a Reverend Brown and his family. He was one of many missionaries sent to New Zealand to attempt to bring Christianity to the Maori people. The main buildings were made from local cowrie tree wood, and have survived the years. This wood is very hard, and as there are no termites to eat it in New Zealand, most of the buildings are still the original wood.

A lot of the pictures, furniture, and personal bits and bobs have been retained and the guide explained a lot about the family history, and their lifestyles.

Outside in the gardens are a separate church and library, plus a selection of local trees including an oak, and of course an elm. They are all decades old and even in the annoying rain this garden was a true pleasure to walk around. As with so many tour visits, there wasn't time to look around the house and the grounds properly, and the rain didn't help.

It was time to get on the coach for the drive back to the harbour.

Just to round off the story of our tour, we arrived back nearly 30 minutes later than advertised…and those same people were still moaning about being 15 minutes late starting.

After a quick snack Deb and I went into the town on the shuttle bus. It isn't a town packed with great tourist attractions but there are lots of places to eat, and nearby there is the spectacular Mount Manganui for a lovely walk, if it is dry. We went shopping, and bought a couple of souvenirs, including a tee-shirt for Deb and a replica All Black shirt for me. On the more unusual side of shopping we bought a little cat collar to keep Deb's rucksack straps tidy, and some insoles for her trainers. Finally my rucksack was weighed down with a new supply of coke.

Back to the ship, and we had an hour or so relaxation before getting ready for dinner

The evening entertainment was a singer/pianist in the theatre. We actually decided to go and watch him. His name was Peter Cutler, and the act was modelled very much on Sammy Davis Junior but without the same level of panache, or to be honest, same quality.

He was acceptable as a singer, quite good as a pianist, a reasonable tap dancer, and included a little bit of humour. He was enjoyed by most people, but to me he didn't manage to show the 'star appeal' that his write-up had suggested.

After the usual late night quiz we all made our way to bed (without a bottle of wine).

Aurora was rocking around again as we make a very short, and slow, overnight sailing to our final stop in New Zealand at the port of Auckland….where it had been raining for the previous four days.

Sunday 12th March – Auckland, New Zealand

The temperature rose again, with a maximum of 22°C on the balcony, but the warmth was overshadowed by rain.

After a good night's sleep I woke to the sound of Aurora's side thrusters edging her into a berth at the city of Auckland, at the far northern end of North Island. It is the largest city in the country and was once the capital, but geographically the capital role was passed to Wellington.

It was 7:30 and it was raining.

Being a Sunday we had no intentions of going out until the shops opened, and hoped that the rain might stop.

A lot of people were leaving the ship today at the end of their adventures on Aurora. They would be replaced later by a similar number of strangers, giving us lots of new faces to spot.

Deb took the opportunity of having a swim in the open Riviera Pool. When she came back just before 10:00, she excitedly reported that the rain had actually stopped.

We had no concrete plans for the day, but the idea of a ferry to nearby Devonport was on a mental list. There were also some thoughts about visiting a museum perhaps, but much depended on the weather.

At 11:30 in the morning there was no obvious sign of rain so we left Aurora for a walk around Auckland. We passed through the entry security and reached the doors out from the terminal.

It was raining again.

In fact it was raining so much that we couldn't see more than a few metres. The scene in front of us was a mass of umbrellas everywhere, and a stream of dripping wet passengers returning to the ship.

We turned around and went back through the security screening and onto Aurora again.

The rain was pounding down on this beautiful city. Apparently there was a threat that the residents would have to boil their drinking water soon, because so much of the fertilisers in the soil had been washed out and drained into the water system.

We had another cup of tea, and on the way back to the cabin had a chat to one of the crew who laughed at us walking down the corridor with a gentle rendition of "Singing in the Rain".

Looking out across the harbour there was a suggestion that the rain might be easing, but I still couldn't see the island of Devonport that would normally be in view. We decided to make our minds up after lunch about going back into the city. Whatever we decided, we didn't think that wandering far from the ship would be a good idea, as the rain was coming and going on a regular basis.

Thank goodness we had a wonderful day here on our visit in 2012.

At just after 2:00 we spotted some blue sky. The rain had stopped, and it had stayed dry for 30 minutes. So we took the chance and rushed away from the ship towards the shopping streets of Auckland.

The city was bustling with tourists and presumably some locals as well, enjoying a moment of dry weather to stretch their legs. The weather really had been bad here, and we heard a news report on a shop radio describing an incident where residents had to be evacuated from their house as the rain was washing away the foundations.

We did a little shopping including yet more toiletries from a chemist: before coming on this cruise, we tried really hard to estimate how much 'stuff' we would be using, but there always seemed to be something running out.

After some 90 minutes wandering around the city shops, we noticed that the wind had suddenly increased, and our suspicions were that a shower might be coming. We made our way back to the quay, and were back on Aurora by 4:30.

As it happened, it stayed dry for the remainder of our stop in Auckland. I even sat on the balcony to look at the city…but as usual, I fell asleep.

The ship was filling up with new passengers during the afternoon, and as we had seen at an earlier port, they all seemed to be wearing Hawaiian leis. This would only be a temporary display of excitement, and they will soon fall into the laid-back relaxation of the ship as we sail towards some sunshine and warmth.

... hopefully

There was a chance to go and watch a folkloric show from a local group in Carmen's late in the afternoon. We didn't go and see them as the earlier show from the Maori group had already left us with good memories of this wonderfully friendly country.

It was soon dinner time, and the six of us caught up with our experiences of Auckland. There was lots to chat about as this is another beautiful city with so much to see. The people of New Zealand are friendly and really want visitors to enjoy their culture and their country. One example of their caring attitude was experienced by Robin and Rosemary. They had a tour which included going to the top of the Sky Tower for a scenic look out over the city. Their visit was during the rain, and there was no chance of seeing anything. The person in charge of the visit told people to hold on to their tour stickers and come back later. He assured everyone that the weather was going to improve.

I have my doubts if this would always have been offered back home in Britain.

When dinner was over, the six of us strolled to Masquerade's for another quizzical challenge. This one was hosted by DJ Martin and it was quite an interesting challenge to find the solution to 20 questions, that had the name of a fruit or vegetable in the answer. Of course we didn't win, but it was a good laugh.

We were all very tired after a couple of busy days, so we didn't make any plans to meet up again during the evening.

Deb and I considered going to a 60s and 70s party in Carmen's, but in the meantime, we lay on our bed catching up on the news with our e-newspaper, and checking Facebook. At 9:00, we decided to skip the party, and just went for a quiet drink in Andersons. Soon Captain Dunlop announced that everything was ready for us to leave Auckland and just after 10:00 a slight rumble and rattle heralded our departure. A lot of people were on the Promenade Deck watching Auckland disappear, and we joined them for a while. The rain had spoiled our plans but fortunately we have wonderful memories of this city from our visit here in 2012.

It was time to make our way back to the cabin. I looked at the weather predictions for our upcoming stops in Fiji and Samoa, and it suggested the sun and warmth was going to return. So I went to bed with high hopes that after two days at sea we might finally get some summer weather again.

We read our books as Aurora gathered speed and headed north toward Fiji.

Our journey home had really started now, and it was time to say goodbye to two countries that I fell in love with five years ago. Australia and New Zealand still leave so many lovely memories in my mind, and have a wonderful spot in my heart.

Two Sea Days towards Fiji
Monday 13th March
Hey, it was 24°C on the balcony today, and the sun shone.

It had been a jiggly night on board Aurora as we sailed almost due north from Auckland towards the Pacific island of Fiji. The trip would be over 2,000 km, and with some warm weather expected, the passengers were looking forward to a couple of days relaxing in the sunshine.

I woke at 7:30 and the view out over the garden suggested a better day ahead. There were breaks in the cloud, blue skies, and although we were on the shaded side of the ship, the temperature was already at 24°. As we drank our morning tea in bed, the Officer of the Watch came on the TV to announce the usual early morning navigation news. As well as *"we are due east of Sydney"* and *"we are going northwards at about 20 knots"*, he said that it should be a good day.

At breakfast the Horizon buffet was rather quiet: a lot of familiar faces were missing and several slightly confused new people were trying out the food. Once Deb and I were fed and clean we did a bit of office work, and then sat down in the theatre to listen to a port talk on Apia in Samoa. The outcome of the talk was that we decided to simply explore Apia by ourselves.

But we did go to Explorers to book a tour for the following stop in Hawaii. The chosen one was a walk (well actually more of a climb) up the Diamond Head volcano to see some wonderful views down over the island. There was method in our choice here, as the tour would be an early one, meaning getting officially immigrated early by the USA officials.

While at Explorers we also booked a tour for our first day in San Francisco. We chose to take a ride on the 'Magic Bus'. This is a restored bus decorated in psychedelic colours, and it would be taking a trip around the areas of the city where the hippy generation had their fun. By having an early tour it would also give us time to walk around the city, and possibly try and book an Alcatraz ferry for the next day.

By now it was time for a morning coffee, and we found a comfortable spot in Raffles. It was always busy here in the mornings and there were often people waiting to find a table to themselves. We quite regularly sat down with other friendly-looking passengers and attempted to strike up a conversation. This usually resulted in several minutes chat about our experiences, but sometimes there was an obvious icy atmosphere because we had invaded their space.

Raffles was also a place where we spotted the same people sitting at the same table day after day. The dance instructors grabbed a coffee before they began their class, while others read the ship's newspaper or tackled the sudoku challenge for the day. There were always conversations going on between people who had become new friends on the cruise, or were regular world cruisers who met up year after year.

One such group included a very recognisable man plus his son and a couple of friends. He always had a large glass of red wine while the others had coffee, and they chatted about the weather, the news from home, or what they had planned for the next port. When his glass was empty, he would catch a waiter's eye and another would appear. He spent most of the morning there and I saw him once at 8:30 with his first glass of the day, and he didn't leave until lunch approached.

"Red Wine Man" never appeared to be affected by his alcohol intake, and his mind was definitely clear and active. Occasionally he looked a little unsteady on his feet as the day progressed, but he never appeared to be drunk or even tipsy. Perhaps he should have been told to reduce his drinking, but he was getting on in years, and perhaps there comes a time when having an enjoyable habit is worth the risk of potential health hazards.

It was late morning by now, and the sun really was smiling down on Aurora, and it was warm. The wind was still a bit keen on the open decks, but after many days in the cold, people were gladly stripping off and enjoying some summer weather again.

The manic midday mania had arrived. Deb went to Battle of the Sexes, and I was soon away to choir practice. This was a fun session with a new song to learn. "Love Changes Everything" had been arranged with multiple harmonies, and after the men had sung, there was a round of applause from the ladies. Of course we responded in the same way when they sang their verse. With all the harmonies backing the melody, I have to say this sounded rather special. But the high notes are at the top of many peoples' vocal range, and beyond others.

I returned to the cabin at 1:15 and after a quick chat to Deb I rushed off for a spot of lunch. Then Deb was away to her Salsa session, and I finally returned to a game of cricket. To be on the safe side, I applied a liberal coating of the painkilling cream to my knees. I used the lift to go to the top deck, and the one I used had a gentleman already in it, and a Japanese couple came in behind me. As the doors closed, the Japanese lady turned her head and sniffed with a look of disgust on her face. My rather pungent liniment smell was obviously the culprit, but I did my best to confuse the situation by similarly looking around and sniffing suspiciously. I don't think anyone really knew who the offender was.

Anyway, the exercise and competition of the cricket was good, and although I didn't excel at either batting or bowling, I thoroughly enjoyed the 45 minutes. There was a strange moment when an Australian passenger was going to bat. He removed his watch and asked someone to hold it, but then removed his cochlea implant from his head, and handed it for safe keeping as well. He then made it clear that he was no longer able to hear, and went into the court to smash the ball around. After his batting time, he came back and casually replaced the little object and said *"thank-you"*.

That was another first for me.

I was back at the cabin at 3:00 and had a quick rinse of my head and body before putting on a clean tee-shirt. Goodness it was such a change to feel true heat again.

Deb came back and we quickly grabbed our towels and went up on deck for an hour to worship the sun.

…wonderful

While we dozed, the Officer of the Watch announced that we were about to pass close by a whale. Everyone on the deck rushed to the appropriate side and stared in anticipation, but we saw nothing. After a very long few minutes everyone trudged away disappointed, and settled down in the sun again.

Later, Richard and Angie said they had seen the whale clearly with a water spout and a perfect dive. They were at the stern of the ship when the announcement was made and saw the creature immediately. It appeared the whale had already gone by us at the bow end of the ship by the time the officer made his announcement.

Tonight was Formal dress code, so we both had quick showers and got our posh outfits ready before going to the individual quiz. After that we dressed and had a pre-dinner drink in Anderson's with our table mates.

The dinner featured a Marco Pierre White Gala menu, and to be honest these were no longer very spectacular. I hope the statistical results of *'how many passengers selected the different choices from the menu'* will lead to an improved one soon. The service was a little slow tonight as well, so we skipped the early evening quiz with an agreement to meet up later. We also avoided the main entertainment which was a group of New Zealand girls singing under the name of The Lady Killers. I am sure they were very good…for those still enjoying vocalists.

As well as being a formal night, it was also themed on James Bond. There were themed games and singing in Champions and a similar theme to the late evening quiz. Considering none of us actually like or watch many James Bond films, we did quite well. Feeling good (but wine-less) we moved on to the Syndicate Quiz and amazingly came a clear second, just a single correct answer behind the winners. They were our Nemesis team called 'Densa' again, who regularly pipped us by a single point in the team quizzes.

That was enough for us. We left the quiz on a high with coming so close, which gave us hope for the future.

The sea wasn't so jiggly as we went to bed, and after a short read I put out my light and snuggled into the pillows and quilt.

Tomorrow would be another sea-day and the weather forecast was extremely positive. We also had a lunchtime invitation to the Peninsular Club meal for Baltic and Ligurian-tier members. This is usually a very special lunch with an officer at the table and lots of wine to enhance a usually very good menu.

Goodnight everyone.

Tuesday 14th March

It was still warming up, and the back garden bathed in a maximum temperature of 25°C

When we woke, it was a pleasant surprise – no, it was an amazing surprise – to discover it was a warm sunny morning. The balcony thermometer was already showing 24°, and the Officer of the Watch promised a lovely day.

It was the second sea-day between Auckland and the island of Fiji, and we had nothing to do this morning, although we were going to the Peninsular Baltic/Ligurian-level lunch at midday. After breakfast we sprayed our skin with sun protection, grabbed our towels and made our way to the Sky deck to enjoy the sunshine.

It was a little breezy up so high, but that wasn't a problem. Deb had her book to read, and I listened to my music system for the first time in probably two weeks. An hour later, having toasted both sides satisfactorily, we packed up and returned to the cabin. It was so hot by then we were ready to cool down.

There was a short break when we had a cup of tea in the buffet, but we spent the rest of the morning relaxing in the air-conditioning. Of course we had to rinse our hair of sun screen, and a little later we got dressed for lunch.

Many of you will be regular P&O cruisers, and will have sampled the loyalty lunches, so you'll have an idea of what to expect. Well, today's was a bit of a let-down. The menu had changed since our last loyalty meal, and even our host (the senior doctor) was surprised, and perhaps a little disappointed by the choice on offer. Fortunately the wine was good, and all nine of us at our table enjoyed themselves chatting, but the food was less than special.

Later we heard similar comments from others who'd been at the lunch, so maybe the feedback would get back to the people deciding these menus, and some changes made. To be honest, I found most of the menus for meals had gone down in choice and appeal. Yes there are always fish, meat and vegetarian dishes each day, and several popular starters and main courses were always available. But we are having random, less than enjoyable, surprises such as salt and vinegar Ice-cream, and crème brulée that have soft tops. The root vegetables were now in chunks, the potatoes not particularly well cooked, and the infamous P&O green beans made appearances regularly. On the plus side we now get mangetout quite often…but that was no longer such a surprise and beginning to rate alongside the green beans. Oh, and we were also undergoing a glut of sweet potato that appeared in different forms at almost every meal.

At dinner it was quite common for at least one person at the table to have the standard prawn cocktail or tomato soup as starters, and the steak or chicken for the main course. I presume that the kitchen managers will be taking note of the lack of interest in certain dishes, and the amount being returned uneaten.

Anyway back to the loyalty lunch, and after consuming half a bottle of wine each, we left the restaurant at about 1:45 quite merry.

Then I made a mistake.

I decided to play cricket in the now very hot sunshine. I became dehydrated and burnt the top of my head in the fierce sunshine. Of course at the time I was enjoying the game, and it was one of the closest matches we had had. The last ball of the match was hit for six runs just out of reach above my head, resulting in the opposition winning by 116 to our 114. With the euphoria of competition over, my error of judgement became clear.

When I got back to the cool cabin, I already had a headache, and my neck was also aching. I put the neck issues partially down to sunbathing on my front with my head in a strange position, but most of my problems were due to a lack of water, too much wine, and getting overheated.

I drank a glass of coke, plus some water, and lay down to try to ease my head. I even put a cold flannel on my neck and forehead to cool down. Sadly by the time we had to go to dinner, I was still in discomfort although the worst of the aches had subsided.

My dinner was a blur, and I remained quiet, just eating some tomato soup, followed by fresh fruit and ice-cream…plus drinking a lot of water.

Things finally started to ease after a further hour on the bed in the cool, and I felt a little human again.

Table 228 did join up again later in the evening for a quiz about the 1980s and 1990s, but we left (wine-less) when it had finished and got some sleep before our arrival in Fiji in the morning.

During the night the clocks went backwards to GMT +12, so we had an extra hour in bed with a calm and quiet sea. The Captain promised earlier that we were going to have an enjoyably warm day when we arrive in the Fijian port of Lautoka.

Wednesday 15th March – Lautoka, Fiji

The balcony thermometer showed 24°C at breakfast time and rose to a glorious 34° as a maximum during the afternoon.

At 7:15 we woke to a sunny morning. Aurora had ceased jiggling during the early hours, and we had a quiet and comfortable night's sleep. Out on the balcony the air was very warm, and our back garden was a beautiful Pacific vista with little golden sandy beach islands covered in palm trees.

This was a part of the nation of Fiji, and we were some way from our destination at Lautoka on the western coast of the island of Viti Levu. This is the largest of the Fijian islands, and the word 'Viti' is the local name for Fiji, and 'Levu' means largest.

Our tour this morning was called '*Fijian Tradition and Beauty*' and was leaving at 9:45, so we had plenty of time for breakfast, and to gaze at the sights from the deck as we began the approach to our destination. Even though it was little more than an hour from when we got up, it was getting very hot, and without a breath of wind.

After waiting in the cool of the theatre for a few minutes, our tour group was called, and we shuffled off to the quayside. Deb quickly located the coach, and as we boarded, we were welcomed by our local guide who wore a sarong and blue tropical shirt. He welcomed us with the familiar "**BULA**!" that we remembered from five years ago. To be more accurate, he shouted "**BULA**" at us, and to all his guests. Once we had settled into our seats, our guide shouted his welcome even louder, and we quickly realised we had to shout "**BULA**" in return. He repeated his gesture of friendship at any excuse during the next three hours, and although we did our best to answer accordingly, our responses became less energetic and significantly quieter, but we did our best to appear enthusiastic.

Our tour began with details about the Fijian island archipelago, its population, the education system, and the very important wheat mill, all before we even left the port area. But soon it became more about our tour, and the beautiful countryside.

We passed by fields of different vegetation on the way to our first stop at an orchid garden called the Garden of the Sleeping Giant. The sleeping giant is actually three rock formations on the towering volcanic mountains above it, resembling a giant man, woman, and child.

The garden was created for Raymond Burr who was an American TV star in my childhood playing leading roles in "Perry Mason" and "Ironside", and his botanical legacy is stunning. We were guided along a pathway with brief (too brief, really) descriptions of the different examples of orchids, plus the other flowers and trees. To be honest this guide was less than useful, and little descriptive notices would have been far more informative.

Eventually we were left to stroll and enjoy this beautiful oasis by ourselves. It was so quiet, but our eyes rarely stopped flitting from one side to the other at the colours and varieties that begged to be looked at. Our cameras were busier than they had been for quite some time. The woodland trail was busy with tourists from Aurora, and another ship, so the pathways were congested, but that couldn't detract from a lovely 45 minutes. Our visit ended with a cool fresh fruit drink before we gave our final farewell "**BULA**" to the garden's staff, and one more as a welcome back to our driver and our guide.

It was time to move on, with more facts about Fiji before arriving at the small town of Nadi, where we had a 30-minute shopping session in one of those favoured shops that tour guides happen to know. As we got off the coach, a small group of men and women in traditional warrior clothing stood at the shop's entrance singing with accompanying drums to greet us. The shop was better than average with a fair selection of departments selling normal clothes as well as souvenirs. I am sure they made a good return from the three coaches on this tour, judging by the carrier bags that were stored on the coach's luggage shelves.

Our final stop was at a small village where the locals gave us a show. Sadly they tried to squeeze probably 100 of us into a small marquee, with rows of chairs that only allowed about twenty people a clear view of the action. Many of us stood outside the marquee in the unbelievable heat, as we took photos and videos of the action.

It started with a welcome ceremony where a chief was selected from the visitors, who shared a coconut shell of a local drink called kava with the head of the village's welcoming committee. The rest of us were also given a chance to sample the drink, and I was of the opinion that it resembled muddy water, but apparently it supposedly has quite mind-scrambling properties.

Our drink of muddy water was followed by several songs and dances from the traditionally-dressed village entertainers. I would like to point out that traditional costume for the men didn't mean very much. They waved spears as they danced to the drums and guitar, and it was really rather special.

At the end there were a few minutes where we could take photos of the dancers who smiled (with many "**BULA**" moments of course) and thanked us for coming. As we made our way back to the coach, some of the village women tried to get us to buy local craft items of jewellery and woodwork, but I think most of us just wanted the cool air-conditioned coach and a quick return to the ship by now.

So, about 30 minutes later we were back on Aurora after a final back and forth round of "**BULA**"s!!' and applause for the guide and the coach driver. It had been a short, but very sweet tour that I think most people found enjoyable.

Well, that is apart from the usual small group of whinging people complaining about too much heat, too short a time shopping, not being able to see, too hot, too much Bula, Bula, etc. etc. etc.

Five years ago our visit to Fiji was cut short by torrential rain that soaked the island for many hours, so this was a real delight. Deb and I thoroughly enjoyed the tour, and our time looking around this hot and sunny, and friendly island.

BULA!

Thursday 16th March – Sea Day

The balcony temperature didn't let us down, and it rose to a lovely 29°C during the day.

As we moved to the north-east, the sunrise was getting earlier, and this morning I saw the daylight through the curtain gap at 6:00. It didn't take much effort to roll over and stay in the comfortable bed for another hour, but then it was time to put on the kettle. A little peek through the curtains revealed the thermometer was already displaying 27° and the sea was almost flat calm with a dimpled surface that just wallowed gently.

Deb had done some washing the previous evening, so after breakfast she completed it by ironing the small number of garments requiring a little extra attention.

This didn't take long, and by 8:45 we were on our way up to Sky deck (above deck 13) to soak up the sunshine. There was a gentle breeze up there that took some of the edge off the intense heat. As Deb read her book, I lay listening to my music which has extremes of genre from Led Zeppelin to a brass band. As that stimulated my ears I also stared up at the blue sky with occasional fluffy cumulus clouds drifting over. The Officer of the Watch had described them as *"fair weather cumuli"* and they only briefly blocked the sun every now and then.

About 45 minutes later, my music suddenly stopped...the battery had gone flat.

It coincided with Deb saying she had had enough and we returned to the cabin to dump our towels and bits.

The morning port talk was about to start, so we hurried off to the theatre to listen to Crystal describing Hawaii, and the port of Honolulu. We had booked a tour there that would involve walking up the side of a volcano that is said to be a 45-minute trek up, and then down again. It seemed we would get a certificate to prove our achievement if we succeed in conquering the volcano.

From the theatre we went to the buffet for a drink, plus a Danish pastry (well actually two for me). We were approaching the manic midday moment again. The clocks went forward another hour (GMT + 13) and we split up towards our various midday activities.

Deb and I met up again at 3:00 after I returned from cricket. Playing in this heat meant a full change of clothes before we went to the buffet for a drink and a couple of sausage rolls.

The afternoon was rounded off with a spell of relaxation on the balcony, with the nearby relief of a cool cabin for cold drinks. Deb was painting a scene of an island we saw in Fiji while I stared at the sea. A flying fish woke me from my doze as it skimmed across the Pacific Ocean. This was my first sighting of the creatures for several days. The sea itself had become even calmer during the day, and now looked like a large silk sheet that just crumpled slightly as if being wafted by a gentle breeze. I remember describing a similar seascape to you many weeks ago. To enhance the scene, there were sometimes diamond sparkles from the sun reflected off any rare splashes of water. A little later we saw clouds building in the distance, and signs of showers on the horizon.

In his late afternoon announcement, Captain Dunlop described the sea as being *"mill pondishly calm"*. This triggered Deb to ask how a mill pond would be so calm, considering it would surely be disturbed by the mill's water wheel. Our Captain never expanded his statement, and also didn't mention anything about the rain showers that I had seen.

Must be OK then.

The navigation information on the television pointed out that we had gone beyond the 180° Longitude today, meaning we had travelled half way around the world.

As Deb and I arrived in Champions for the Individual Quiz I spotted drops of rain on the sea, and soon a dark cloud passed over Aurora, giving us a short sharp shower. Yes this was the tropics where you don't get much warning of rain, so I wasn't annoyed with Captain Dunlop for not predicting this change in the weather.

We had no rush this evening as we were having dinner in the Beach House for a change. So after a shower, we went for a pre-dinner drink in Andersons. The barman and waiters in there now recognised us as regulars, and quickly took our order, and brought the canapes and the little bottle of salty snacks. The canapes were rarely very interesting, but the salty nibbles were hard to ignore.

Just before 7:00 we picked up a bottle of quiz wine from our fridge, and made our way to the stern of the ship and the lovely Beach House restaurant.

Being early we had a choice of table, and picked one at the extreme stern to watch the sunset as we nibbled our shared starter of nachos. Sadly there were some clouds on the horizon blocking what should have been a wonderful sunset. Never mind we thought, the view was still sensational. Then the clouds increased, and it became darker. And yes, it started to rain.

We got up, grabbed our drinks and escaped inside. The guys found us another table and then ordered another plate of nachos for us. We could have done without any more, but of course we couldn't refuse to at least nibble a few. The rest of the meal passed beautifully with glorious food including my favourite of sizzling chicken, while Deb cooked her own steak on a hot lava rock. For pudding we had a huge slice each of key lime pie, and all this was accompanied by superb service, and of course the bottle of house red wine which went down very smoothly.

With the meal finished, we went back to the cabin and lay down, and we both quickly dozed off. We had arranged to meet up with Richard and Angie later, and fortunately woke up just in time to join them for the usual late night brain teaser.

That was all we could manage for the night, with all four of us tired and looking forward to our beds. Just one last twist to the day, was putting the clocks forward yet another hour (GMT + 14) to match the time in Samoa for tomorrow.

We had been told that the sea would be calm tonight, but Aurora was wallowing around quite noticeably, and not helping my slightly overindulged stomach from too much food and a little too much wine.

Perhaps that slice of pie was just too much.

Friday 17th March – Apia, Samoa

Our balcony started the day at 27°C and quickly rose to 32°.

We had no need to get up early but unfortunately when I had changed the time on my clock the previous night, I'd forgotten to put the clock settings back to normal. This incorrect setting meant the alarm became active, and we were woken by it at 7:15.

Deb and I did our best to stay asleep, but it was soon time to make the tea. To be honest the sounds of others around us flushing toilets and banging drawers and doors, was not going to let us doze any longer.

Today we would be in Apia, the capital of Samoa. We came here five years ago and had a wonderful day on a beach, but we never saw anything of the city. So today we hadn't got a tour booked, and just intended to look around the city of Apia later.

Aurora started her docking procedure around 8:30 when the temperature had already risen to 29°. That was when we went to breakfast, and as we hit the air of the open deck, the heat, and more importantly the humidity, hit us. I was leaking sweat before I had walked the length of the Riviera Pool.

The harbour at Apia is small but busy, with a container area, ferries, plus our cruise ship mingling with a police boat, tugs and local small craft. With breakfast over, we looked around as Aurora was being tied up and preparations beginning below to get gangways and secure areas sorted. Looking out to sea there was a wonderful view of the calm sea, and about 250 metres from the harbour, a ridge of coral just below the surface created a long length of breaking waves as if it was an invisible beach.

We were having our wash in the cabin when I heard singing. I went out on the balcony and saw group of locals on the quayside in traditional dress of grass skirts, and plaited grass tops for the women. The men did most of the dancing while the ladies sang and swayed, and the group entertained the balcony passengers for about fifteen minutes. As they left to applause from above, the first of the passengers on tours were on their way to the buses, and other people were beginning a walk into the city centre.

Then, with almost no warning, it started to rain. It wasn't heavy and only lasted a few minutes, but it soaked the ground and reminded us of 2012 when we had rain for all of our time on this island. We decided not to even consider going out yet.

Deb went for a swim in the deserted pool and I caught up on my diary entries.

At about 10:30, with the ship almost deserted, we made our way to shore for a walk. The heat and humidity were even worse, and I felt the instant outpouring of sweat. We fought our way bravely through another flock of taxi drivers that stretched for 100 metres from the port gates down the road towards the city centre. After half an hour of walking without finding more than a photocopier sales showroom, and a local supermarket, we called it a day. There was still a long way to walk before getting to the centre, with things to see, and possibly some shops, and it was horribly hot and sticky.

The walk back was energy-sapping from the uncomfortable heat, and those same taxi drivers continued to offer us tours of the island. There were some souvenir and clothing stalls in the harbour that amused us for a few minutes, but we only added $5 to the island's economy.

The cabin's air-conditioning was a real relief as we peeled off our sweaty clothes and found some fresh ones to wear. It was lunchtime, and although not feeling particularly hungry we both had a plate of fish and chips, and they were delicious. In fact they were probably the best we had had in over ten weeks. Even more enjoyable was an ice-cream on the way back to our cabin.

Although it was still hot and humid, we had three quarters of an hour in the sunshine. My iPod was recharged, and I continued to work my way through the music of my younger years, and Deb immersed herself in a book again.

Hot and sticky once more, we returned to the cabin's air-conditioning to find comfort again. The thermometer was showing 30° on the balcony (which was out of the sun) and it was still rising.

We stayed inside.

Tonight's entertainment was once again less than sparkling for our tastes.

In Carmen's, one of the orchestra members (Les) demonstrated his musical virtuosity, while the theatre featured a couple showing off their dancing skills. Called Epic Moves, they certainly interested us a bit, and we thought they might be better than the Masquerade's gameshow based on "The Chase" TV show.

We were on the way to Curzon's at the end of the first theatre show, and we met Robin and Rosemary as they came out. They enthused about the dancers, saying we must see them.

So after watching the gameshow for a little while we made our way to the theatre to watch the late night show from Epic Moves. It was fantastic, and the couple were extraordinarily good. It was a fusion of traditional ballroom and Latin styles of dancing, mixed with some fantastic gymnastic moves. The dancers used video clips from popular films and danced to the theme tunes with their own interpretation. It included the "Dirty Dancing" moment with the run and lift above the head. There was a hum of anticipation for this one, followed by a gasp of amazement when the girl soared into the air. The audience around us were cheering every sequence of dance, and audibly "***ooh-ed and aah-ed***" at the spins, lifts, and throws. It was also obvious that a number of the people had been to the earlier show, as they were anticipating the special moments before the rest of us knew what was coming. Deb and I had been attempting to improve our dancing skills for several years, and this was a wonderful demonstration of skill, as well as being an energetic and truly artistic show.

It was bedtime by the time we left the theatre.

During the night our journey would reach a special landmark. We would be crossing the International Date Line, so when we wake up tomorrow, instead of being 13 hours ahead of Britain, we will be half a day behind, and it will be the 17th March again.

Yes we were getting an extra day!

I despair

I struggle to comprehend some people.

I will go back to yesterday afternoon in Apia, but it could probably be any cruise terminal throughout the world.

Aurora was due to leave Apia at 6:00, and the *"be back on board"* time was 5:30. I was watching proceedings, and at 5:15 there was a rush of passengers on the quayside to be on time.

Now, Apia is a city where the port is at one end of a bay which carries on around for at least a couple of miles to the city centre. There is a footpath that follows the shoreline, and from the balcony I could clearly see a part of that path at a spot several hundred metres away from the ship. I noticed there were still passengers making their way back at that point, with a 10 or 15-minute walk ahead of them. I remarked to Deb that these people were pushing their luck to be back on-board on time. I leant on the balcony rail in the sunshine and continued to notice people walking along that pathway. These people were now almost certain to be late, but none of them appeared to be in any hurry.

The time moved on to 5:30 and I could still see people strolling without a care in the world with 15 minutes of walking to go.

Now, we have never been anywhere near to the *"back on board"* time except when on delayed tours. I would be in a blind panic if I was that far away from the ship with less than 30 minutes before scheduled sailing time. These people must have an assumption that *"the ship would never go without me if I'm late"*.

To cut my story short, the last passenger finally walked up the gangway at 5:55. In that period beyond the final boarding time, over 30 people made their relaxed way back to Aurora. Among them were the Spanish teacher and his partner, who rightly had a ticking off at the gangway. One of the ship's security crew on duty at the gangway was trying to instil a bit of urgency into these people, as they strolled along the quayside: several stopped to admire the flowers from the morning's welcome show, others stared at the water in the harbour, or stopped to take photos of the ship. It was as if they were competing to be the last person to get back on board. The stevedores had long been ready, the tug had been ticking over its noisy engines below our balcony for half an hour, and I assume the pilot had been on board for a similar time.

We were late leaving, OK perhaps not by many minutes, but certainly later than scheduled. These thoughtless passengers had had eight hours to explore and enjoy this city, but without any concerns had left themselves less than enough time to get back.

I am sorry, but I no longer have any sympathy for people being left behind by a ship without a reasonable reason. Although rare, there are moans from people who have been stranded in ports around the world for being a *"little bit late"*, and then expecting sympathy from the hundreds of passengers who make it back with plenty of time to spare. I am sorry for those who have valid reasons through sickness, but it clearly states the times in the ship's newspaper, and on signs at the gangway.

For all those who were late that evening, and who didn't even show any concern ....SHAME ON YOU!

Tuesday 17th March – *Again!* – At Sea

At last the tropical warmth was making the balcony more tempting, with temperatures up to 29°C.

I had a restless night, and as I lay awake hoping I could get back to sleep, my mind began to wander through the phenomenon called 'Crossing the International Date Line'. Yesterday morning (17th March) we woke up at our usual time and we were 14 hours ahead of our friends and relatives back home in Britain. Now I was about to get up on 17th March again, but we were now 10 hours behind those same people. Even more peculiar to some, yesterday was St Patrick's Day but it wasn't officially celebrated on the ship, now a day later it had suddenly become St Patrick's Day.

It was another lovely morning as Aurora sailed virtually due North with just a slight bit of east thrown in. We were now on a five-day voyage from our Samoan stop to the port of Honolulu in Hawaii. As I suggested, the weather had improved over the last few days, and today brought temperatures into the late 20°s with just a few clouds occasionally shading us from the sunshine.

This morning Deb started with a swim while I worked in the office. Later we had half an hour in the sunshine as well as checking in at Raffles for a mid-morning coffee. Midday approached, and with the clocks stable for a little while, we had time to have lunch together, before choir practice, quiz commitments and exercise. It made a change to not have the manic frenzy of late.

After getting together for afternoon tea Deb and I relaxed in the cabin, and I dozed on the balcony in the warmth.

Our evening was rather enjoyable. Dinner was the usual hour of chatter and gossip, and then we had the first of the quizzes. We hadn't won a bottle of wine for many days, but it was no longer because of our bogey team (Densa). A new person had become the wine cellar champion, and was becoming far too predictable with his amazing knowledge of film, TV and music, plus a pretty good general trivia recall. Even he was aware of his reputation among the quizzers, with his quiz team name being called *'**Brian…..go away!**'*

After that disappointment all six of us went to the theatre to watch a show from Robbie K who described himself as an 'unusualist'. It didn't disappoint us. He started with juggling at which he is good (not brilliant), accompanied by jokes and banter that got our attention. Then there were a couple of magical tricks, plus more jokes. By now the audience were right with him, and it was a superb 45 minutes. He described his act as pure variety that he enjoyed as a child, and I think many of us yearned for more of that style of entertainment as well.

As expected the show finale involved audience participation. This began with a woman throwing juggling balls to Robbie while he balanced on a toilet seat rolling on a tube. This was greeted by much laughter and applause. Then I was dragged up to join them on the stage. We were both asked to play a simple tune using tiny bells...more laughter and applause from the audience. The woman was then allowed to return to her seat with a balloon toy, and it was my turn to assist him.

Initially I had to catch hoops on my finger thrown from half way across the stage. I managed to catch all five and got a round of applause. Then I had to throw them back to be caught on a spike attached to his hat...three out of five, which brought more applause. My reward was a ridiculous balloon hat with a pair of eyes and a heart. I was supposed to wear it for the rest of the evening and be loved by everyone.

The show ended with a deserved standing ovation (for him, not me!) and the audience left the theatre with smiles and positive comments ... well from most people, anyway.

Elsewhere around the ship there were singers in the different bars, plus Caravan in Carmen's performing their tribute to the Bee Gees ... again.

Caravan had finished in Carmen's so we all went to Vanderbilt's for the St Patrick's Day themed quiz. I was ordered by the others to wear my hat and look stupid, and one woman did come up to me and gave me a hug and a kiss to **show the love,** as commanded by Robbie K.

Of course we were humiliated in the Irish themed quiz. The only good thing was that we scored more than the only Irish team in the room.

Bryan and his helpers won again.

Robin and Rosemary had gone to the cinema before the quiz ended, but the remaining four of us weren't disheartened, and we went upstairs for the syndicate quiz. We didn't win but Deb came up with some amazing guesses that brought us to one point behind the pair of teams who had the highest scores. This time it wasn't Bryan….who was probably drunk from an excess of free wine. The winning team were Densa again.

We were quite content with our performance and went to bed happy.

Aurora was still sailing on her north-north-east course at a little under 20 knots. The wind was light, and the sea calm. There were another four days and nights at sea before we would arrive in Hawaii, and the forecast was for the weather to remain good for this journey.

Saturday tomorrow, and our floating home would be crossing the equator back into the northern hemisphere.

What an amazing voyage.

Four Further Sea Days towards Hawaii

Saturday 18th March

Today it was 28°C on the balcony during the afternoon.

Late up again, but that meant 7:45 rather than 7:15, so we were still vertical and mobile before many hundreds of the other passengers. It was slightly cooler at 27° early on, but the sun shone through the breaks in the clouds making us all happy again.

Following an early morning worship of the golden globe in the sky, we went to the port talk for San Francisco.

It started with quite a surprising discovery.

Crystal asked how many people in her audience were leaving Aurora in San Francisco. Amazingly the majority of the people in the theatre put their hands up. Ok, so the majority will be replaced by new passengers, but it was strange to see the percentage involved.

Anyway, we listened to the presentation just to get ideas for the rest of our stay as we already had a tour booked on the *'Magic Bus'*. This is a vintage coach decorated in 60s style which tours the city looking at the hippy places of that era.

Having been through most of the highlights and tours of the city, Crystal added another one to the list that had only just become available. This featured a ride on a restored luxury train to the Napa Valley, with wine tasting and a meal on-board. It looked rather special, and when I turned to Deb she agreed with me. So after leaving the theatre we rushed to the Explorer's Desk and asked for more details, and the price. We had been warned by Crystal that the places were very limited, and it was expensive.

Twenty minutes later we came away with our new tour tickets. It cost over £200 each but we reduced the price a little by the *'Magic Bus'* tour refund. This would be a luxurious and special tour, but we hadn't been extravagant anywhere else.

After coffee we relaxed for the remainder of the morning. It was hot and sunny outside but lunchtime wasn't far away followed by our busy time again.

While we were relaxing in the cabin, a plumber arrived to sort out our sink which wasn't draining very well. This was the second attempt at fixing this in two weeks. To put it into context, apart from the creaking in bad weather that everyone suffered from, this minor sink malfunction had been our only issue.

The lunchtime refuelling visit to the buffet set us up for our afternoon activities. With the Headliners performing the ABBA tribute show late in the afternoon, the singers and dancers had rehearsals. This meant choir practice had been early, and Deb had no Salsa class after the Battle of the Sexes quiz. She had an hour on the stern deck enjoying the sun while I sweated away in the cricket nets. There were over 20 of us there today, including two girls joining in. That calmed down the language, and DJ Martin was unusually quiet.

Exhausted, I joined Deb and we went to the buffet again. Once we had finished our cup of tea (and a scone for me) we went back to the cabin to cool down. Well actually I went out on the balcony in the sun, and my chest quickly took on a pink colour. The sun was very intense, and it didn't take long to doze off to the gentle lapping sound of the sea.

Tonight was a formal night, and it was soon time to begin our preparations for the evening. With showers over, and our formal clothes hung up ready, we went to the individual quiz.

Dinner was from a special menu, and we all ate at least one item from the featured chef choices. This had been one of the better meals.

After dinner all six of us made our way to Carmen's for the second 'Around the World Passenger Cocktail Parties'. Let's just say that although we hadn't expected to drink much, it became a very alcoholic party. The Captain made his speech, and introduced us to the senior officers from right across all the ships areas. Then as second sitting passengers went towards their dinner, the cocktail waiters had to get rid of all the glasses of wine that had already been poured. Oh dear, we were all holding two glasses of drink for nearly half an hour.

Sadly, at some stage of this party, I had again spilt some red wine onto my dress shirt. This was really annoying, as I had been trying to be extra careful. Rather than going off to change my shirt, I simply returned to the cabin and put on a waistcoat to hide my embarrassment. Of course we were nearing the equator and it was a hot evening, and that extra layer didn't improve my body's temperature.

The entertainment that evening was quite limited. There was a Ball in Carmen's, and in the theatre someone called Peter White performed a tribute to Kenny Rogers. Of the two, Carmen's was our preferred choice, but the dance instructors hadn't enthused us enough to rush and join in with their evening Balls. To be honest, I didn't rate them as suitable for beginners, and they appeared happy to concentrate on a small group of people who had been going regularly to their lessons, rather than anyone wanting to join in as the cruise progressed.

Perhaps I was hoping for the same level of fun and teaching we enjoyed five years ago with Alan and Ginny.

We avoided both venues, and the evening turned into a slightly tipsy and unsuccessful quizzing session. Somehow we had found ourselves some balloons that followed our progress from Masquerade's to Vanderbilt's. Our brains were cumulatively not working, and scores were pathetic.

Did we care?

Well not knowingly at the time.

Now here is a little fact about the day. We hadn't seen anything outside but the sea. There had been no ships, whales, or dolphins. Our only company had been the occasional flying fish and some lonely birds.

What a very big ocean we were sailing across.

Well that was the second of our sea-days before we would reach Hawaii on Tuesday morning. As had become a regular feature of the cruise, the sea became a little lumpier as we went to bed, and the wind was buffeting the ship a bit. Never mind, the forecast was for the sun to continue shining on us, and the temperature to be in the late 20°s.

……………………………………………..

Sunday 19th March

It had warmed up again, and the temperature in our garden managed to get to 31°C.

The sea was noticeably lumpier this morning, and with an even stronger north-east wind. Aurora moved around more than we had come accustomed to since leaving New Zealand. It was still warm but there were very few people on the deck when we went to breakfast.

Except the Mayor and Mayoress of the Riviera Pool of course.

After breakfast we parked ourselves on deck 13 in the sunshine. The blustery wind was obvious, but it was warm so didn't put us off. We had an hour out there as Aurora woke up and passengers began to choose from the abundance of unused loungers, the one that best suited their preferences. There was a problem with my iPod again, and my audible entertainment stopped. Presumably the battery had gone flat once more, but it wasn't long since I charged it. I had a suspicion that my trusty little music player was wearing out, and that a replacement would need to be sought out.

After sufficient sunshine we went for coffee, and then returned to the cabin to cool down. There was no port talk today, and although the guest speakers had some fascinating subjects to listen to, they didn't appeal enough to tickle my fancy.

For the second day in a row, the clocks have remained at the same time.

Our choir was polishing off a medley of songs from "Singing in the Rain" for our performance at the end of the sector. And many of you will know that the title song involves whistling at the beginning. Now, earlier in the cruise I complained to you about people whistling, but now I had become one of them. I decided that in this instance, whistling is permissible in public as "artistic enhancement", and not simply producing weird notes in no particular order and not to any recognisable tune.

Oops, sometimes a little like us then.

Anyway, when singing was over, I got myself some lunch before going back to the cabin for a relaxed 15 minutes. Then I said "cheerio" to Deb as I went to play cricket. Deb was going to her Salsa class very soon after.

There was a re-run of the 'Crossing the Line' ceremony in the afternoon, and all the entertainment team were involved. Hence DJ Martin wasn't at cricket to supervise and shout at us in his very special way. Apparently, Martin was always right, always saw exactly what happened, was the only one to understand the rules, and always made new rules if something went wrong.

Oh, and he always had the last say.

Anyway, back to today's cricket match. Because Martin wasn't there, it was an "un-hosted" event, and so just for fun. During the afternoon of the first 'Crossing the Line' ceremony many weeks ago, I hurt my little finger during the cricket. It still hurt, and I hadn't been able to catch the ball with any confidence, so I regularly dropped the ball because I couldn't grip it properly.

Well, luckily there were no injuries today.

Unfortunately my batting was a little disappointing as I was out twice during my innings. That cost our team 10 runs, and my final score was just two runs. On the plus side, I actually managed to hold one catch, and helped the team with my bowling, when I had a batsman out three times in three balls...a hat-trick, and 15 points for us. The team I played for won by over 100 runs.

When I re-joined Deb, she was in the laundry waiting for the washing cycle to finish. It finished moments after I found her, and the clothes were loaded into a dryer. That allowed plenty of time for an afternoon cup of tea. No cakes today, but I did have two small tuna sandwiches.

When the washing was dry, we both sat and dozed in the cabin. I went onto the balcony where the wind was quite buffeting, but the sun was strong and the warmth delicious. Deb tried to read her book, but just like me, found it difficult to stay awake.

The evening entertainment was a second show from Epic Moves in Carmen's, and in the theatre, was Peter Howarth, a singer who had been one of the Hollies. We were already aware of the wonderful Epic Moves brilliance, and but also wanted to watch Peter Howarth following some very positive feedback about his singing. So to fit it all in we went to the buffet for a much quicker meal, and were sitting in Carmen's for the first performance at 7:00.

It was another terrific show of dance and gymnastic moves, and we left with smiles on our faces as we rushed the length of the ship to get a seat in the theatre. The feedback about Peter Howarth was right, and he sang several memorable songs from my youth. He also played the guitar for some of the act and I thoroughly loved the show. Deb was positive about his singing as well, but not quite so over the moon with the act as many of the watching passengers, who stood and applauded him at the end.

There was time after the shows to get to Masquerade's for another quiz disaster, before we went to Vanderbilt's, where we were pathetic, and one of the lowest-scoring teams in the syndicate challenge.

It was late by then and our bed was calling out our names to come back and get some sleep.

It had been a hot day again, with more of the same promised for tomorrow. The wind was getting a little wilder, whipping up a few waves and making the ship jiggle. I returned to the little white pills to ensure my head, eyes, and stomach were kept synchronised and happy.

……………………………………………..

Monday 20th March

It was a delightful 28°C on the balcony during the afternoon.

Today was our son's (Andrew) birthday. We couldn't phone him to wish him many happy returns, but did send him a text at midnight yesterday (our time). The price of satellite calls is ridiculous, so a text message was the only sensible option.

It had to be sent last night, as ship's time is now 10 hours behind Britain.

Bringing our progress up to date, we were on our fourth of five sea days from Apia to Hawaii, and I had to think carefully about what day it was. Aurora had crossed the equator during the night, and we were back in the northern hemisphere. The sun was shining and it was 28° outside. The wind continued to strengthen and was up to a Force 6. Apparently, the sea was only slight, but Aurora rocked and juddered enough to make the water in the Riviera Pool create waves, that broke so violently on the pool's edge that there were plumes of water going over anyone sitting nearby. The couple (you can guess who by now) who had occupied that same position every day on the little deck by the pool, were still there. They refused to move even though the water was drenching them as they tried to eat their breakfast. Yes, they got there early enough each day to secure their thrones, and eat breakfast no matter what the weather was, apart from a small number of days when we were around New Zealand, when the rain was just too heavy, even for them.

They hadn't done anything wrong, but they had caused quite a few passengers to remark on their quest, suggesting they were just a little bit over the top.

Anyway, the wind was a little bit much for sun-bathing at the moment, but we hoped things would improve later.

There had been a change in the Headliners' dance classes. They were now alternating Salsa on one sea day followed by tap dancing the next. Although Deb had been told she could learn the basics of tap dancing wearing trainers (much quieter I imagine) she wasn't sure if this was something she really wanted to do.

Moving forward to 3:00 I was back at the cabin with Deb. She had enjoyed the tap dancing lesson but still prefers the Salsa. We would have to wait and see what happened with this change to her routine.

My cricket wasn't as enjoyable as it used to be. The strong wind made it difficult to maintain balance, but that wasn't the problem. Matches had become more and more argumentative, with more shouting and barracking than getting on with the game. There were still young and perfectly fit men throwing the ball at the batsman as if it was target practice. It was becoming more and more difficult to enjoy in the same way as I remembered from earlier cruises. If this is the way cricket is run on the P&O ships in future, then a traditional cruise ship game will have been ruined.

Oh, and to make it worse I fell over and hurt my knee and wrist. I decided to give it a rest for a few days.

It was a casual dress code night, and we met up in Anderson's for a drink before dinner with Richard and Angie. We told them that we had looked at how much it would cost to change our booking for 2018 on Aurora, to join the cruise that they are on. Sadly, the prices of the cruises to the USA East Coast had gone up dramatically, and we would be keeping to our original plan.

With dinner over, four of us went to the early quiz, and then had a few minutes of Trivial Pursuit. Then Deb and I said goodnight to Richard and Angie as we went to Carmen's to watch the second show from Robbie K. It was another 45 minutes of his 'unusuality' with lots of old fashioned variety style-entertainment plus non-stop humour throughout.

This is a good act to go and see if he turns up on your holiday ship.

From Carmen's we walked to the forward end of the ship to the theatre to watch the Headliners with their show called 'New Romantics', which is a fast-paced tribute to artists of the 1980s. I also enjoyed watching and listening to the Headliner singers who had helped with the Aurora choir over the last three months.

We'd already seen the show once on this cruise, but it was well worth a second time, as this music was from my growing years, and features on the music favourites that I have on my iPod.

It was late when we came out of the theatre, and time for bed. Aurora was moving even more erratically with the strong buffeting wind, and a sea that seemed to be getting angrier as we moved nearer to Hawaii. I hoped the weather wasn't about to turn bad for our visit to Honolulu.

We would have a final sea-day tomorrow before arriving in the American state of Hawaii. On the day we arrived in Honolulu we would be having a face-to-face interview with the American immigration authorities, before being allowed to go ashore. Fortunately our early tour meant an early interview. We'd had to complete the forms today, and they had now joined the mass of reminders, programmes, lists, and notices that are stuck to our wall with the fridge magnets accumulated on the voyage so far.

....

Tuesday 21st March
Just a maximum of 25°C today on the balcony.

What an awful night. I struggled to get to sleep, as my leg had gone into the restless state that I sometimes get. When it happens I have to bring the leg out from under the quilt to get it cold, then after a few minutes bring it back into the warmth. Well, after repeating this several times without relief, I then tried stretching the muscles, which made me go into cramp a couple of times. Still suffering, I tried going to the bathroom and putting cold water on the offending leg. That really felt cool, and I was hopeful, and after another dose of leg out, leg in.......ZZzzzz.

It was still a disturbed night, as Aurora was really being told off by an angry sea. We were banging and bouncing and rolling around, and there were moments when I had to bend my leg as a brace to stop myself falling out of the bed.

Eventually dawn came, and the ship felt slightly more stable. The Officer of the Watch reported a Force 6 wind, and the sea state was classified as moderate. It was only 24° with some sunshine, but lots of heavy clouds threatening rain. While we were having breakfast a very vivid rainbow appeared which seemed to be ending on the sea just below us.

Well, this morning we listened to the port talk for San Diego, which is the first port on the next (and final) sector of our world adventure. After that we had a coffee before getting prepared for our midday round of activities.

Deb only had Battle of the Sexes because the Salsa had been cancelled. The Headliners' dancers had been given more preparation time before an afternoon matinee show. This was their tribute to Queen. Sadly, they only had two options for matinees in Carmen's: Abba and Queen tribute shows, and we had seen them both several times.

My leg and wrist were still in a bit of trouble so I gave cricket a miss.

The evening entertainment was a little limited again, with a second show from Peter White singing songs by Kenny Rogers. I hadn't heard any glowing reports about him, and we politely declined the invitation to be a part of his audience.

While we were in Auckland, Paula from the entertainment team went home and wasn't replaced. Then in Fiji or Apia, Danny had had to rush home for "*personal reasons*". The team was depleted and Abby would be getting off in San Francisco. Her replacement as Deputy Entertainment Manager was already on board and having the handover, but he hadn't been passenger-facing very often. Two brand new entertainment team members were due to board in San Francisco, but apparently they are really new, and will take a few days to go solo.

The entertainment situation was really disappointing.

On a world cruise we expected more than quoits, shuffle board and quizzes. Yes, there were other choices for specialised activities such as dance, bridge, and art classes, but in all honesty, they only appeal to quite small numbers. The advert for this world cruise said there would be traditional games and activities that cruises have had over its 180 year history.

I somehow think that as well as other changes that have happened over 180 years, the level of entertainment has reduced significantly, and now the numbers involved in providing and overseeing the entertainment are dropping to ridiculous levels. Just to put it in context, there were as many, if not more, people in the youth crew who looked after the children, and I believe the maximum number of children on the cruise at any time was just ten. Don't get me wrong, the children had to be looked after, kept amused and safe, but the adult passengers should have been equally as important.

The day ended with the dinner table six being frustrated once again with a quiz. We all went to bed early because tomorrow morning we would be docking in Hawaii, and there'd be an early start to life on the ship. The US Immigration authorities would be carrying out a face-to-face inspection of paperwork with all of us, before we would be allowed to go ashore. That process would begin at 7:15am, and we all wanted to get ashore as soon as possible.

The alarm was set for 6:15am and after just a quick read, Deb and I snuggled into our duvet and pillows.

Wednesday 22nd March – Honolulu, Hawaii, USA

Our balcony managed to warm up to 27°C today.

We were woken by my alarm, and got ourselves ready for a day on the wonderful Pacific island of Oahu, which is just one of the Hawaiian islands. It was warm (and would get hotter) with blue skies and light winds. We had a tour booked to go up to the top of an extinct volcano, and that meant an early start.

Initially the most important thing was to get our paperwork ready to be inspected by the United States authorities, and because of our chosen tour, we were one of the first to go through the process.

It was fast, almost friendly, and all over for us before 7:30am.

Just after 8:00am we went down to get to our tour coach, and once on board the driver (who was also our guide) said how sorry he was for the terrorist attack in London.

WHAT!!

He was talking about the attack in the Westminster area of London, killing four and injuring scores of other innocent people.

We were isolated from most of the world on a cruise ship, and this was a total shock for us. Very few passengers turn on televisions to get the news first thing in the morning, and like Deb and I had no idea anything had happened.

The news may not have stopped us doing what we had planned, and we had a wonderful time, but thousands of miles away in London innocent people had been killed in a cowardly attack by a terrorist, who had been convinced that his religion would reward him for taking the lives of people, who possibly knew, and had access to more truth about his beliefs, than he was ever told.

I think the British people knew it would eventually happen, but those were just people going to work, maybe going shopping, or perhaps tourists going to see the heart of a democratic government, where people have the freedom to say *"we don't like"*, or *"we don't agree"*, with the views of others. Can the cowardly leaders of the organisation involved with this attack say that they allow their people that same level of freedom?

My thoughts go out to those who died, those who were injured, and also to the relations and friends of those innocent people. There are also those who were lucky and survived without injury, but witnessed an atrocity that will never leave their minds. And then there were the people who helped the hurt and the dying.

Our nation would think and wonder and possibly fear for what else might happen.

May your gods bless you, and give you peace and the bravery to continue life without blaming anyone…

…except the people who indoctrinated that killer to do what he believed, in ignorance, to be right.

....

Life, and holidays, have to go on

Hundreds of us on board Aurora that day were dumbstruck by the tragedy at home. We couldn't do anything about it, and it would appear no-one on the ship had anybody caught up in the mayhem.

So life on the ship, and ashore in Hawaii, continued.

We had a wonderful morning. Deb and I, accompanied by Richard and Angie walked, or more accurately clambered, up the side of the Diamond Head Peak from the extinct volcano crater floor below. The walk is around a mile and at times is very steep with rough stone pathways. It took us about 45 minutes to get to the highest point where we had tremendous views over the island. Waikiki was just one of the stretches of golden sandy beaches below, and the shallow coral seas were very beautiful. In the distance I saw our ship which was a tiny blip amongst the Honolulu cityscape of shimmering glass towers.

We had been told to look out for whales in the vast bay, but none of us saw any. Sadly the passengers on expensive whale-spotting trips were also disappointed.

Having got our breath back, and rested aching legs, we began the slightly easier downward trek. It took a little over 30 minutes this time, but progress was still difficult on the steep and uneven paths. The paths were wide enough for two people to pass, and by 10:30am it was packed with hundreds of walkers. Some were athletic and enjoying a gentle workout, but others (like us) were challenging ourselves to do something different, and we panted at times and swigged regularly from our water bottles in the hot sunshine. Shade was rare, and rest points with benches a pleasure to find.

Back at the bottom we congratulated ourselves, and after buying a fridge magnet we waited in the shade of the trees for our guide to appear. He had stayed with the last person from our group on the trek, and now handed out certificates to remind us of our morning.

Our guide was exceptional, with a tremendous knowledge of the island, especially Honolulu. On the journey to and from the volcano site, he pointed out and named trees and birds that we passed, and even showed us where Hollywood stars lived, or where different television programmes were filmed. He made the morning a pleasure, and took away a little of our aches (and thoughts) with his stories.

We were back on Aurora in plenty of time for lunch, and soon we were on our way off the ship again to go shopping.

The shopping trip was to the Walmart store that our free shuttle bus serviced throughout our stay in port. It was enormous, and very different to similar hypermarkets in Britain. The pharmacy wasn't a small counter hidden away in a corner of the store like in Britain; it had pride of place at the entrance with perhaps four aisles of medicines, supplements, cough medicines etc.

The shop even had a huge souvenir department, which I have to say was amazing, with items similar that we usually buy, but at far lower prices. It even sold ukuleles, and in hindsight I wish I had bought one.

We got a lot of things from an extended shopping list, but one thing remained. My trainers had begun to fall apart and I really hoped to find some that day, but the vast footwear shelves were almost empty. I was also looking to get a new iPod if the price was better than home, but although it was certainly a little cheaper, the exchange rate for sterling didn't appear to make it attractive enough. This was another "in hindsight" moment as in reality it would have saved me a significant amount.

Anyway, we came away with both our rucksacks full, plus a carrier bag (6 cents) with a large multi-pack of chocolate-covered macadamia nuts.

On the bus back to the ship there was a group of Australian passengers who were quite loud and outspoken about their holiday. Their discussion centred on the bargain they had got for this sector of the world cruise. Now many people suggest that British cruisers always like to talk about prices, but these Australians were really making their good fortune known.

Eventually one of the ladies realised we were British and decided to bring us into the conversation. She asked what we had paid to go around the world, and I declined to answer, so she suggested it must have been in excess of £30,000. Well without saying exactly what we paid, I nodded, and she then asked if I would like to know what she had paid. I politely said *"**NO**"*!

My response was apparently not heard, and she said the trip had cost the equivalent of £1,500 and included the flight back to Sydney from San Francisco. They laughed in delight, and added that they even had special parties laid on for formal nights to avoid having to dress up.

I was seething about their rudeness, but we ignored them for the rest of the shuttle trip.

Australia is one of my favourite places in the world, and the Australian people are generally wonderfully friendly, but these bargain-hunting morons needed to think a little before upsetting British passengers.

Back on Aurora by 3:00pm, we were shattered and our legs needed to be supported on a comfortable bed for a while. That was enough for the day, and finally we had a chance to watch the TV News Channel to discover just what had happened in London. We couldn't do anything about it, but it did spin around in my head for quite a while. When I worked at Goonhilly Satellite Station we often saw news broadcasts arriving from disasters and tragedies all over the world. We saw horrible pictures and scenes that the public wouldn't see until many hours later, if at all. Some of the news and pictures we saw made us go silent at times, and today this news from London had made me reflect on how horrid and evil some people can be in this otherwise wonderful life.

In the evening the dinner table gang did the early quiz and lost once again to a couple from Densa. They apparently do not drink wine, and offered it to us. This was quite strange as we actually came third and the second place team got nothing. Thanks very much!

After that we all trooped along to the show from a comedian called Jeff Stevenson. None of us had seen him before, and I have to say he was really good. It was a very fast patter act based on reality situations (sort of) with the odd bit of banter with the audience, especially with a number of late comers.

That was enough for us after a long day, and we trooped off up the stairs to Deck 10 and our beds.

North-east across the Pacific

Thursday 23rd March

It was just 24°C today on the balcony as we headed northwards.

Having had an early night yesterday, we slept and fully recharged our batteries after several days when we had felt exhausted.

We woke to another sunny day with a bit of a breeze across the decks. It was only in the low 20s at 8:00am, but still a lot warmer than back home in Britain.

It was medicine day, and after breakfast, time to refill our little pill pots for another week.

Aurora was ploughing her way through a lumpy, but not a rough sea, heading north-east across the Pacific Ocean at about 20 knots. This was the first of four days sailing before we would reach San Francisco on Monday morning. Last night the Captain told us that we had over 2,000 miles to go, and warned that there were some "nasty depressions" heading east from Japan that would give us a rough time tomorrow. If the Captain suggested *"rough times"* then I assumed to land-lubbers it meant really, really, rough, so best to make the most of today's relative calmness.

After watching the port talk at 10:00 about Cabo San Lucas in Mexico, we relaxed in Raffles for a coffee and a cake. We had no plans to book a tour for the Mexican stop as nothing jumped out at us as being special, but instead we planned to look around the town, and maybe even have a paddle at the nearby beach. Without any doubt, there would be lots of local tour companies offering trips if we change our minds on the morning.

But hey, Mexico was ages away yet on the next sector!

At midday the clocks went forward again to GMT-9 hours, so Deb and I would be having a late lunch. It was the final choir practice before our concert on the 25th, and Deb had the Battle of the Sexes before going on to Salsa or tap dancing (she wasn't sure which yet), and I trotted off to cricket.

The highlights of the midday mania included a very successful choir practice where Paul (the pianist and arranger) didn't pull us up on any mistakes. We went right through the programme of eight songs, plus the encore, without stopping. We now know that the concert will have about 35 minutes of singing.

In cricket I was chosen to be a captain. This was a purely random thing, and I had no control over who was in my team. Anyway, we were not the best at batting, although I was second highest scorer, and I feared a bit of a disaster as we began to field. But we produced a real grafting display of fielding and catching, and won the game by three runs.

Deb was annoyed to discover that her class was tap dancing again. It was supposed to alternate on sea days, but someone had forgotten that the previous sea day, which should have been Salsa, had no session because of a Headliners rehearsal. So to be fair, Salsa should have been today but instead it was programmed to be tap. Tomorrow the room would be busy with talent show rehearsals, so Salsa will probably be cancelled again and the next day will be tap once more.

Methinks the left hand doesn't know what the right hand is doing here.

Deb wasn't really enjoying tap, as it is not as energetic as Salsa. To make matters worse, a large number of the people in the class were already quite experienced in tap dancing, and had even brought their tap shoes with them. Deb and some of the others were beginners, and Kemal, the instructor, struggled to keep the session as a beginners' class, because the more experienced tappers used their power of numbers to move on to more complicated stuff.

Once again, the lack of available entertainment hosts has resulted in removing the fun from some people, to try and satisfy others who shout louder. In the past the instructor would have been one of the official entertainment hosts and there would have been separate lessons. Now P&O have cut their costs by using the Headliners as instructors who were not expected to do more than one session of extra work a day.

To be honest, I have to say that having professionals helping the passengers with dance lessons and singing was a wonderful improvement, and it was great to have interaction with these hard-working boys and girls, but using the opportunity to reduce staff is a bit naughty.

Mid-afternoon, and we were back together in the cabin after a cup of tea and a scone in the buffet. Deb and I relaxed for a while before shower time and dinner. We often used this time to bring our diaries up to date, or to just sit back and doze – well I do anyway. Outside it was cloudy, and although the sea looked to have calmed down, the wind continued to remind us of its strength. The temperature outside was only 24° and forecast to get cooler as we headed northwards.

Talks around the ship today were from a Dr Richard R Rubin discussing US Democracy, and another from Karen Hardy, the professional dancer who took part in Strictly Come Dancing. I would have liked to have gone to her talk, but she was on at a time when we had other things on.

This evening the Entertainment Team were performing their show in Carmen's, well what was left of the team, anyway. This was followed by a trio of singers called The Flyrights in the theatre, and they have been recommended to us by Richard and Angie.

Well, we went to watch the show from The Flyrights, and it was amazing. Featuring a mix of soul, Motown, and swing, these three young men from South London were very good. They also danced and performed some moments of acrobatic magic. The audience needed no coaxing to stand up when asked to wave, sway, and sing along to their songs. There was even a bit of nostalgia for me when one of them sang a solo with his version of "Mr Bojangles". I have loved this song since Gary Wilmott sang it on our very first cruise 17 years ago. OK, personally this version wasn't the best I'd heard, but it still brought the wonderful memories back.

Of course, they had a standing ovation at the end and I was sure we would be going back to see them again on the second show.

That was just about it for our evening, and we ended it with a final nightcap in the comfortable surroundings of Anderson's, while chatting, and listening to the pianist gently playing outside in Charlies.

Friday March 24th

Just 20°C today, and the back garden wasn't very inviting.

It was the second day of four on our lonely crossing from Hawaii to San Francisco. The ocean was still being kind to us with quite flat seas, but during the morning there was a light wind and a hidden swell that made Aurora roll gently from side to side. It was cool, but we had to accept that this was the northern hemisphere again. The clouds were trying to break, but there were also several showers, and if the Captain was correct yesterday evening, the wind would be getting up during the day, and the sea creating a roller coaster for us tonight.

So what was going on today as we sailed at 21 knots north east towards the USA mainland?

Deb and I were hoping to have an hour in the sunshine, but with the weather turning much more towards winter again, we just took to the Promenade Deck for some exercise in the morning.

After a mile's walk we went for a cup of coffee, and it was strangely quiet in Raffles. I put it down to people still being at breakfast, even at 10:15 am.

Our next stop was the Crow's Nest to sit and relax for a while. The art class had just begun, and today the subject was a picture of a puffin. Now this art teacher made life very easy and only seemed to ask his students to paint birds, faces, and still-life objects. Surely on a world cruise it should have been about capturing images from the places we had visited, and then painting them? When Deb did the classes five years ago she came home with images of Vietnam, Sydney, Athens, Istanbul and scenes of tropical islands, and mosques. These people went home with puffins, penguins, and a lady's face obscured by a mask. How will this bring back memories of where they had been?

He might be a good teacher, but he was actually telling his class the exact paint mix to use at the exact spot, and for the exact distance. Is this teaching to paint, or simply recreating something? An interesting comment he made: *"If you follow my instructions carefully, you will always get it 80% correct"*. In other words, copy what I am doing, and yours should look similar.

There had been the odd glimpse of sunshine during the morning, but suddenly at 11:00 am the view from the Crow's Nest became a blanket of mist. The weather had really changed over the last few days.

During the day there were talks in the theatre from Karen Hardy (dancing), Dr Richard R Rubin (US Politics), and Gillian Perry (the life of Anne Frank). This was quite a mixture and kept people culturally happy.

In the afternoon there was the Passenger Talent Show, with several singing acts as well as at least one from ukulele players who had somehow decided to bring their instruments with them. Later in the evening, one of the Headliner Singers (Lucy Aniston) performed her solo cabaret act in Carmen's, while in the theatre Julie A Scott sang a tribute to Cilla Black.

Anyone notice the abundance of singing again?

A week ago, those of us on the full world cruise were given some vouchers for different treats. One of them was five internet packages. Obviously a lot of us went for this treat, but ever since the internet speed had slowed to virtually snail's pace. Hopefully by San Francisco these packages will have run out, and we can start to use the internet properly again.

While online today I (very slowly) checked my electricity and gas bill for the last quarter. Interesting logic has been applied. Over three of the coldest months of the year, we have still paid in slightly more than necessary for the estimated amount power that we would have used. We were also in credit following the summer's lower energy use, but for some unknown reason our energy supplier had **increased** our standing order by just over 20%.

Unfortunately it would cost us a small fortune to speak to them and sort it out while away. This was even more annoying, as while we had been away from home, our energy usage would have been minimal.

The lunchtime period began with Deb at the Battle of the Sexes. I stayed in the cabin, but the ship's movement was beginning to get to me, so I moved to Carmen's and watched the quiz from the back. I always find the cabin a bad place to be when the sea is moving, as there is no escape from the shifting horizon without drawing the curtains. A little white pill was taken, although I had hoped to wait until later.

When Deb had finished battling, we had an unhurried lunch. No time changes today to confuse activity timings, and I had no choir practice either, so we had time together until Salsa and cricket sessions at 2:00 pm.

I was absolutely thrilled today. Our team lost the cricket match, but I scored the most runs for the team and won my first gold sticker. I still didn't like the way the cricket had been changed, but this cheered me up a bit.

As the afternoon drew to a close, Deb decided to do some more laundry, and amazingly a washing machine was available. To fit this in we went to the buffet for dinner, where there was a chicken-themed menu which we had sampled before.

By 7:00 pm the washing was dried and back in the cabin. There were a few items to be ironed but Deb left them for tomorrow. We went down to Masquerade's to begin an evening of quizzing.

The evening entertainment featured a female vocalist and was of no interest. We also avoided the late evening game show based on "Mr and Mrs", and played Trivial Pursuit up in the Crow's Nest instead. That was until the karaoke queen (Lyn Frederick) arrived. We gave her a silent standing ovation and went to Vanderbilt's to continue our game in peace. After a full team effort in the late-night Syndicate Quiz we gave in to give our brains a rest.

It hadn't been a very dynamic day, but we were building up to an active time in San Francisco in two days' time.

Contrary to what the Captain predicted yesterday, the wind didn't become too bad, and the sea was actually classed as just "slight to moderate". It actually looked almost flat and calm, but there was still an underlying swell that rolled us around quite dramatically. I wasn't too worried about the movement, and went to bed without any topping up of white pills.

Postscript 1 - I saw a ship on the horizon today. This was the first thing I had seen since Hawaii, except for occasional birds, and unidentifiable fish jumping around many miles away. This really is a vast ocean, and must be a lonely place for yachtsmen and women.

Postscript 2 - Just in case you think we were not enjoying the cruise, I must make it clear that we may not have been too happy with the entertainment, but Deb and I were still having a wonderful time as we approached the last sector of our adventure around the world. Once again we had seen so much that had made us smile and gasp in amazement, met so many people that we have laughed with daily, and stored away many memories that will last forever.

....

Saturday 25th March
Sadly it only warmed up to 17°C today.

It was a sunny morning, but the temperature never tempted us to lie in it, and the forecast suggested this would be the best we can expect until we head southwards again.

On the way to and from breakfast, the Riviera Deck poolside was deserted, except for the Mayor and Lady Mayoress who were fully wrapped in their tennis towels trying to enjoy their cornflakes. I had no doubt they would still be there late into the evening unless a thunder storm disrupted them.

We did a bit of housekeeping after breakfast by checking our account, and completing the Customer Satisfaction Questionnaire for the sector. Our only moans were really the entertainment, and the ship's retail outlets. They contrived a daily special sale, and advertised their bargains on tables spread out around the narrow area by Charlies. This created massive congestion which was a serious obstacle for those with disabilities.

And the bargains weren't that good anyway!

It was going to be a busy day with our choir performance in the theatre during the afternoon. Ship clocks were going forward at midday again, and the final rehearsal would be just as the clocks move to GMT-8. Our rehearsal would include setting up the standing positions on the stage, so quite hectic.

Over the last couple of weeks we had been annoyed by a heckler who popped into the rehearsals and shouted abuse before running away again. He had been in the choir but had an issue with the way a song had been adapted, so decided to be a nuisance. Anyway, today we hoped he would leave us alone.

With no sign of any warm sunshine, Deb and I took an early morning walk around the Promenade Deck. Just like yesterday we walked a mile, but this was no longer a part of my personal marathon challenge. As we walked towards the stern of the teak highway, we caught sight of some gull like birds flying close to the ship. They looked like albatross, but perhaps were a little too small, and certainly a long way north of their traditional territory.

Well, they were confirmed as albatrosses (or albatri or simply albatross) and there were several of these graceful birds, and an amazing spectacle. Anyway, they stayed with us throughout the day, keeping close to the ship so as to use Aurora's drag to pull them along.

Why didn't they just land on the rails and have a ride?

And I'm sure they would have been fed by the curious passengers.

After our walk we had a drink in the buffet and I had a cake to keep me going until the choir rehearsal ended. Then there was time for an hour in the cabin catching up on the television news.

As the clocks jumped forward an hour, the choir assembled in the theatre. There were several new members on this sector who needed to fill out the Health and Safety form, allowing them to go onto the stage. Then we lined up and sorted out our positions for the performance. There were really a lot of us this sector, and we spread right across the stage. We had time for just one song to get us in the mood again, and then we were told to go and get some lunch.

Two hours later I was putting on the approved clothing of white shirt and black trousers, having my final sip of water, and sucking a "just in case" throat sweet. My second choir show was about to start.

We were late getting onto the stage because Karen Hardy (dancing person) had overrun, and was having a photo opportunity by the stage. Karen appeared to be a nice lady, and apologised profusely as she walked by us, but I am sure she had no intention of missing out on her fans.

Eventually our performance began, and maybe there were a few mistakes and occasional dodgy notes, but it went very well, and yes it was without any heckling. I was roasting hot after 45 minutes under the stage lights, and from the adrenalin rush from the effort of singing.

It was all over again, and now I had to get the tunes out of my head which had been constantly there for the last couple of weeks.

In less than a week we would be starting again with new songs, and probably a much smaller band of singers as we begin the next sector.

I absolutely loved this experience.

Deb and I went to the buffet for a drink, and then returned to the cabin. I considered getting my iPod out to listen to some different music, but I realised it was time for a shower before the evening began.

We had a pre-dinner drink with Richard and Angie before the six of us enjoyed a noisy table chat while we ate.

Aurora was still on a North Easterly direction across the Pacific, but she had slowed to less than 20 knots. Earlier in the day we had been hurtling along at over 23 knots, which is almost Aurora's maximum speed, and certainly above her fuel efficiency speed. I can only assume the Captain was trying to outrun the bad weather, as the predicted doom and gloom of a storm hadn't affected us.

I had a feeling the high-speed run probably meant the Captain lost out on his fuel efficiency bonus.

The evening entertainment was the comedian, Jeff Stevenson, and he was tremendous again. I know he wasn't everybody's cup of tea, but most of us thoroughly enjoyed laughing for 45 minutes at his observations and jokes.

He even used the flock of albatross in his act, describing them as a new surveillance weapon commissioned by Donald Trump. Fitted with communication equipment, they left their base and went to look at approaching cruise ships to detect unwanted visitors, or sniff out drugs. Of course I am not against Donald Trump, as he has been democratically elected just as we have democratically decided to go down the Brexit route.

But he is an unusual person to become a President of the (supposedly) most powerful nation in the world, and some of his ideas are (to put it mildly) downright weird.

We rounded off our evening with some mind exercises, and once again it was more about having a laugh rather than the winning.

Tomorrow would be our final sea day before San Francisco where 900 passengers would be disembarking, and replaced by 900 new ones. The atmosphere on the ship would change again, especially as many of those leaving will be the Australians who have been so obvious for the last three weeks.

……………………………………………..

Sunday 26th March

Mothers' Day, and it was even cooler at just 15°C.

We enjoyed another wonderful night's sleep. The usual dawn chorus of drawers and toilets woke me just after 7:30 and we had our first cuppa of the day 15 minutes later.

Outside it was foggy and rather cold on the balcony. The garden was looking quite untidy and the confused grey sea reminded me of Biscay on a good day. It wasn't overly rough, but Aurora was moving around enough to remind us we were at sea.

The sun was trying to peek through the clouds above the fog, but this wasn't the sort of weather we had a week ago. Even the Mayor and his wife were missing from the throne above the Riviera Pool as we went to breakfast, and this was the first time this had happened (apart from port days) since we were in the Atlantic Ocean three months ago.

When we had finished breakfast we returned to the cabin too quickly, and our steward, Lloyd, hadn't finished it. We went for a walk again, but only did a couple of laps in the cold weather.

With the cabin clean and tidy, it was time for housekeeping. This involved opening our third and final tube of toothpaste, plus the weekly charging up of the electric toothbrush.

Mid-morning and we went for another walk, completing another two laps to make it over a mile this morning. Having used up a few calories we went to Raffles for coffee, but no cake this time for either of us. From there we ventured up onto the Lido deck to see what the weather was like. It had improved, but was still too cool for us to strip off in the sunshine, and the same applied to the majority of the passengers – except for the Riviera Royalty who had returned to their thrones to survey their empire.

As morning turned towards lunchtime, the familiar *'bing, bong'* heralded an announcement from the bridge. It was given today by a passenger who had paid a lot of money at the Macmillan coffee morning to do it. He spoke very well and told us that the clocks were going forward yet again, and ship's time was now GMT-7. Of course, the clocks back in Britain also went forward an hour last night, so we are still 8 hours behind home. There were just some 200 miles to go before we would reach San Francisco tomorrow morning, and the television navigation channel was now showing the US coast. Our trip across the Pacific Ocean was nearing its end.

By the time of the announcement, Deb had gone to the final Battle of the Sexes challenge of the sector, where the men were the overall winners of the challenge. I went for a spot of lunch before going to the final cricket session, and today I was on the winning side. A few days from now all the organised activities would start again, and the passengers arriving in San Francisco would have a chance to join in.

It hadn't really warmed up much at all today. The sun had peeked down on us a little, but the chilly wind from the north-west reminded us that we were well back into winter.

Through the morning we had missed talks from John Graves discussing exciting cruising destinations to 400+ passengers who were already on a world cruise, many of whom had cruised around the world several times. Karen Hardy had another session in the theatre with an interview, and questions from the passengers. After lunch we avoided Gillian Perry telling people about the 'afternoon tea' custom – once again to cruisers who have probably been enjoying this tradition for a decade. Then to round off the afternoon there was Dr Daniel R Rubin hoping to wake up the passengers as he talked about contemporary American politics.

I am sure all of these speakers were absolutely fascinating, but five years ago we had a mix of such speakers, together with comedians and actors who entertained us with stories and anecdotes to break up the serious cultural talks. Have they all put up their charges so much that P&O are no longer using them?

That evening the theatre had the Headliners performing 'Stop in the Name of Love', while at the other end of the ship Julie A Scott sang another selection of "diva" songs in Carmen's. I believe this was the fourth female vocalist to feature the "diva" word as a part of the act.

As an aside, while I was at lunch I interrupted Jeff Stevenson (the comic from last night) to thank him for the temporary break from the abundance of female vocalists.

Caravan was performing in the Crow's Nest, and Lyn Fredrick was giving her interpretation of background music in Champions. Personally Deb and I had decided that the pianist David Taylor is more entertaining, with his gentle music in Charlie's just outside of Anderson's.

Late afternoon saw the return of the Albatross Stealth team. They must have detected something suspicious and gone back for a closer look.

Wow, these Americans are cunning!

As usual the Captain made a 6:00 pm announcement of where we were, and initial details for tomorrow. He finished his speech by giving us the total distance we have sailed since Southampton. As we come to the end of the penultimate sector, we have travelled over 24,000 nautical miles.

We went to bed at just after 10:00 pm having not bothered with the Headliners show. We played Trivial Pursuit with Richard and Angie as well as losing a couple of quizzes.

We will have an early morning appointment with the Golden Gate Bridge.

....

Note to self, and anyone preparing for a long cruise
If you buy a new pair of sandals to replace some perfectly good, but older ones, buy them early enough to fully test that they are correct and comfortable.

My previous pair, which I had been wearing for 15 years, were getting old and a little tatty, but were very comfortable. I decided they should be replaced. The new ones were also very comfortable, but the Velcro straps had stretched and work loose, allowing my feet to move around inside the sandals. Now when I went walking I had to make regular stops to try and tighten them.

Monday 27th March – San Francisco, USA

Although it felt warm while we were out walking, the balcony only managed to get to 15°C.

After a night without much sleep, I finally gave up and peered out through the curtains at a little after 7:00 am. The Golden Gate Bridge was in view on a sunny horizon. I put the kettle on, and then put on my dressing gown to step outside onto the rather cold balcony to take the first pictures of the bridge.

This was my third visit to San Francisco. I flew here back in the early 1980s, and then five years ago came here on Aurora. This was the first time I had seen the bridge clearly, and I finally got a photo of it. Five years ago we arrived in the dark, and it was shrouded in mist for the two days.

Deb and I dressed and took a series of photos as we neared and then passed under the beautiful bridge. Then it was time for breakfast as we approached the dockside. The Horizon Buffet was packed with people who had rarely seen bacon and egg before 10:00 am. The queue for hot food was ridiculous, but that didn't worry us, as we continued with the fruit and croissants start to our day.

Our plans for the day were to wander the streets of the city, and let our footsteps and eyes decide what to do. Of course we had a shopping list to sort out, and we hoped to book a trip to Alcatraz if possible, but that wasn't a priority as we'd visited the island back in 2012. Another wish was to get on one of the cable car trams and actually get a seat. I had been on them twice before and both times stood clinging to the strap of the little rollercoasters.

Well, before 9:00 am we were docked and the sunshine was streaming down on us. Our garden had the Bay Bridge in the distance to our left, and if we looked past the slightly unsightly quayside piers to the right, there was just some of the glittering glass cityscape. Unfortunately the most obvious buildings we could see were under construction with cranes spoiling the skyline, but hey ho, that's what happens in a bustling city.

We had to wait for a while before getting the all clear to go ashore, but that wasn't a surprise for stops in the USA. I didn't think we would be delayed for too long once the officials gave us the all clear.

Hang on now, just what did the Albatross Squadron find? No, there wasn't a problem and at 9:00 am the Deputy Captain gave the all clear to go ashore.

By 10:00 am we were bumping along the air-bridge to the terminal building of this amazing city. The officials in the terminal were friendly, and pointed us in the right direction through quite a maze. We had already realised that this wasn't the terminal we had arrived at five years ago, and it seems that Pier 27 is now the first choice for cruise ships.

It was dry and sunny, but we had taken a jumper with us in case the wind proved to be chilly. I felt warm enough, and the extra layer wasn't needed, but Deb (unusually) felt cooler than I was, and she put on her jumper after we had walked around the waterfront to Pier 39.

For those who don't know the arrangement in San Francisco, the waterside has a series of berths labelled as Piers. They run as odd numbers from the starting point at the old Ferry Terminal in one direction, and even numbers on the other side. We hadn't investigated the even number side as the bigger cruise ships dock on the area to the Golden Gate side. Aurora was docked at one of the bigger berths numbered as Pier 27. We walked past 29, 31 etc. and eventually reached Pier 35 where we were docked in 2000.

Adjacent to that pier was the ticket office for the Alcatraz tours that we hoped we could fit in. On this Monday morning we were politely told that the first available tickets were on Saturday. OK, this wouldn't be something we would be doing.

We carried on along the busy sidewalk to the Pier 39 shopping and amusement area. One of the first things that caught our eye was the Alcatraz souvenir shop, so rather than going to the island, we looked around the shop. Deb bought a book about Al Capone, plus a convict tee shirt for our grandson, and of course, a fridge magnet of a cable car as well.

Our next stop was an Information booth, where we hoped we could find out the location of a couple of shops which Angie and Richard had recommended we visit. A young man asked if he could help us, and came up trumps with the location of both marked on a map, and they were only a couple of 'blocks' away.

Before beginning our shopping, we continued our walk around the pier and found a possible restaurant for the evening as a change from eating on the ship.

Then it was time to look at the famous San Francisco sea-lions. They were lazing on the pontoons at the side of Pier 39 and had an enormous crowd of visitors watching their antics. Most of the lazy animals simply lay quietly relaxing in the warm sunshine, but two or three were trying to raise their profile by barking (or honking) at others, and pushing them off the pontoon. The response was for the defeated sea-lion to swim under or around the pontoon and slither back onto it. The two sea-lions then honked and battled again until one or the other was pushed back into the water. This went on for quite a while to the amusement of the watching crowd.

It was a wonderful scene to get engrossed in, but we had other things to do.

Back to the city sidewalks, and we went along a street past several 'blocks', and easily found the shop ("Trader Joe's") from the young man's directions. Well it wasn't what we thought it was going to be and was fundamentally a cut-price grocery store. At least we found a cheap bottle of prosecco, and a bar of chocolate. Richard and Angie were also in the shop and they pointed out the other shop called "Ross" just across the street, in the same 'block'.

This was more like it, and here I found some suitable trainers to replace my rather bedraggled cricket ones, and Deb found a pair of dresses at a very reasonable price.

Our shopping list was now down to a few painkilling options for my knees and one or two random bits that had eluded us so far. My knees were at a critical point this morning. My shoe laces came loose, and when I bent down and knelt on the pavement (sorry, sidewalk) to re-tie them I discovered I was struggling to get back up again. Anyway, we found a sort of pharmacy where I managed to get a different cream for my knees, which hopefully won't leave the stench of a sports centre changing room behind me.

Deb and I were now carrying rucksacks and bags full of 'stuff', so it was time to stroll back to the ship and store away our purchases. On the way we stopped for a snack, and had a hot dog. Sometimes you have to do things, and eating a hotdog in San Francisco was one of them. With those treats polished off, I spotted some Ghirardelli chocolates that Deb had picked up, and we greedily ate them as well. I had been told this chocolate wasn't as nice as the European versions, but a wafer-thin chocolate filled with salted caramel convinced me not to listen too much to other peoples' views on American chocolate.

Our last task as we walked back was to investigate a possible pleasure cruise around the bay. This seemed a good idea for an afternoon adventure. There were regular trips around the San Francisco Bay going as far as the Golden Gate Bridge and circling Alcatraz Island. So with that stored in our minds, we completed the morning walk and entered into the hands of the US Security officials between us and Aurora.

They asked to see our cards at what felt like every turn, and then it was time for the scanner. I failed, and had to undergo the polite but thorough hand scan to assure them it was just my hip. Over the two days in this city I became a regular of the hand scanners, along with several other titanium-filled pensioners from Britain.

Back in our cabin we unloaded our treasure, and had a drink while we discussed what to do next. My first thoughts were to plaster my knees in the latest potion. Well, I have now learnt that the US instruction to 'liberally apply cream to the affected part' is actually a little over the top. I rubbed the white paste into my knees for several minutes and it wouldn't disperse. Next time I will use the more typical British instruction to "apply sparingly….."

We were ready to go out again, so I changed footwear to try out my nice new soft trainers that gave me something between the sole of my foot and the ground.

As we left Aurora, we saw a hop-on-hop-off bus approaching and we asked the saleslady about it. A man on the top deck from Britain shouted down to us that it was wonderful, so we decided to use the bus ride for a panoramic view of the city.

OK, it was expensive, but it turned out to be a lovely trip that lasted nearly three hours. We went around the city, learnt about some of its history, saw the steep streets used to film many Hollywood epics, glimpsed the twisting Lombard Street, and had descriptions of hordes of old and new buildings that stretched upwards to the blue sky above us.

We stopped at various places of course, for people to get off or join, but we stayed for the complete journey. We sat on the top deck of the bus: it was cold, especially as we had no warm clothing with us, but it was a good view. As passengers got off we took the opportunity to make our way forwards until we had front seats.

As the journey progressed to the outer areas of the city, we viewed the areas frequented by the hippy colonies of the 1960s and then we wound our way towards the Golden Gate Bridge, and the vast garden area associated with it.

The Bridge was the turnaround point of the tour, and after stopping for a few minutes we began the return journey. We saw many of the same streets again, but also many other landmarks of San Francisco. I don't know how much of the commentary we will remember, but it was certainly a lovely way of spending the afternoon, absorbing just a small fraction of what San Francisco has to offer the millions of tourists that have come here.

At about 5:00 in the afternoon our bus dropped us off back at Aurora. We were hungry, but it was too early to have a meal yet, so we made do with some Australian potato crisps, and a couple more Ghirardelli chocolates from our snack reserves. As we came through the terminal building we had spotted a free Wi-Fi sign, so we dashed back there in the hope of making contact with home. Although we managed to get onto Facebook, we failed to get to any of our other favourite sites.

We were soon going back via the security scanners again, for the third inspection of my lower limb.

Now our stomachs told us it was time to eat. We put on some clean and less scruffy clothes, and I swapped my comfortable trainers for a pair of shoes. We walked back along the waterfront to Pier 39 again, and the Italian restaurant we spotted earlier. Deb chose a pizza, and I selected an Italian sausage sandwich with fries. We'd both forgotten the size of American portions and neither of us managed to complete our meals. Both rather bloated we walked slowly back to the ship, looking at the busy scene as the dusk brought a different atmosphere to the sidewalks of San Francisco's Bay area.

The day had been so lovely.

We'd had some minor disappointments with the weather taking away some of the 'wow factor' in Australia and New Zealand, but San Francisco was proving to be delightful. The weather wasn't hot, but warm enough to allow comfortable strolls without coats. The fog had stayed away, and we had had some beautiful views of the Bridges and Alcatraz Island. And that panoramic trip on the bus had been better than we had anticipated.

After a final pat down and hand scan of the foreign body in my thigh, we had a cup of tea to round off our day, and then it was an early bedtime.

We had been up since our first views of the Golden Gate Bridge just after 7:00 in the morning, and we hadn't relaxed properly since. We would have another day in this city tomorrow, and we would be setting off on the most expensive tour of our adventure early in the morning.

Tuesday 28th March – Day 2 in San Francisco

The balcony was slightly warmer today with 17°C during the afternoon.

I woke at about 5:30 am and looked through the gap in our curtains at the rising sun, just lighting up a clear blue sky. The only thing that I could see in the Californian sky were vapour trails of jets coming and going. Soon the sun began to stream through the curtain gap, and I had a warm glow inside with the memories so far, and in anticipation of the day to come.

When I eventually got up to make some tea, I looked out for a better view at the scene in our back garden. It was fantastic with the sun creating gold and diamond sparkles in the water of the Bay. It was so bright that it left the Bay Bridge virtually a silhouette in the distance, and to our right the sky-scrapers were absolutely glowing as the sun said hello to them.

Once again it wasn't hot, but the warm spring sunshine was enough that we had no need of jumpers. Deb and I were on the quayside before 8:30 am to board our rather luxurious coach for our trip. Initially today we were going to be driven to the Napa Valley where we would board a restored 100-year-old train for a very special journey along the wine growing valley. We set off, and the guide, Jason, gave us a wonderful friendly commentary during a 90-minute trip from the city of San Francisco out over the Golden Gate Bridge, and then northwards to the valleys where some of the most expensive wines in the world are produced.

We even saw San Quentin Penitentiary in the distance, where Johnny Cash made a live recording of his concert in 1969 including the famous "A Boy named Sue" track. The jail was probably the only ugly building or landmark we saw during the day. We were soon entering the Napa Valley region which had lush green vegetation, similar to what can be seen in Northern Europe, and its micro-climate is also very similar. After about 45 minutes we began to see the grape vines in rows stretching away on both sides of the road for as far as the eye could comfortably see. The vineyards bore the names of famous wines and we realised that this area was responsible for millions of US dollars-worth of red, white, rose and sparkling wines enjoyed all over the world.

After about 90 minutes we came into the City of Napa where our coach trip ended. We went into a specially constructed railway terminal to be greeted by smiling staff of the *'Napa Valley Wine Train Experience'*. It was luxurious in the vast lobby area, with shops selling high-end ranges of clothing, plus souvenirs, and of course wine.

This was just the start of a wonderful three hours.

The train is over 100 years old and has been restored lovingly to attract passengers that want a truly luxurious experience. We had an old diesel locomotive pulling the ten carriages over the 36-mile journey from Napa to St Helena and back.

Depending on what package you buy, you get a different lounge to sit in, and there is a spacious dining carriage for those having a meal. There is even one carriage called the 'Champagne Vista Dome' for those who are really after something very special. We were in the 'Chardonnay' carriage at the front on the outward journey. It has rows of comfortable armchairs on both sides that face the windows and swivel to allow the lucky passengers to capture beautiful views of the Napa Valley.

As soon as we had settled into our chairs, the waitress (known as a Captain) asked for our choice of a welcome glass of wine: either a red Merlot, or Chardonnay for those who preferred white. Next they asked what wine tasting selection we wanted. These were called 'flights' and consisted of three glasses (small but far from tiny) of a selection of white, red, mixed, or sweet wines. To accompany the drinks there was also a tray of nibbles with cheese, ham, biscuits, fruit, and honey-covered salted walnuts. All the food on this tray was delicious, but those walnuts were sensational. The snacks were designed to enhance the wine-tasting experience against different sweet and savoury nibbles.

Deb and I chose one white and one red wine flight, giving us a chance to sample six different wines. Initially we behaved ourselves and tried to remember what we had been taught about tasting wine, but it wasn't very long before the wine-tasting went downhill as our palates lost the ability to compare the taste of the different wine, and we just drank to enjoy, and became just a little tipsy. In addition, the snacks were really enjoyable, and the views from the window were sensational.

Jason, our guide, patrolled up and down answering questions about what we were seeing, and showed that his knowledge of Californian wines was quite extensive. The carriage 'Captain' also gave bits of information as we passed vineyards owned by various wine brands that occupy prominent places on shelves at the expensive end of the market.

We also broke away from the wine glasses for a look around the rest of the train to see the various lounge themes and furnishing. We even got a glimpse of the restaurant car, and the galley where our lunch was being prepared. One of the waitresses let us know that we would soon be called to eat, so we returned to our lounge carriage in anticipation of our three-course feast.

To be honest, the wine and the nibbles had taken the edge off my appetite, but I did my best to do justice to the meal that appeared before me. There was a choice of salad, or asparagus soup to begin, followed by beef, pork, chicken, a fish dish, or gnocchi for the vegetarians. For a sweet course there was a choice of a chocolate dish or carrot cake. The meal was rounded off by a cup of coffee. Some people had another glass of wine which they had to pay for, while others brought one of the wine tasting glasses that they had saved. Deb and I didn't bother with anymore wine, as we were contented with what we had had already,

All the food was good. The only reservation was that Deb did not enjoy the sweetness of the main course. They obviously season the food with salt, pepper and sugar, which was noticeable, but I thoroughly enjoyed the fresh tasting vegetables, and beef cooked to my well-done preference, which our waitress described as being "to European taste".

While we were eating, the train reached the end of the line at St Helena, and began to come back the other way again. As lunch came to an end, the train was just ten minutes from where we had started and our delightful experience was coming to an end.

This had been a special treat, and although it cost us over £200 each, I believe it was worth it to have a little bit of luxury.

On the coach ride back to San Francisco, Jason told us more wine-based facts, more details of California, plus some amusing stories. Much of it fell on sleeping ears as we tried to digest the meal, and sober up from the wine. Our return journey took a different route, and instead of going via the Golden Gate Bridge, we came back over the Oakland Bay Bridge. This had been a huge circular trip around the Napa Valley and the San Francisco area, and it was even better than we initially expected it to be.

Back at the ship we went through the security for the last time, and my hip was patted and scanned for the final time in the city.

Having asked a few questions, we did go back to the terminal building to try the internet again. It seemed we had to enter a valid zip code (postcode) to get a proper connection. Our advice had been to try 90101 which was accepted, but although we managed to connect to most of what we wanted, the speed was slower than on board the ship – and that is really saying something.

Back on the ship we decided not to go out again. We had enjoyed a lovely day, and had eaten plenty, although we did have a plate of cheese and biscuits from the buffet.

Our evening was rounded off by a quiz, and then we took a last look out from the balcony at the Bay Bridge with a colour-changing light show making it even more spectacular. Aurora was due to leave the city at around midnight, but there was no chance of staying awake for long enough to watch what was probably a wonderful sail-away from this beautiful and friendly city.

I don't suppose I will ever come back here, but I left with so many memories that will stay with me. It is most definitely one of my favourite cities in the world, and the terrific weather really helped to make these last two days perfect.

Goodbye San Francisco, you will always have a place in my heart.

That was the end of the fourth sector of the world cruise, and Aurora was now going to sail southwards again, and back to the warmth …. we hoped.

Sector 5 – San Francisco to Southampton

The countries we visited:

- USA
- Mexico
- Guatemala
- *Transit of Panama Canal*
- Colombia
- St Lucia
- Barbados
- Portugal (Azores)

Wednesday 29th March – Sea Day to San Diego

As we sailed south again, the sun shone, but with a chilly wind, and it never rose above 17°C on the balcony.

We were slightly later getting up this morning. Our new neighbours didn't rise as early as the previous ones, so there was less drawer banging to wake us up.

When we braved the open decks towards the breakfast buffet, the Riviera Pool wasn't overly popular …. except for the Mayor and Mayoress.

This was the beginning of the final sector, and we decided to try and do as much as possible over the next three weeks. Of course, that meant a congested morning programme.

10:00 – Port Talk on Puerto Quetzal in Guatemala

11:00 – Dance instruction covering the cha cha cha

12:00 - Battle of the Sexes where Deb was made captain of the ladies team

12:30 – Choir Practice

Lunch to fit in with our schedule

14:00 – Deb's Salsa class

15:00 – Part 2 of cha cha cha dance class

16:00 – Afternoon tea followed by a rest

You will note that we went to the dance class. As it was the beginning of a sector, the instructors would have a batch of new people, so our thoughts were that if we joined in now, we might get a better chance of learning something. We already knew the basics of the cha cha cha, but it was good to discover our bad habits and learn a few new steps as well.

While at the Battle of the Sexes, as well as becoming the ladies captain for the sector, Deb discovered that DJ Martin had found out that we were posting regular blogs, and so had read the comments I made about the cricket sessions. I was perhaps a little embarrassed, but certainly not sorry, as these were my honest views based on many years of playing the game on P&O ships. And I have certainly played this game for more years than Martin has been involved.

It was a Formal Evening so after having a rest, it was shower time, before putting on the traditional evening clothes. It was also the 'Welcome on Board' cocktail party, only this time the six of us from the dinner table rebelled.

We were fed up continually having our cocktail party in Carmen's. It's a dark room and is always packed, so we decided to invite ourselves to the Crow's Nest party instead. This was a brighter room, with more room to stand, and had much better views.

The Captain had a cold and sounded quite poorly as he made his speech. It was sad that he was ill, but good to know that the ship's crew also catch the bugs that float around this vessel.

Suitably tipsy, all six of us returned to the dinner table after two nights away, and discovered we had new guests in the spare seats. They had actually joined the ship in San Francisco and now had the difficult task of being accepted by us. Hopefully they will soon be brought into our little friendly group …. but definitely not the quiz team.

The entertainment tonight was Zoe Tyler singing in the theatre, and a formal night ball in Carmen's. There was also a new classical duo (Sfordzandi) with a concert in the cinema. I never did find out how to pronounce their name.

We were quite tipsy after the wine at the cocktail party and obviously didn't go to the theatre. We met up with Richard and Angie for a game of Trivial Pursuit, and the late quiz in Masquerade's before having an early night.

Well, it had been a busy day.

Thursday 30th March – San Diego, USA

The sun was shining and the sky was blue. It was a little warmer on our balcony today, and the temperature managed an agreeable 19°C during the afternoon.

I was woken by a strange noise that seemed to be a police siren. There was no way of getting to the balcony to see what it was, but I suspect it was the coastguards showing off their toys to us strangers, and emphasising their power.

We got up early as we had a tour today that left before 9:00.

There was time to have a look around at our back garden, and the view was a little strange. Our berth allowed a view of some ships that were a part of the San Diego Maritime Museum. Square-rigged vessels sat side by side with a paddle steamer called the Berkley, that helped rescue people after the San Francisco earthquake in 1906. There was a rusting, but still menacing, Russian submarine near to an American one, both of them surrounded by various other boats of all sizes and shapes.

Aurora had unknowingly become a temporary exhibit, as beyond us on the starboard side, the museum continued, including the retired US aircraft carrier USS Midway.

Also from our balcony we could see the airport in the distance, and later in the day I watched planes arriving and departing every few minutes.

San Diego is the southernmost city in California, and is just 100 miles or so from the Mexican border. It has its share of skyscraper office blocks and some amazingly vast and beautiful modern hotel complexes. It also has history, and our tour guide told us lots and lots of stories as she described the city's buildings and parks. This lady was proud to say she was 81 years old and a lifelong San Diego resident.

Once we had moved away from the dockside our first stop was a car park adjacent to the USS Midway carrier. This ship is gigantic, and a major attraction to visitors wanting a really unusual experience. It wasn't for us today, but we did get a photo opportunity and a chance to look at a huge famous statue of a sailor holding and kissing a girl. Just to the side of this colourful statue was a small garden with more statues (bronze this time) of Bob Hope at a microphone with a group of sailors positioned around him. It has a recording playing of a few minutes from a concert he made to sailors during the war.

I have to say that the Americans are really good at this type of display.

Back on the coach we passed by a few of the enormous hotels, the city's convention centre, and numerous vast office blocks of course. Then we drove along a street in an area known as the Gas Lamp district. This has many of the city's original, and much lower buildings. We had Wyatt Earp's hotel pointed out to us, and stories of how the city was developed. One of our guide's stories was about a stray dog that acquired a severe drinking problem in the bars, where he was given beer by the locals.

After this street drive we went to the old ferry terminal which has been developed into a small park, with a few little shops and cafés for locals and visitors to enjoy. Unfortunately, we were rather early and hardly anything was open, but here was a good view out over the harbour area.

Our next highlight was the city park which doubles up as a major complex of museums. There are sports halls, and an outdoor music venue with the world's largest outdoor pipe organ. It's a beautiful place with trees from all over the world to tickle the visual senses, alongside the cultural venues and athletic opportunities. We didn't stop here, but the coach did drive slowly enough so we could see how good it is.

The morning was moving on and there was a further drive along the waterside and beaches, with a lot of history of how it was developed. Our guide was excitedly name-dropping throughout the morning, and some of the information sunk into my mind, but much of it went in one ear and then rushed out the other.

A combination of an enthusiastic guide and a newish driver now resulted in us going along a series of roads and avenues to get to our final stop. We were not lost, but certainly spent quite some time in residential areas. We went along one avenue with side roads alphabetically named after trees, hence we had "ash", "beech", etc. It was quite fun to guess and then discover what the next tree would be. Sadly, they couldn't find anything for 'V', and ran out of streets after "walnut".

Meanwhile the guide had rambled on about something that neither Deb nor I absorbed.

Finally we reached the tour highlight with a stop at a district called The Old Town. We had no idea what it was going to be, and were quite surprised by a reconstruction of an area that reflected how the original settlers of San Diego had lived.

It was a lot like a cowboy town from Hollywood film sets, but with a serious degree of Mexican influence. Most of the buildings were reconstructed shells from the mid-1800s which now housed modern day souvenir shops. Others were little museums depicting the wild west era with a restaurant, Wells Fargo office (complete with stagecoach), a jailhouse and so on. It was really rather nice and easily occupied the hour that we had there. We could have done with more time, but to be fair, many of the shops were selling Mexican style items, and we would be visiting Mexico next. Our suspicions were that the prices might be cheaper there than in this expensive US city.

And yes, we were proved right.

Our trip was over and we were back on Aurora by 1:00. It was time for lunch and although we had plans to go out again, it would have only been to visit the shopping mall. Our shopping list was still active, but nothing too urgent. We relaxed in the sunshine instead.

San Diego had been another wonderful visit. In fact, all three of the American ports had been superb and now with delightful weather, all the passengers were smiling again.

The evening entertainment was a male saxophone/piano player that didn't appeal, so we quizzed again and even got very close to the top in the syndicate challenge. We now had two novice entertainment hosts on the ship, and they appeared occasionally to gain experience of the different activities. They were really brand new to the job and still very much apprentices, requiring one of the experienced hosts alongside them. It would be several days before they actually became active on their own.

Tomorrow Aurora would be at sea again sailing further down the western coast of North America. On Saturday we would be arriving in Mexico: another new country to add to our list of worldwide experiences.

Friday 31st March – Sea Day to Mexico

It was a little windy on the balcony today but it warmed up to 18°C in the afternoon.

As I woke up, I was aware that the sea had calmed since our departure from San Diego when the ocean was rather lumpy. It was a sunny morning with a blue sky, but a breeze was keeping it cool. By late afternoon that breeze also subsided, and the open decks finally had a few people worshipping the sun again.

We had another full morning of activities:

8:30 – Office work to get diaries and journals up to date

10:00 – Port talk on Cartagena in Colombia. We already had a tour booked and it appeared perfectly adequate after hearing Crystal's talk.

11:00 – Cha cha cha part 3. It was going well, but after an hour of repeated twisting it made my hip hurt just a little.

12:00 - Deb went off to Battle of the Sexes, and I had a rest.

12:30 – Choir practice. This was my last session of singing. I had loved doing it, but the time had come to think about other things, and perhaps spending a little more time in the sun.

13:30 – Lunch time for the both of us. Then 45 minutes in the sunshine. This was the first time in weeks that we lay in the golden glow.

15:00 – The final part of the cha cha cha lessons. We were very pleased with the instructors and had learnt a new move as well as getting ourselves back into the dance.

There was one slight annoyance: the instructor said he was going to spend a moment revising a move for people who had been before. We had not done this move and wanted to learn it, so I pointed out that this was advertised as a beginners' class, so surely it should be from the beginning. He wouldn't budge, so I sulked for a few minutes until he moved on to teach a new move from the start.

This backs up my comments from earlier when he ignored beginners in another class which stopped us going back for the rest of that sector.

16:00 – Dance over, so we had a chance for afternoon tea with sausage rolls.

Our busy period was over, and we had time to relax in the cabin …. but not for long.

We showered and then went to the Individual quiz, before beginning preparations for the evening.

Today was our table-mate Robin's birthday, and the six of us went to the Beach House for dinner. It was a lovely evening with delicious food and wonderful service. There were steaks cooked on lava stones at the table, sizzling dishes and a kebab hanging on a huge hooked stand. We chatted and laughed as we washed the food down with three bottles of quiz wine. There were photographs taken on all our cameras by a waiter, and four of the Headliners eating nearby sang "Happy Birthday". It was rounded off by a delicious chocolate cake that was huge, and which we shared with the Headliners.

While we had a wonderful evening, the other entertainment around the ship was from Zoe Tyler singing in the theatre again. The Headliners had the evening off after performing a matinee in the afternoon. I can't get my head around this new afternoon matinee idea. After a very special evening, it was time to put our rather tipsy heads on our snuggly pillows. Aurora was sailing at quite a rate in order to arrive in the Mexican Port of Cabo San Lucas by the morning.

The sea was smooth and we were soon fast asleep after a truly lovely evening with our new close friends. We had all booked another cruise over the last few days, and we will be meeting up again in January 2019 for a two-month trip to the Caribbean and along the River Amazon.

Saturday 1st April – Cabo San Lucas, Mexico

What a delightful day in the warm sunshine that managed to heat up our balcony to 22°C.

This was our first visit to Mexico and it was a tender boat port.

The daylight woke me early at just after 6:00, but this was far too soon to get up. Eventually as the sounds of anchors heralded our arrival, I peeked out of the window to see a beautiful view. We were at rest in a bay and our vista was a cliff formation that reminded me of the 'Needles' to the west of the Isle of Wight, but even more spectacular. It's called Land's End, and is a famous tourist sight for visitors to Cabo San Lucas. Boat tours take visitors to look at the cliff formations all day, and some drop them off on a tiny secluded sand bank, known as Lovers Beach, while others go in search of whales and dolphins. We had the view for free …. well apart from the cost of the cruise of course!

We had no tour today. There was very little left by the time we considered one, but we were quite happy to go ashore when the rush hour was over, and have a look around what had been described as a very pretty town. From the starboard side of the ship we could see hills behind the port area and away into the distance. The hills were different colours with greys and browns, and reminded us of our stay in Jordan with similar craggy mountains. Some of the town's houses and hotels were built and painted a similar colour to the hills behind them, but not everywhere.

Just after 10:00 we were boarding the tender for the short ride to the harbour. The sea was quite calm but with just enough swell to make the ride interesting. Aurora had three of its boats out, and there were also two local craft helping to ferry passengers back and forth.

Once ashore we began a battle to ignore the continuous questions asking if we wanted a taxi to tour around the islands, or a trip on a glass-bottomed boat.

We went into an arts and craft market which turned out to be less 'arts and craft', and more a typical tourist souvenir and 'tat' market. Never mind, we had at least escaped the glass-bottomed boat offers, which were now replaced by *"come in and look"*, *"you want a tee shirt"* or *"jewellery for the pretty lady"*. Well we didn't respond very favourably, but did buy a fridge magnet, a Christmas tree bauble, and a top for Deb.

Back outside to the "g*lass-bottomed boat s*ir" brigade and we walked around the harbour for about half an hour looking for anything else to interest us. We looked in numerous souvenir shops which all seemed to sell the exact same ponchos, sombreros, and holiday keepsakes. I did eventually find something that caught my eye – a shop with some quite elegant white summer shirts. Unfortunately, they were just about the most expensive thing on sale in Cabo San Lucas, and I quickly returned my gaze to the endless numbers of sombreros.

No, I never bought a sombrero or a poncho!

Forgetting the shops and the annoying boat trip pimps, the town was actually very beautiful. The houses were typically Spanish, and it was very clean. There was music playing almost everywhere, and the people were polite and cheerful. Many locals and tourists were enjoying beers, tequilas, or coffee in the different cafes and bars, and I couldn't really fault the place. The water in the harbour was clear and clean with beautiful tropical fish swimming around to delight the European visitors, and the sun shone brightly to warm and cheer us up.

After perhaps 90 minutes of shop-gazing and gentle strolling we were back at the tender jetty and soon bouncing our way back to the ship.

We indulged in a naughty lunch of a burger and chips, before changing into sun-mode and lay on the deck for an hour. Today was finally a true holiday moment of sunshine and souvenir-hunting again. We had not had this weather very much as we travelled around the world, so this was a pleasant change.

The temperature mid-way through the afternoon peaked at 22° …. delightful.

Back in the cabin I spent a long time on the balcony just watching the pleasure boats, yachts, catamarans, and even replica galleons slowly moving around the Land's End headland. There were occasionally "honks" of seals or sea-lions from their rocky sunbeds, but it was sad to see the pleasure boats getting so close to them. The secluded Lovers' Beach in that same rocky complex was now crowded with people enjoying the sun-drenched sand, and the calm waters to snorkel, or just swim in.

Sometimes a pleasure craft that had been taking tourists fishing returned towards the harbour, and they were followed by birds hoping (and getting) scraps of fish. There were pelicans and other birds I didn't recognise, but they were all larger than the average seagull that scavenges fishing boats around Britain's coastline.

From the beaches on the shoreline of this beautiful little port we had a constant sound of disco music, and the afternoon partying attracted holiday makers to make the most of the sun, sand and alcohol. This is a lively place, and probably enjoys the arrival of cruise ships to swell the tills of the souvenir shops and bars.

The on-board entertainment later was a singer called Donny Ray Evins, who has a tribute act based on Nat King Cole. He had been seen previously by some passengers, and they gave a very good recommendation. Maybe we would go and watch a singer tonight.

After that a deck party was scheduled up beside the Riviera Pool with a 60s/70s theme. The weather forecast looked promising, so we tentatively planned to get out our fancy dress gear again for the last chance to wear it on this cruise.

Well, we watched the show and he is a really good singer. But he has spent a lot of time in the USA doing the cabaret circuit, and insisted in asking us if we were having a good time after every couple of songs. It's as if these people are frightened that they are failing, and need the reassurance of forced adulation every few minutes. The majority of British audiences are uncomfortable with this outpouring of unnecessary and quite often dishonest choruses of "yeah".

We weren't sure if we would be going to see his second show.

It was time for the deck party which began with Caravan repeating their 'Eagles' tribute show. This was very good, but many of the people watching left as soon as the act was finished. As the deck party started the Riviera Pool became almost deserted. Sadly, it didn't get much busier and our 60s/70s costumes were once again the only ones, apart from the entertainment team.

Along with Richard and Angie we had a few dances to try and stir up some enthusiasm, but there was rarely more than a handful of people on their feet. By the time we gave up at about 11:00 there were more bar staff and waiters than passengers, and if you counted in the entertainment team and Caravan there was almost a 2:1 ratio. What a sad response, but I have to say it wasn't very warm. This had been one of several deck parties, and there had only been one that was a well-attended and lively evening.

Unless the entertainment team are keeping the attendance information to themselves, P&O needs to rethink these deck party evenings. Something needs to change to make these more interesting rather than sticking to the tried and tested format, that no longer appeals …. well, not to this age profile anyway.

To be honest, I think this comment could be directed at a lot of the entertainment.

Two Sea Days to Guatemala

Sunday 2nd April

Warm again today with the balcony getting up to 24°C.

Aurora was on the first of two days sailing along the coast of Mexico before our next stop in Guatemala at Puerto Quetzal. I woke early again with the sunrise at 6:00. Never mind, I rolled over and stayed in bed until our neighbours turned on Sky News just before 7:00. Whenever they were in the cabin (and awake) they had the television on this channel, and loud enough that the sound could be heard by us, and even some words were recognisable. To make matters worse, with the television sound up high, they had to shout at each other when talking.

I considered going to reception about this soon, as their regular bedtime appeared to be after midnight, and only then did the television go off.

After breakfast we went up onto the top deck and lay in the sun for an hour. It was wonderful with the edge taken off the heat by a gentle breeze.

Deb and I survived the sunshine torture for quite a while, but I was eventually quite glad to go. It wasn't because of the heat this time but something which made me feel slightly queasy.

One of the familiar characters on the ship arrived close to us and prepared himself to enjoy the sunshine. He began a long-drawn-out preparation by laying out various towels on his lounger. Next, he stripped down to the smallest of posing pouches, before oiling himself all over, very thoroughly. That deep oiling stage took the length of the "Ommadawn" track by Mike Oldfield that I was listening to, and that is over ten minutes long. Finally, slippery man rolled and pulled his posing pouch tightly before laying on his lounger displaying virtually all his oily body to the sun, and leaving nothing to imagination for anyone passing by.

Yuk!

When Deb said she had had enough of the sun, I was more than pleased to pack up and go.

We refreshed ourselves with a cup of tea before spending a few minutes updating diaries etc. Then it was time to put on our dancing shoes, well flat shoes actually, and then we were off to Carmen's for our dance lesson. Today was the social foxtrot for beginners, which we had touched on before but never got very far with it.

After a pleasant 45 minutes we left the venue as they began setting up for the choir practice. It was unusual not to be grabbing a seat, but I think the time had come to do other things, and perhaps consider joining our local community choir when we get home.

At midday, the clocks bounced forward another hour to GMT-6 and Deb had rushed off to continue with the Battle of the Sexes.

I had a relaxed lunch before dozing back in the cabin.

Deb came back at 1:00 after finishing the quiz (which the ladies won today) and grabbing a quick lunch in the buffet. We shared a piece of chocolate each, and then Deb changed back into her dancing shoes and disappeared to Carmen's for her Salsa session. I put on my dancing plimsolls and followed her after 30 minutes, to meet up for part two of the social foxtrot at 3:00.

Today's dancing lessons had been very enjoyable, and we learnt a great deal. We had enough steps now to dance a social foxtrot if we felt so inclined. The downside was that my knees ached very badly. I took some painkillers and put on a knee support that I brought with me, but my legs seemed a bit fatter than the last time I wore it, and hence the support was very tight.

The weather remained warm and there was what I call a "big sea" today. It was calm and just looked like a flattened piece of crumpled paper stretching miles away to the horizon, where it had been possible to see the hazy mountainous coastline of Mexico for most of the day. Even better, the temperature was up to 24°.

We were sailing south eastwards at just over 20 knots and the ride was quite smooth with just a little jiggling from an almost following north wind.

Tonight was formal dress code, and I would be sending my dress shirts to the laundry for one final clean in the morning. This would give me enough dress shirts to get me through the rest of this sector. This wasn't as extravagant as it might seem, as we had 50% off laundry charges, plus it gave Deb a break from ironing the complicated pleats.

There were two shows on the evening's entertainment list that we wanted to see. In Carmen's Adam Hepenstall was performing a comedy magic show, and in the theatre a comedian called Phil Melbourne was performing.

After a bit of discussion about how to fit in both shows, we made a radical decision to ignore the dress code tonight.

Shock and horror!

Instead of going to the main dining room we would eat early in the buffet and then dash off to Carmen's for the early performance by Adam Hepenstall.

Things just about worked perfectly. We had a rather enjoyable plate of fish and chips in the buffet where we also saw Richard and Angie, who had similar plans. We were away from the buffet first and arrived at Carmen's just as the doors opened, and we grabbed front seats for us, as well as for Richard and Angie. The magic show was very good, and although I had seen most of the tricks before, they still amazed me. There was also a superb trick to end that flummoxed almost everyone. I won't describe his act any more than that, to allow you to enjoy it if you come across Adam.

The only problem was that he finished late. Ten or twenty of us rushed along the deck to get to the theatre where Phil Melbourne had just started his act. We ran the risk of abuse from him as we piled in to the few available seats left. He did eventually ask what was happening, and his only reaction was to say he would have words with his magician mate later about running over time.

Anyway, the comedy was good. There were a few jokes that might have offended some people, but they weren't bad enough to offend the majority. He also finished his act with an escapology trick that was close to being a Tommy Cooper impression. It was purposely going wrong, but at the same time showing his escapology skills were very good. There was laughter throughout his act, and we would be going to the return shows from both of these amusing men later in the week.

With the formal entertainment over, the four of us took to quizzes, expecting Robin and Rosemary to join us. They had enjoyed the Beach House so much a few days ago, that they went there again. We'd also booked a table there for Tuesday evening to use up our remaining Around the World treat voucher.

Well Robin and Rosemary never showed up as they went to the shows after their meal. This was probably a wise decision as the quizzes left us wineless and confused, even coming last in the Syndicate Quiz. I don't think that had ever happened before in all the years we have been doing it.

Meanwhile I was beginning to think I had more wrong with me than aching knees. I started to cough far too regularly, and the aches and pains were from my head down to my legs. The latest virus (or whatever) appeared to have come and visited me. I dosed myself up with painkillers and was soon fast asleep.

………………………………………..

Monday 3rd April

Today it was hot and humid with a sticky temperature of 25°C on the balcony.

I woke with a headache, and felt very sorry for myself. My throat was sore and the cough told me, and everybody around me, that I had 'The Bug'.

The day was warm and humid now that we were back in the tropics, but that didn't help me to feel any better. While I relaxed in the cabin with "man flu" Deb went for a swim. My whole body was aching and I didn't feel like doing anything today. Without a shadow of a doubt, the dancing over the last few days hadn't helped and had seriously affected my knees. I knew they were bad when I came away, but had no idea that they would get this worse in just three months.

When Deb came back from her swim and opened the balcony door, I felt the humid heat come into the cabin. I broke out in an instant sweat.

At 10:00 there was a port talk on our stop in St Lucia. This Caribbean island was a long way off yet, but with nothing booked, we had to go along.

Before we went to the port talk, Deb took a look through the tour options for St Lucia, and she came across a boat trip to see the island's Piton Mountains. The trip also included swimming time and free rum punch cocktails. This seemed a good idea, especially as we promised ourselves we would swim in the Caribbean Sea this time, having failed five years ago.

Now armed with ideas we went to listen to Crystal's thoughts on St Lucia. While in the darkened theatre I attempted to cough as quietly as I could while we listened to what Crystal was offering. The talk presented a lot of tour possibilities, but I saw little to better the boat trip.

Well actually, I slept through a lot of the talk but Deb was still happy with our choice.

From the theatre talk we went for a cup of coffee in Raffles. Quite a weird moment as one waiter took the order, and then a waitress delivered our drinks. A couple of minutes later the original waiter appeared with our coffees and looked totally confused. For a moment I wondered who was still waiting for their latte and cappuccino.

I was still feeling poorly (aah!) and decided not to bother with the morning's dance class. Instead I sat on the balcony for a few minutes while Deb went and booked the St Lucia tour. Just before midday, she went to the Battle of the Sexes and I lay down on the bed, and instantly fell asleep. When Deb woke me almost an hour later, I wasn't totally sure where I was, but managed to struggle up to the buffet for a very light lunch.

Back from lunch I surprised my lovely caring wife by suggesting that we go and sit in the sun for an hour. I think this must have done me a bit of good, because when we returned to the cabin Deb said that while I was looking pale at lunch, I had now got some colour back. And yes, I was actually feeling a little better.

We both sat on the relatively cool balcony reading books, while keeping a watchful look for passing wildlife. Having gone three-quarters of the way around the globe, the best I had seen was sea-lions in San Francisco, fleeting glimpses of passing dolphins, plus numerous flying fish, one or two albatross, masked booby birds, and pelicans. Almost everyone else on the ship had seen whales and dolphins performing their tricks, but these beautiful creatures had just about avoided my gaze for more than 25,000 miles. Then just as I was feeling hard done by about this lack of wildlife, Aurora overtook a turtle just a few metres away from the ship, swimming peacefully down the coast of Mexico.

Finally, I felt I had seen something special.

My excitement was short lived as it appeared that many of the passengers had spotted sharks and seals today: I felt such a failure

There was still a lot of mist in the distance, but fortunately the ship had been sailing through a clear patch since late morning, and the temperature was deliciously warm. The open decks were covered in semi-naked bodies with all shades of skin from a light beige through to walnut and teak. Deb and I had acquired some tan and we described ourselves as cappuccino coloured, although my legs were definitely getting to a shade of light oak.

Although not feeling 100%, I felt well enough to at least go to dinner with the others. I just had a bowl of soup, followed by a salad as the main course, and finished with fruit salad and ice-cream. Tomorrow we would be going to the Beach House, so we let the waiters know we wouldn't be at the table.

Tonight, the entertainment was Donny Ray Evins in the theatre with more songs, but not Nat King Cole this time. In Carmen's the Headliners were performing the Abba tribute again. I don't understand why they hadn't performed the Queen tribute, and even when we spoke to the boys and girls, they seemed just as confused as us.

Deb and I didn't go to the shows, and simply relaxed with our books. My head was still feeling as if it was full of cotton wool, and the cough had got worse.

Tomorrow we would be landing in Guatemala, and I was hopeful that a good night's sleep would see me OK for our tour in Puerto Quetzal in the morning. Luckily, we wouldn't have an early start, as the tour wouldn't be leaving until 9:45. The tour was called *'Macadamia Discovery'*, and yes, it was about the nuts.

Aussie Complaints

In our brief moments when connected to the internet, I read a post on Facebook from an Australian who had been on board Aurora for a previous sector of our cruise.

The theme of the post was that she vowed never to join a P&O World Cruise again because the ship was full of old British people who complained all the time.

I responded, as politely as I could, that this person didn't really know what they were talking about.

Aurora is a British ship, and the majority of the passengers on the voyage were British. The ship was on a World Cruise lasting over three months. A World Cruise is a special cruise aimed at people who can afford the time, and money, to come away during the winter months from Britain to see faraway and exotic places. Many of us were seeking sunshine and warmth, but most of all we were having an adventure. To be able to enjoy this style of thrill, the majority of the British passengers were in the more adult age range.

Sadly, the ship could never be full of passengers who were able, or wanted, to go all the way around the world. Hence like all world cruises it was split into a series of sectors which could be bought as separate cruises. There were just over 400 passengers going all around the world, but to make it financially possible, the sectors had been eventually priced quite attractively in an attempt to fill the ship for every sector.

Many of the sector passengers were more inclined to party for their three - or four-week holidays, and without a doubt, the long-stay people appeared rather less active. We didn't drink and party every night, as we wanted to go home with our livers intact. We sometimes preferred peace and quiet as an alternative to disco music. We wanted to spend time in the sunshine, and liked to go ashore to look at the places we may never visit more than once in our lifetime.

Now we get to the Australian interest. Along with some who did complete the whole circumnavigation, or at least a couple of sectors, there were a small number of these wonderful people who had secured unbelievable bargains for single sectors, or even just parts of sectors. Their aim was a short holiday full of partying, drinking, laughing and shouting loudly for every available moment they could.

But they couldn't understand why the rest of us weren't joining in.

I am not trying to be rude about the Australian passengers, as my comments are targeted at those long-weekend bargain-cruise people. They had been openly shouting about what they paid. As well as the incident in Hawaii when the loud-mouthed lady insisted on telling us how much her holiday had cost, there had been similarly ridiculous figures being banded around the ship. What we suspected to be simply laundry rumours, appeared to be true.

A world cruise is special, but passengers wanting the experience have to pay a lot of money, and there are fewer able to afford the adventure as the years pass. Hence instead of the traditional two ships making these voyages each winter, P&O have decided that there will be just one for the foreseeable future.

Of course, the alternative to try and stop this happening would be to reduce the cost of the full world cruise, and then fill our British ships with more British people …. but that will never happen.

To the wonderful Australians that we met, and in fact all of the different nationalities that sailed thousands of miles around the globe with us, thanks for your company.

To that small band of loud, rude, and thoughtless bargain-hunters, I hope you continue to have fun cruises, but hopefully not on British ships.

Contrary to what you might have thought, we were having a really good time, in our own way, and when we got home we had a wealth of tremendous experiences from around the world.

Plus a few ridiculously funny memories of you as well!

Tuesday 4th April – Puerto Quetzal, Guatemala

It was incredibly hot here, and our balcony was a roasting 30°C.

I had a bad night with my virus, bacterial infection, or whatever it was. Our neighbours didn't do me any favours by having their television on until well after midnight. I heard the "Coronation Street" theme tune three times, so I had no idea what channels they were looking at. To be honest the background babble of sound probably didn't affect me at all, but I became angry that people didn't realise how easily sound can travel between ship cabins.

Eventually I got to sleep, but it was only until I woke again at 6:00. Lying there dozing got me through to 7:30 when I finally got up and put the kettle on.

It was already 27° on the balcony, and a layer of mist was disguising the horrendous humidity that we discovered later. This was the tropics again and northern Europeans are not used to this form of heat for long periods.

Aurora was nearing our port for the day which was Puerto Quetzal in Guatemala. This was another first for us.

After breakfast I had to log on to the internet to check the bank. We had paid the deposit on another cruise at the same moment as the last sector bill was due, and we were very close to the credit card limit. Realising the possible issues, I changed the on-board account to my debit card yesterday, but there was still a potential problem. Fortunately, the previous bill (sector 3) had been cleared giving us some leeway again. Panic over.

Soon Aurora was moving into her berth for the day, and we had our first proper look at what the port offered. It was very much a commercial port, and to our left were huge piles of what I think was anthracite for the power station. A coal ship was offloading throughout the day to make the black mountains even bigger. To the right was the usual container area with two huge cranes and at least four mobile container-moving vehicles roaring around the dockside.

Our berth was actually a floating metal pontoon, with walkways to concrete rope-tying points on either side. It took several minutes to manoeuvre our ship along the pontoon to allow our walkways to clear smaller tying points. This made us slightly late getting the all-clear to leave the ship, so tours were delayed.

On a slightly more passenger-focussed note, at the end of the walkway from the pontoon to the shore was a large circular thatched terminal building in a small area of palm trees. Between this building and the tour coach park was a quite large tourist-trap market with a café plus stalls selling leather, wood, and local craft goods, plus all the usual souvenirs. It was amazing that so many stalls could somehow make money when they all seemed to be selling the same range of products.

The shiny bits and pieces were ignored for now as we made our way through to the tour bus.

Today we were going to a macadamia nut plantation. Our road journey took us across the flat coastal strip towards the hills and mountains several miles away. This pleasant air-conditioned ride took over an hour as we passed a countryside that was mainly agricultural, although there were a few holiday resorts as well. This country looked to be poor, and with little organised services. It was dusty and covered in litter wherever you looked. We were told that the vast majority of the population work on the land, planting, tending, and harvesting crops.

Our guide expanded on the country's agriculture, describing the regional split of the country and how each region specialises in particular crops. Near the sea it appears the soil is perfect for sugar cane, and we saw fields with the remains of last year's crop being cleared, and another being planted. A little further on the vegetation changed to bananas and plantains on either side of the road. On the roadside were regular markets selling fruit and vegetables for communities that lived in simple block buildings hardly bigger than a large garden shed. Even worse, some of these huts were internally split to support multiple families in spaces we would assign to a single small bedroom.

As we got closer to the mountains, the crop changed again to coffee. As the soil or availability of water changes, so do the crops.

We passed by a complex of hills that were revered by the Mayan population of the country. There were rocks at the top that had been weathered, making them appear like little heads. This is where the Mayan people used to make sacrifices, but now limit themselves to praying, although apparently some of them still live in the caves in the hills.

Next were two volcanoes that are still active on a regular basis and they dominate the landscape visually, and presumably have quite an effect on life in general.

The roads we had come along so far had been generally ok, but now we turned off the main highway. The surface became dusty, and the carriageway narrower. Even on the busy main road we had been on earlier there were places where it went to a single carriage to cross bridges over dry river beds. I assume these revert to torrential rivers during the winter as the water drains from the mountains, but now with the short rainy season over, these beds were dry and we could see huge boulders that had been washed down the valleys.

Finally, we turned off into an even narrower road, and then stopped by a dusty lane that was the entrance to our macadamia plantation. We strolled up the lane and were greeted by the owner and his wife. He was once a fireman in the USA but retired in his thirties and eventually moved to Guatemala to buy a series of farms to grow the macadamia. Our group was split into two, and while one half went on a tour of the farm, we went with the owner for a breakfast of pancakes made with 20% macadamia nut flower, spread with macadamia butter, and topped with his own grown blueberry marmalade. It was delicious, and washed down by superb coffee that he grew and processed as well.

While we ate and drank his products, he talked to us about his organic farming techniques, and his 'back to nature' style of farming. He was very philosophical and expressed anger at politicians and experts, who are killing the world by not addressing the causes of global warming, but simply trying to control it. He believes that the worldwide vegetation gene pool is being eroded to maximise efficiency, with the result that basic 'survival of the fittest' and natural adaptation of plants is being stifled. Lots of his ramblings were a little wild, but his primary thoughts were very straight forward and correct.

I enjoyed the half an hour listening to his assessment of our world going into a nose dive to destruction.

Soon we swapped to the show-around tour. The owner's wife described the ethos of the farm with the trees simply being planted and then left to look after themselves. There is no mechanised harvesting, and as the nuts drop naturally, local people are employed to pick them up off the floor. The nuts are then allowed to dry before grading and processing. There are no chemicals used and everything, other than the actual nut, is returned to the soil to complete the cycle of nature. As well as packaging and selling the nuts, they also extract the nut oil to create skin creams, butter and wax. On the farm site they also give massages to visitors using their own products to relieve and relax aching muscles.

The farm is a small business, but rather than using machines, they employ a local workforce who can earn enough to send their children to school. This enables the children to get an education, and those who don't go into more skilled careers become the next generation of farm workers. Without these jobs the families remain poor and uneducated, with no way of breaking the cycle of poverty. Eventually the current farm owners hope the locals will expand the macadamia forests and become self-sufficient.

One statement the owners left us with was simple and to the point:

" What can I do to help the world?"

The response from an eminent scientist was *"plant a tree"*.

"Yes, but what else can I do?"

"Plant another tree".

We left the farm with the sweet taste of macadamia in our mouths, and the confusion of ideas about the world's problems.

Back at the port we had time to wander through the little market, and to buy just a couple of memories of this country. With nothing else to amuse or interest us on shore we retired to the air-conditioned cabin to relax.

Deb went and did some washing while the ship's laundries were quiet.

I wasn't feeling much better but refused to give in to the cough and sore throat. In the evening we went to the Beach House for a delicious meal as Aurora sailed away from Guatemala on the next stage of our adventure. We would be at sea for two days now passing several countries before arriving at the Panama Canal on Friday morning.

That would herald the end of our Pacific Ocean travels, and returning to the Atlantic Ocean for the crossing towards home. We had just four more ports to visit, and just over two weeks to go of the spin around our world.

Pacific Sea Days to the Panama Canal
Wednesday 5th April

This morning it was 30°C on the balcony at 7:30, and it stayed this hot throughout the day.

I woke with a horrid sore throat: clearly, I am no better yet!

The ship was wobbling around but not too violently. It was misty, but as I stepped out on the balcony at 7:30 the heat hit me in the face, and the humidity was stifling.

This was the first of two days at sea while Aurora sailed south-east towards the Panama Canal. Over the next 48 hours our ship would be passing by the coasts of El Salvador, Honduras, Nicaragua and Costa Rica before we reached the coast of Panama itself.

After our daily office chores, we met up with Richard, Angie, and Robin to sort out details of the Amazon cruise in 2019 which we have all booked. After five minutes talking with the future cruises people, the six of us are now linked and we are assigned the same dinner table. I doubt we will get table 228 again with its superb views from the window of the wake, but we will be together.

In just over two weeks we would be saying goodbye to each other, but hopefully we would be keeping in contact until our reunion on this beautiful ship again in January 2019.

It was now port talk time and this one covered our visit to Barbados. This would be another new destination for us, and we needed to know something about the island before booking a tour. Still not feeling too well I quickly lost interest and dozed off, but I did register the main points about this Caribbean paradise. Eventually Deb and I decided on a '*Best of...*'-style tour to look around the island and visit one or two special places.

With that booked, it meant we had our final tours sorted for the cruise.

After our short stop at the Tours Desk it was time for morning coffee, plus a muffin to keep us going until lunchtime. From Raffles we went to Carmen's to see what the dance instructors were doing. I was in no fit state to take part, but we wanted to see what they planned to cover in the waltz, which was the subject for the next two days. Hopefully by tomorrow I would be well enough to join in and perhaps discover all our bad habits in this quite familiar dance.

At 12:00, the clocks went forward to GMT-5, and it instantly became 13:00. Deb went to Battle of the Sexes, and I sat at the back for some of the quiz before joining up with Deb for something to eat. It was soon 2:00 and time for Deb's Salsa while I spent an hour in the Crow's Nest.

The Crow's Nest was a popular venue throughout the day. The prime spots with a view out over the bow of the ship were usually grabbed before 10:00, and couples read, or did puzzles for what seemed like hours. It was reasonably quiet in the daytime, apart from the art class that created a bit of louder chatter. There was morning coffee, or a pre-lunch beer, and then a quieter period while people ate, before the seats all filled again for the afternoon.

And yes, a lot of people found time to have a doze, and several drifted into full sleep.

The men were the worst examples of sleepers, and they often enhanced their experience with increasingly loud snoring. Usually the wives managed to stay awake, and give a gentle prod occasionally to stir their embarrassing snoring partner.

In the evening the Crow's Nest was a venue for cocktail parties, or just a lovely place for a pre-dinner drink with little savoury nibbles, and background music from the pianist. Later there would be more informal music from the different musicians, as cocktails were replaced by more serious drinking and louder chatter.

And some people sat and played Trivial Pursuit rather noisily!

I often spent time up there enjoying the glorious views. I liked to sit and read, with the odd catnap as my eyes struggled to maintain focus on the words. But I also inadvertently tuned in to conversations around me that captured my interest.

That particular afternoon my doze was interrupted by a pair of women who came in and sat close to me. They appeared to be sisters, with one in a pretty impressive mobility chair. The older one, in the chair, was occupied with a book of sudoku puzzles while the other sat quietly reading. Occasionally there would be a short conversation, and my interest was grabbed when I realised the one in the mobility chair had not switched on her hearing aid.

She initiated one short discussion by asking the other if they were going to bingo later. The younger one responded that they certainly were, to which the other seemed to ignore the answer and return to her puzzle. When her sister tried to converse a little louder, she eventually realised the lack of hearing aid.

After another peaceful few minutes, I was stirred again by the younger woman asking *"whose turn is it to pay for the bingo tickets tonight?"*

No response.

Five minutes later she tried again, with a similar lack of answer.

She shrugged her shoulders and returned to her book. I was able to return to studying the inside of my eyelids, with a little smile on my face.

After several silent minutes the older one suddenly stirred and asked her sister *"whose turn is it to pay for the bingo tickets tonight?"*

Younger sister responded *"I don't know…who paid last time?"*

Silence.

The younger one gave an audible sigh of frustration, and returned to her book. The older one was oblivious, and turned to a new puzzle.

I was afraid I would give away my amusement by giggling, so I grabbed my e-reader and went back to the cabin, knowing that Deb would be back there soon.

At 3:00 we met up again for a cup of tea, before dropping in on the dance lesson to see what they had achieved so far. We wouldn't have any problem joining in with them tomorrow if my throat and knees felt better. The waltz routine was at quite a basic stage, following a series of steps that we were quite familiar with.

On the way back to the cabin I bought some new throat sweets before we ran out. I really had to get rid of this bug!

Time for some more painkillers, and a rest on the balcony.

Late in the afternoon I spotted a squadron of masked booby birds flying alongside us as Aurora disturbed the fish. These birds were using the air pressure and turbulence created by Aurora to give them an easy flight while they searched for unsuspecting meals in the sea. They are so graceful as they glide, and they occasionally came up to our balcony level to show off and no doubt to check us out.

Still no whales or dolphins!

I think it is time to update you with my shaving adventures since my electric razor was damaged. I persevered with the disposable razors, and managed to speed up the process of getting a reasonably smooth chin. But there was an unusual problem.

When I was a teenager, I was threatened by a slightly miffed young man with a knife. He did me no physical injury but left me with a phobia about knives and blades. Every time I put the edge of the razor onto my face, my legs trembled, accompanied by a feeling of dread in my stomach. This might seem stupid after 45 years, and especially when I was the one in charge of the sharp edge, but it happened, and I was looking forward to having a regular electric shave when I got back home.

To put this issue into context, in perhaps six weeks of using these razors, I only managed to draw tiny specks of blood on two occasions.

What a wimp!

During the day there had been a talk from a chap called Tony White discussing drug culture and consequences, and another from Adam Hart-Davis about seafaring explorers. I recognised Adam Hart-Davis from his television appearances where I always thought he seemed surprised by what he said.

He was also a very loudly spoken man and sat at a dinner table quite close to our own. He dominated conversations at the table and his voice carried sufficiently for a large area of the restaurant to eaves drop on his views …. whether they wanted to or not!

Dress code this evening was formal, and there was a gala Marco Pierre White menu for dinner. This was one of several of these gala menus, and after three months they were becoming just a little disappointing compared to the special menus of years gone by.

To be honest the main dining room menus were all becoming disappointing with rather bland flavours (in my opinion) and a very obvious bias towards fish. If you took away the *"always available"* steak and chicken, there was just one meat choice and a speciality dish for myself and others who preferred not to eat fish …. Unless fried and covered in a crispy batter.

Of course, none of us ever went hungry.

From the dining room the six of us legged it to Carmen's where we had been invited to a cocktail party. This one was quite exclusive, and only for passengers who had booked major cruises whilst on board for the spring of 2019. It seems the Future Cruises team had surpassed themselves with bookings for the World Cruise on Arcadia, and our adventure to the Amazon on Aurora.

We mingled with the Officers as we drank a couple of glasses of fizz, and politely listened to the Future Cruise team's speech thanking us for our loyalty to P&O, and wishing us the best with our cruises in almost two years' time. Eventually the numbers of passengers in Carmen's reduced to the point where we realised it was time to go. For us, it was off to Masquerade's for the first of the two evenings quizzes. The early one was all about television programmes and we did well enough to feel happy with our efforts.

The entertainment tonight featured a singing duo called The Sounds of Simon, with the music of Simon and Garfunkel. This sounded quite interesting, but as these are some of our favourite songs, we worried that it might be a disappointing 45-minutes if their versions might prove to be painfully different.

For the cultural music listeners there was a classical concert from a pianist and a clarinettist.

The only other alternative was a Las Vegas themed evening in the Casino and Champions.

At least we had some quizzes to amuse us.

At the late-night syndicate quiz, we started rather badly, and were last after half a dozen questions. Then it all clicked together and we managed to be second behind a runaway winning team. We felt very proud of ourselves after our best ever result.

It was bedtime and the sea had calmed during the day promising a smooth night. I had been coughing quite regularly during the evening and felt embarrassed about my illness, and extremely sorry for myself. After a last dose of painkillers, I lay in bed and finished the final book that I had downloaded onto my kindle reader before leaving home.

As I rolled over onto my pillow I hoped for a good night's sleep and to feel better in the morning.

....

Thursday 6th April
Still hot and humid, reaching 30°C on the balcony.

Well, the first half of the night was very peaceful and I slept. Then I woke with my throat screaming for me to cough. I fought the tickle and wheezes for as long as I could but the battle was unwinnable.

The intermittent dozing and coughing continued until 7:30 when I got up and made some tea. It was another very hot and humid morning with the thermometer telling me that it was already 29° on the balcony. This sort of weather wasn't helping me to feel any better.

Aurora was continuing south-easterly at a relaxed 15.5 knots. The official conditions were that the sea was calm, with just light airs. In other words, we were sailing across a near-flat sea with a shiny surface and just a hint of dimples. We were passing by the coast of Panama and on schedule to arrive at the canal early tomorrow morning.

Late in the morning we were at latitude 7° north, meaning we were almost back at the equator again. We wouldn't be going much further south before we turned northwards to the entrance of the Panama Canal later in the day.

After breakfast we went up onto the very top deck to have an hour in the hot sunshine. I don't suppose it did my man flu/bacterial infection/nasty bug any good, but it was very hard to ignore such wonderful weather. I was without my little iPod this morning as it had decided to lose all the music, for the third time. It looked like it was nearing the end of its life and when we get home I will definitely be replacing it. My music is too important to not have with me when I relax in the sunshine either on a cruise, or back home in the garden. Fortunately, I managed to make the other music machine play a Moody Blues album to keep me amused as I absorbed the sun's rays.

NEWS FLASH - I saw a pod of dolphins. They weren't very active but one did a perfect flip to say sorry for ignoring me over the last three months.

OK, where are the whales?

At about 10:00 as we slowly got off the loungers to make our way back to the air conditioning, we saw a squadron of the masked booby birds resting on the prow of the ship waiting for their next meal to appear. Several of them were "scrambled", took off and peeled away to starboard. The remainder kept watch to port for any signs of prey.

Back at the cabin we relaxed in the cool, but were interrupted several times by the birds screaming as food was sighted. Their squawk is something akin to that of a crow or a goose. As one shouted its delight, the rest accompanied it, diving like arrows into the sea. They rarely failed, and would quickly bob up to the surface again to swallow their meal. Then they returned to the sky, regaining their composure alongside Aurora with their heads twitching from side to side for any hint of a tasty fish. Over the previous few days more and more of these birds had joined our ship, and I counted a dozen of them on our side of the ship, and suspected a similar number were patrolling to starboard.

Deb and I had a brief stroll up to the buffet for a cup of coffee, but the sticky heat was just too much for me, and I was much happier back in the cabin. The cough wasn't improving and Deb gave me instructions to go to the doctor this afternoon unless I showed a significant improvement.

I reluctantly had to agree with her, as I really felt unhappy.

Midday was approaching and Deb would soon be away to the Battle of the Sexes again. That was our only commitment for the afternoon, so once over, we went for some lunch. I didn't feel hungry, but I knew I had to eat something.

By late afternoon we were just less than 7° from the equator, and had changed to an easterly course towards the Panama Canal maritime car park, more officially called the canal's pilot station. The Captain reported that the temperature had reached 31° during the afternoon, and he promised the same, or even hotter, tomorrow. And the humidity was likely to be around 95%. That meant it would be almost raining at the same time as being flipping hot!

It seems the canal transit action would begin tomorrow morning at about 6:00 when the first of the pilots would be on board, and making decisions for the Captain on how to drive his ship.

The birds remained with us throughout the day, and as I relaxed on the balcony they continued to give us demonstrations of gliding and fishing. I am not sure if they ever really caught enough fish, as none of the squadron appeared to be getting any fatter.

These birds were of two different colours. They all had a white belly and head, with quite a long-pointed beak. Most of them had dark wing feathers and dark upper body extending to just above the eyes. This layer of dark feathers above the dark eyes make them look as if they have a hood on.

…. hence hooded booby birds.

But there were also other birds with light coloured feathers on most of their wings and head. They looked identical in shape, so I wondered if they are simply juvenile hooded boobies, rather than a completely different species. They all seemed to work quite happily together when fishing.

It was superb watching them dive, with their wings folded close to their bodies as they speared into the water. Sometimes they went down deep and left a bubbling inferno of water, before bobbing up after a few seconds. Other times they made a much shallower dive to chase the fish going sideways, before bobbing up much quicker. Sometimes when they surfaced they shook their feathers before quickly taking off to re-join the gang. Other times when they came up, they sat on the surface for a while before catching up with their mates again.

Sadly, I could never actually see if they successfully caught anything.

It was Angie's birthday today and we ate in the main dining room with balloons and cake to celebrate. Before that we had a pre-dinner bottle of Prosecco between the six of us while chatting in Anderson's.

The evening went very well with delightful waiters singing slightly out of tune at the dinner table. From the dining room we went to the early quiz in Masquerade's, and then to Carmen's to watch the second show from comedian Phil Melbourne. He was really enjoyable, and had most of the audience eating out of his hand. OK, so some of the jokes were a little familiar but many of them were new to us.

He ran over time and when he eventually completed the act, Richard scampered off to Vanderbilt's ahead of the rest of us to get a table for the syndicate quiz. Unfortunately, there were no tables available, and the questions had already started.

We gave further quizzing a miss and had an early night.

Tomorrow Deb and I will be up early to watch our arrival into the Panama Canal, so the alarm clock was set for 6:00.

Friday 7th April – Panama Canal

When we got up, the temperature was 24°C on the balcony, but by the afternoon it reached a hot and sticky 32°.

The alarm clock wasn't needed, and I got up at 5:45 to make a cup of tea. Various unidentifiable lights had woken me much earlier, but I couldn't lie there any longer. This wasn't just because of the spectacle of the Panama Canal, I was also suffering badly from the cough, and I had a headache that needed some attention.

At 6:00 it was just about light, and near to Aurora were many ships of different sizes and colours, all waiting their turn to pass through the canal to the Caribbean Sea, or onwards to the Atlantic Ocean. Out on the balcony it was obvious the humidity was high, and my body instantly let out a burst of sweat. Deb was also up and took her camera outside to capture the first images of the day. As I poured the tea I saw a pelican fly close by Deb at head height, and she jumped in surprise.

There were vast numbers of these birds, which are so graceful when in flight, but sometimes not so elegant when on land. They seemed to have formed up into groups that were patrolling the waiting bay, swooping down close to each ship to inspect what the day had brought to their home. Quite often they lined up one behind the other and then flew past us without a sound.

As the light increased and the mist burned away, there was a moment when I could see the cityscape of Panama in the far distance. Then more birds appeared. These were black and flying in at low level, just grazing the sea like an attack from bombers below radar detection levels. They might have been the booby birds we had been seeing daily, but now there were hundreds of them in flocks arriving as the sun rose. Other flying visitors came and took a look at Aurora. Some flew around above us like condors, others with different tail shapes and longer necks, came lower. Smaller black birds and gulls of varying sizes also introduced themselves to us, as a welcome to Panama.

At 6:15 after we had finished our tea and had a wash, Aurora slowly began to move and turned towards the canal entrance. I counted over 30 ships waiting in this holding area, and one, a red bulk carrier, was sailing in front of us. This would be with us for the day as we made our progress during the transit.

By now we had already been up on the top deck of the ship, and it was packed with excited passengers catching their first views, or perhaps just catching up on previous memories of this maritime spectacle. It was obvious now that we were on our way into the canal, and a visiting speaker came over the PA system, giving the first information about our day. His voice was very familiar, and he was almost certainly the same speaker as we had five years ago when we came through the canal the other way. The first landmark he told us to look out for was the Bridge of the Americas, that we would pass below about an hour before the first set of locks.

Deb and I had returned to the cabin as we had a breakfast tray arriving at 8:00. We now parked ourselves on the balcony to watch the action on our side of the ship. The guide was continuing his commentary and gave us the history of the canal plus descriptions of what would be visible on either side of the ship.

Sadly, our neighbours preferred listening to Sky News or whatever channel they felt important today.

At 07:45 we passed under the Bridge of the Americas, and a few minutes later our breakfast arrived. The first lock system was visible in the distance as we nibbled our croissants. It was a lovely day, but I felt awful. I realised I was going to have to visit the doctor today and get myself checked out. This was a horrible bug and I knew that many others on this ship were suffering in the same way.

At this point in the canal we caught our first sight of the waterway that connects with the new lock system. This allows even bigger ships to pass through this incredible short-cut between oceans. Of course, the gigantic ships have to pay for the privilege, and are charged upwards of $1million a time. We would be charged less than half of that to use the older, narrower, and less efficient lock system.

By 08:30 it was our turn for the Miraflores lock system where we would rise 26 feet, through two locks to the lake of the same name beyond. This would mean 26 million gallons of water would be taken from the fresh water lake to lift us.

And no, I don't know how many Olympic-size swimming pools that is.

For those who have never been through the Panama Canal, the experience and engineering spectacle is amazing. I can't do it justice here, as a full book would be needed to just give the history of its planning, construction, and failures, and more importantly the number of deaths involved to create the canal.

Anyway, the Miraflores lock system consists of two channels with two separate locks chambers in each. Although both channels could operate with ships going in the same direction, they normally have ships going in opposite directions. To lift (or drop) ships the 26 feet difference from the Pacific Ocean to the canal lake, there are two separate lock chambers in each channel.

To cut the lock process short, as Aurora began its lift, she was attached by steel ropes to a number of engines that ran along rails on either side of each lock channel. They are called 'mules' that purred along beside us guiding our ship centrally in the locks to protect the paintwork as we slowly progressed through the two chambers.

If you have ever watched a narrow boat going through a lock you can understand the principle, but these locks are massive, and lift enormous ships.

It took just over an hour to complete this first stage, and there would be two more sets of locks before we returned to the sea at the other end of the canal.

Sadly, I had lost interest by now and went down to see the doctor.

Almost an hour later I returned to the cabin about £80 worse off, with a box of antibiotics, a bottle of cough medicine, and a little bit of sympathy. The doctor described my chest as having *"several rattily areas down there"*.

I was shattered, and after taking my first pill and a swig of cough linctus, I virtually switched off for several hours in an attempt to get some rest and allow the medicine to work.

I stirred occasionally to have a drink, and nibble some food, but the amazing things going on around me really wasn't thrilling me as much as it should have done.

Deb had a break from the canal for the Battle of the Sexes, but that was the only thing that took her away from the canal action during the day.

At 5:00 in the afternoon, the journey was complete. I was feeling slightly more human and took a bit more interest as we dropped back down to sea level in the Caribbean Sea. During the day we had passed through six lock chambers, and used millions of gallons of fresh water to help us on our way, and save us the alternative sea journey of many thousands of miles around South America.

In the evening Angie hosted her birthday meal in the Glass House. This was the first time we had ever eaten there, and it was a lovely evening. The food was delicious and the company was superb. We had become such good friends. I felt much better and certainly considered I was finally on the mend, but I should not have had the alcohol. After just one glass of prosecco I felt light headed, and a glass of red wine later I realised my mistake. For the rest of the evening I quietly watched as the three bottles of quiz wine were emptied, but I was content to simply sip what was in my glass.

After a lovely meal we went to the syndicate quiz, and through a considerable alcoholic-fuelled haze managed to come a credible second. I even managed to give some positive input, but I was ready for bed well before we slowly made our way back to our cabins.

Aurora was now in the Caribbean Sea. She was creaking, jiggling, and bouncing along even though the official sea condition was 'slight'. The forecast was for the wind to get up to Force 6 or 7 during the night, but the movement wasn't going to stop me sleeping.

It had been a lovely day and evening, but I hadn't appreciated it very much. Tomorrow we would be landing in Colombia at the port of Cartagena, and hopefully I would be feeling better at last.

Saturday 8th April – Cartagena, Colombia
It was 30°C on the balcony today, and very humid.

This was our first visit to Colombia, and we woke to another hot and humid day. Our arrival was through a pretty area of waterway with palm trees and what might have been a mangrove swamp, but we soon saw where we would be berthing, and it was another container port.

I was feeling considerably better, but still woke up with a sore throat. The coughing had reduced, so maybe I was getting over the latest cold/cough/bug that the ship was inflicting on its passengers.

Alongside Aurora was the Thomson Dream which fortunately blocked most of our view of the container area. To starboard there was the Norwegian Pearl, and beyond that the Celebrity Eclipse. Today was going to be a very busy day with many thousands of cruise passengers descending on the city of Cartagena.

For those of you with a similar knowledge of Spanish as me, this Colombian city's name is pronounced as **'Cart-a-hay-na'** and requires you to gargle as you say it.

We had a tour booked that looked around the old city and a fortress known as the 'Inquisition'. After our breakfast we looked down to the vast quayside where the tour buses were filling with Thomson passengers, including three very noisy 'fun buses' with drums, whistles and trumpets blaring out music. As I stood amazed at that scene, our own tour buses arrived and soon the quayside was packed with coaches belching out air-conditioning waste.

Just before 10:00 we were away. Our guide was called Rafael and the driver was Rodney. Fortunately, we also had the company of our Port Lecturer (Crystal) as this turned out to not be the best of trips we had been on. The city is one of those that I would describe as dirty, with waste paper and plastic bottles behind fences and on waste land.

There were probably around 5,000 cruise passengers all visiting the same tourist spots during the morning, so it was busy, and it was also very hot.

At the first stop we piled out of the coach and followed the guide to a statue of one of the city's historical heroes. This is where we discovered that Rafael only spoke to anyone directly in front of him, and ignored any possibility that others behind might like to hear his story as well. The amount of traffic noise, and the constant babble from other tour groups (and there were lots of them) made it impossible to hear anything he said, unless it was directed straight at your ears. Add to this the unrelenting attention of street sellers trying to persuade us to buy hats, fans, watches, sunglasses, jewellery, and maracas, and any hope of hearing Rafael was gone.

What little information I did hear suggested that this hero was the Spanish Admiral Blas de Lez, who is revered as the person who defeated attempts by the British Navy to conquer the city. The fortress we were looking at, San Felipe Castle, was built to defend the city after numerous pirate attacks in the 16th Century.

One notable British pirate called Francis Drake, initially did very well as he sailed away with a 10-million-peso ransom after besieging the city in 1586.

Blas de Lez defended the city from the British attempts to take Cartagena in 1741 during a major sea battle with the Spanish fleet. Apparently, that was the end of any British attempts at capturing the city.

Rafael wasn't holding back on his negative views of the British, and was very keen to point out how Sir Francis Drake was unable to make any more money from his country.

Struggling to really understand too much of what was being said, Deb and I simply took some photos of the beautiful scene and quickly returned to the coach, where at least it was comfortably cool.

Our next stop was the old dungeons that sounded a little more interesting.

Wrong!

It may have been dungeons many years ago, but now it is a shopping complex using the old cells. We were steered towards one particular shop and told we had 30 minutes. It was a typical souvenir shop with a lot of imported tat, so Deb and I wandered off to return to the coach. Unfortunately, our cool refuge was driving away to find a better parking space.

After a slight verbal confrontation with Rafael, we gave in and looked around one or two shops, finding nothing to interest us. Outside again and Rafael pointed us towards the coach that was now back, and we went there with several other passengers until time to move on.

While waiting in the coach, an American couple returned and sat in a pair of seats near to us. I didn't recognise them but didn't think any more about it. Then another couple came along and suggested the American couple were in their seats. It appeared the Americans decided to move closer to the front assuming that was the normal thing to do. Well, after a short stand-off, the Americans moved back to their original seats.

Now I know there are no rules to say that the seats you start in are where you should return to, but it is the way that the British do things. Anyway, peace returned and there was no repeat of the incident.

Sadly, when the Americans came back to the coach after the next stop, I heard him say as he passed by, *"We will sit at the back because of that asshole"*. I go back to one of my earlier comments and reiterate: Aurora is a British Ship, and the majority of the passengers stick to our ways of behaving. I think he might have been the *"back-side"* in this incident.

Back to our tour and through the periods of driving we were getting yet more information about the Spanish saviours of Cartagena, as well as the glorious defeat of a British invasion. I think all of us had a pretty good idea where the British stood in the rankings of his favourite nations by now.

Anyway, the third stop was the Inquisition fortress where the Spanish heroes employed the religious leaders to torture anyone they felt to be witches, or people with negative thoughts about the Spanish …. and probably anyone who could speak English. This was the highlight of the tour and very interesting. There were some examples of the torture instruments, as well as the living accommodation of the city's religious heroes, plus a large church.

Eventually the tour group slowly came together outside in the sunshine, and some of us witnessed Rafael being given a serious ticking off by Crystal. She was livid and told him off for not giving clear instructions, and not waiting for everybody to gather, before beginning the next chapter of Cartagena verses Francis Drake.

We had more or less done our own thing for 30 minutes here, and preferred it that way rather than following our less-than-efficient Colombian guide.

Finally, it was time to get on the coach for the cool drive back to the port.

To be honest we weren't impressed by this tour. I think the heat and humidity made us feel negative to start with, but the guide and itinerary were also sadly lacking.

We had lunch and then quickly returned ashore to look around the cruise terminal shops. Here we discovered that there was a small zoo to explore. There were flamingos, parrots, peacocks, small rodents, and even monkeys. What a lovely place. Sadly, neither of us had brought our cameras so we never had a record of it.

Although the main duty-free shop in the terminal was closed, Deb and I did manage to get a couple of souvenirs before going back to collapse in the cabin. I was drained from the heat and humidity following my days of illness, and the effects of the medicine were making me very tired. I dozed for a while before getting enough energy back to go for a cup of tea and a cake.

Refreshed again, the sun was shining on the balcony and it was still very hot, but I managed to sit there for quite a while. The Thomson ship was preparing to leave by late afternoon, but there was some sort of delay. Eventually an ambulance pulled up and took away someone whose holiday had been cut short. Almost instantly the lines were dropped and the ship sped away from the port. That just left us and the Celebrity ship, as Norwegian Pearl had left while we were at the terminal complex.

Aurora eventually sailed away from Cartagena as we finished the individual quiz, where I lost in a tie break. I was just amazed to be so close to winning a sticker. After dinner there was another shock as our table team won a bottle of wine in a quiz where all the answers were numbers. We actually beat 'Densa' by one point this time.

Showtime!

Tonight there was a variety show featuring someone described as a comedian, juggler and magician. His name was Richard Gauntlet, and most of his act was comedy, and he was very good, except that we had heard several of his jokes before. It didn't spoil a very good show and we were already looking forward to his second one.

By the end of the show we all decided it was too late for anything else, and an early night was the agreed consensus. I was actually quite pleased to relax into my pillow at the end of a tiring day, that hadn't inspired us to plan a return to Cartagena.

Aurora was now sailing east across the Caribbean Sea for two days towards the island of St Lucia.

Sea Days to the Caribbean Islands
Sunday 9th April
A little cooler on the balcony today at only 26°C.

Aurora continued to sail eastwards at quite a slow speed towards the island of St Lucia. The weather wasn't quite as hot as it had been, and perhaps the humidity was a little less intense, but it was still a sticky morning.

I felt a lot better and wasn't coughing very much anymore. I was still feeling very tired however and didn't like the idea of going outside in the sunshine. Deb went out by herself for an hour while I caught up with two days of my journal.

We got together for a cup of coffee mid-morning and decided to pop down to the Future Cruises Desk. We wanted to see what the price would be to book the cruises before or after out Amazon trip in 2019. Well, it was quite a shock. The New Year cruise before it was expensive, but by booking the following one going north for 12 nights, the extra incentive discounts meant we only had to pay a seriously low amount. We could even stay in the same cabin. Deb and I went away to think about it, but it was an offer that was hard to refuse.

Back at the cabin, Deb tried to log onto the internet but kept getting a message that it was not possible, and we needed to speak to reception. I said I would go and have a word with them while Deb was at the Battle of the Sexes.

At lunchtime the clocks leapt forward again to GMT-4. Deb went to the Battle of the Sexes and I went down to find out what the problem was with purchasing an internet package. Now things began to turn very sour. It appeared that by changing the card we used to pay the on-board account, the system would no longer allow either of us to purchase internet packages. It was suggested I spoke to the internet manager.

Slightly miffed I went and sat at the back of Deb's quiz until it finished, and we went to lunch. I explained the situation but decided to wait a while before going up to the library and sort out the internet.

Then because our fridge chocolate stocks were all gone, Deb went to buy a bar from the shop. Her card was refused, and she came back feeling embarrassed and furious. We went to reception again, and discovered that changing the payment card meant Deb could no longer use her card to purchase anything.

Now we were both angry and asked if something could be sorted out. In the meantime, we had cabin account statements to see what had been going on since changing our card.

The idea of changing the payment card was to avoid further charges being made to the first card. This hadn't worked, and almost everything had still been charged to the old card. Back to the reception desk and now I was livid that my attempt to avoid an embarrassing situation by changing cards, had turned out to be an embarrassing disaster.

Our next challenge was to sort out the internet in the library, and once again it was all because of changing the payment card, as internet packages are blocked when this type of account change takes place.

After yet another heated discussion at reception three people looked dumfounded with what was happening, but no one had a solution. They promised to look into what was going on, and I assumed they would get back to me.

It was late afternoon by now, and time to begin getting ready for a formal evening. We did at least squeeze in the individual quiz to take our minds off the money issues, but my anger levels were just about at maximum.

Dinner was very nice, and at the early quiz we scored 20/20 on a 'cryptic themed quiz'. Another team also got them all correct, and once again it was 'Densa': we lost to them in the tie break.

We didn't go to the show but after a rest we met up with the others for trivial pursuit and the late-night syndicate quiz. The girls and boys drew one game each in the trivial pursuit, and we were all pretty useless with the quiz.

It was time for bed, and time to forget our payment issues and internet access until the morning.

Surely this can all be resolved?

Monday 10th April

The back-garden temperature sneaked up to 27°C today.

Aurora was jiggling around although the TV navigation page insists the wind was just Force 4 and the sea state 'slight'. On a brighter note, the sun was shining and it was delightfully warm at 7:30 in the morning.

I slept rather well again and suspect the medicines were actually knocking me out, but as I only had two more doses of the antibiotic, and little need for the cough syrup anymore, I don't think I need to worry about being a little dozy …. quite normal really.

To begin our day, we had an hour on the sunny deck. My iPod music was working again and it was a pleasure to be awake enough to absorb the wonderful sunshine.

After a cup of tea to prepare ourselves, we returned to solving the issue of our onboard accounts.

It took nearly three hours of visits to the reception and climbs up to the library. The situation culminated in me seeing the ship's Finance Manager who came up with a slightly convoluted solution, but one that allowed us to have the internet again, and Deb to have a card that works.

In the middle of all this I also paid the deposit on that cruise which followed our Amazon adventure in 2019.

Deb had the midday Battle of the Sexes, and after lunch she went off to Salsa. I remained rather dozy from the medicines so had myself a long sleepy bath while Deb was out.

The rest of the afternoon was relaxation time, and showers before the individual quiz and dinner. The team got together in Masquerade's for the early quiz, and much to our surprise we won a '*lovely jubbly*' bottle of wine.

Showtime in the theatre was Headliners with 'Destination Dance' that we have seen many times, but which we both enjoy. When we saw the boys and girls on the way out, they were dripping in sweat. They really work so very hard.

Richard and Angie came along with us to Masquerade's again and now we were even more shocked, as we won a second bottle of wine for the evening.

That was enough excitement for us for one night, and it was time for an early night.

Tomorrow morning, we would be docking in St Lucia at the port of Castries. We had a tour booked that is really different for us, and we were very much looking forward to it.

Tuesday 11th April – Castries, St Lucia

It remained delightfully warm at 26°C on the shaded balcony, but was much hotter elsewhere during the day.

The alarm clock at 6:30 was a shock, but it was necessary to be ready in time for our tour. We were going on a catamaran trip around the coast of this delightful island. There would be an opportunity for a swim in the Caribbean, plus a view from the sea of the Piton mountains.

As usual we were ready with plenty of time to spare on this beautiful sunny morning with temperatures into the mid-20s by 8:00.

We realised just how hot it was as we queued on the quayside for the short walk to the catamaran. The boat was called Spirit of Carnival and she had plenty of room for our group of passengers. Off we went, and the first fun was watching the crew raising the sail as it flapped and tangled around the ropes. I had never sailed (with a sail) before and it was a delightful experience, even if the sail was mainly just for show, as the boom was tied in the central position.

A guide from the crew told us what would happen and pointed out landmarks as we made our way through the calm Caribbean water. The tour included free drinks with unlimited rum punch, but only after we had stopped for a swim.

St Lucia is a beautiful island with lush vegetation, and wonderful little bays where coconut palms sway gently in the breeze. There are traditional Caribbean villages, along with several exclusive hotel resorts, that are among the most select that can be found around the world.

After about an hour relaxing in the hot sunshine we stopped in one of the bays and it was time for a swim. Five years ago, we missed out on swimming in the Caribbean, so this was a special moment that we thought would never happen. The water was refreshingly cool in the extreme heat. There were fish swimming around our feet and Deb spent as long in the water as she could, to make the most of the opportunity. I had perhaps ten minutes in the water and that was enough as I was still feeling the effects of the antibiotics. I still loved that moment.

Back on the catamaran we turned around and headed towards the Pitons. The rum punch was now being served along with local banana bread, sandwiches and fresh fruit. Without a doubt this was very special. It was hard to beat sitting in the sunshine on a delightful boat, drinking and eating, with Caribbean music playing, amongst a group of fellow passengers who were all enjoying themselves.

The Piton Mountains were a superb sight to round off the outward journey. I had seen them in brochures and on DVDs but this was the first time I had seen for real how they dominated the skyline.

The return journey slowly became more and more lively thanks to the rum, and soon the small open area was full of dancers swaying and jiggling to reggae rhythms, plus a few classic disco sounds. The run punch never ran out, and at least one person was seriously over the limit as he crashed around the dance floor. It was all friendly though, and I don't think I saw anything but smiles throughout the four-hour trip.

We arrived back at Aurora at about 12:30 and we immediately changed our clothes, and Deb even showered off the salt and sand that she had gathered. Then it was time to go out again for a quick spot of shopping. Goodness it was hot as we walked around the shade-less shopping areas of Castries. There was little shelter from the sun, but we persevered and found a couple of souvenirs to take home.

Back on board again it was time to relax in the cabin with our thoughts for the rest of the afternoon. We both caught up with our diaries, but I was exhausted and soon couldn't keep my eyes open anymore. I don't think I have ever fallen asleep while typing on a keyboard before! The hot sunshine, salty air, and rum punch had been very special.

We decided to eat in the Glass House that evening, and Deb took the opportunity to put some washing on. She hoped that this would be the last time doing the laundry would be necessary on the cruise.

Aurora set sail again at 6:00 and hooted a farewell to this beautiful island that had given us all a superb day.

Deb's washing was put into the tumble dryer and we were sitting in the Glass House by 6:45 with our food ordered. We only needed a main course to satisfy our appetite and it was delicious. Then Deb fetched the dry clothes, and we were in time for the early evening quiz in Masquerade's with the rest of our table mates. We were equal with two other teams, but as usual, we lost in the tie break.

The evening was billed as tropical night with a deck party again. The others were off to see the show, but we had a few minutes rest in the cabin. We all planned to meet up later around the Riviera Pool with hopes that the wind would stay away tonight and allow a decent party atmosphere.

Well, it wasn't too windy, and we had several minutes dancing under the stars. But we were all tired, and with another early morning rise for all of us, an early night was too tempting.

Aurora was now slowly making her way eastwards to our final Caribbean stop on the island of Barbados. Our tour meant getting to the coach before 8:30 in the morning, and although this may not sound early to you, the alarm clock would be needed to wake us again tomorrow.

Wednesday 12th April – Bridgetown, Barbados
Balcony temperature registered 27°C today.

It was another lovely night's sleep, and although rather bleary-eyed, I was out of bed just before the alarm clock beeped its good morning to us. The time was 6:45 and Aurora was already just about alongside at Bridgetown, the capital city of Barbados. It was another beautiful morning with bright sunshine from a blue sky and just a gentle breeze.

And yes, it was already warm and would become very hot again during the day.

In the harbour with us today was a little ship called Fairwinds, and later the Carnival Equinox arrived to give Bridgetown a boost to their economy. It was late in the local cruise season now, and the arrival of ships like us was a bonus before the quiet period to come.

After our usual light breakfast of fruit and croissants, we were soon ready to set off on a tour that would be taking us around some of the island. It was named 'The Best of Barbados' and we had stops to come at a sugar plantation house, and orchid farm, and a lookout tower which was used to spot and signal any danger.

The coach was small with a driver called Bernard, and a guide called Mona. We rattled our way through the city where we had the chance to glimpse various places with Mona giving an amusing, and quite thorough description of what we were seeing. Then we turned inland from the southerly port and wound our way through country lanes with crops of sugar cane and sweet potato in the fields around us. Mona was in her element talking about her island and the different parishes that we were passing through. At one point we passed a field where they were actually harvesting the sugar cane, with an impressive machine that sent the cane into a trailer, and vast amounts of dust and rubbish out of the back. Small white birds that looked like miniature cranes watched and then investigated the freshly-cut rows where something tasty must have been.

To my surprise Mona now prompted a discussion about slavery. The subject is obviously raw in the minds of the local people, but the message was that they wanted to move on. I'm not naïve enough to think that this was the view of every

Barbadian, but this was a wonderful sentiment coming from people who suffered so much as they helped to make Britain rich.

After this short stop on the roadside to watch the sugar harvest we soon arrived at our first stop at the Sunbury Plantation House. This complex dated back to 1660 and was another typical colonial house like we had seen virtually everywhere on this cruise. It's another time-capsule of history with lots of furniture and pictures, but I was most impressed with a spectacular long dining table that is still used for exclusive evening meals twice a week. There was also a collection of optical items including glasses, cameras and even eye testing equipment. Upstairs were four bedrooms with various exhibits of clothes and several sewing machines.

Our tour eventually took us to a restaurant area where we rested with a glass of rum punch or fruit juice. Oh dear, Deb and I both chose the rum punch. It was different to the punch we had on the catamaran yesterday, tasting fruitier, and was possibly a little stronger.

Back on the coach again we made a short journey to our second stop at an orchid farm called Orchid World. Mona warned us that it wasn't the best point in the season for the orchids, but there were still plenty of flowers and trees to look at as we walked around the garden and a series of shaded houses. Mona showed her knowledge of the plants in the garden, and also added her personal anecdotes of growing up from the late-1950s in her homeland.

As the walk around the garden ended we were offered another drink of rum punch or fruit punch as we sat in an airy conservatory area. This time I avoided the rum and had a delicious fruit drink to quench my thirst.

It was soon time to go again, to our final stop at the Gun Hill Signal Station. This was one of six such towers built by the British on high points around the island. They allowed a watch of the plantations below for any sign of problems such as fires, or with the gangs of slave workers, and also to look out to sea to watch for any possible invasions.

Mona did her bit again to describe the restored tower where there were magnificent views over the island, and even Aurora was easily visible several miles away. As we made our way to the exit we were blocked by a group of boy scouts on a visit. They wanted to have a photo taken as they stood with us. We duly obliged and with smiles and waves we might just be remembered when the boys look back on their trip out.

We were on the coach again and heading back to Bridgetown and Aurora. There was more to be pointed out to us including a white statue of a lion with one paw on a red ball. This is all about the British rule of the island. Barbados gained independence from Britain in 1966, but they still retain the Queen as a monarch, and still have a love for Britain.

We had yet another national test cricket ground pointed out to us, this time the Kensington Oval. I had seen so many cricket grounds over the last three months.

We were back at the port before 12:30 and spent half an hour looking around the terminal shops. It was expensive there, but we splashed out on a fridge magnet (of course) and a tea towel. This was the last chance of using our stash of US dollars.

It was time for lunch on a quiet ship. After eating Deb converted the remaining US dollars back into sterling. We had completed the visits to countries that accept the dollar, with just the Azores left where the currency will be the Euro. Sadly, it meant we were really on the way home.

The remainder of the afternoon was a chance to relax in the cool cabin. I think we would have both had a doze, but below our balcony a pair of musicians entertained us with steel and percussion drums. I was amazed how loud they could play. It got even worse when a third person came along and added to the sound. To be honest it was actually a very good sound, but it stopped us having any doze time. They continued until just after 5:00 and their money pot was looking very healthy with donations from the returning passengers.

As the last of the stragglers (including two who were rather late) climbed up the gangway, the captain gave his "farewell to the port" speech, and soon the ropes were released and stowed away in their secret part of the ship.

Just beyond the docks from our balcony I could see the cricket ground where the massive floodlights had been switched on and were warming up. There was obviously an evening game, and as we left the port and the sun went down, those lights were like bright beacons bidding farewell to Aurora.

We had a pre-dinner invitation in Anderson's from our new table mates to celebrate their wedding anniversary. They were doing their best to be accepted by us, but it was always going to be a struggle joining our very tightly-bonded group after three months together.

…. but perhaps sharing more bottles of champagne might help!

The six of us did our best to make them feel welcome at the dinner table, but the couple sometimes managed to give off the wrong image. They enjoyed their wine, and always had two bottles at dinner. One would be the remainder of the night before, plus a fresh one each night. The wine was always sniffed, tasted carefully and remarked upon before drinking it with their meal.

One very memorable evening involved them ordering a bottle of Zinfandel Rose from the wine list, but sadly that particular wine had all gone. After much discussion over the wine list they chose another. When it arrived, they went through their ritual and the lady in her finest "Mrs Bucket" voice expressed:

"It's all right… but it's not Zin!"

We somehow managed to keep straight faces, but the six of us giggled regularly about the incident for the rest of the cruise.

After dinner we had our usual quiz, scoring 19 out of 20. It was all about science and we were very good, but we failed on that one question, making us runners up once more.

We'd all had a busy day, in fact two busy days in the Caribbean, and all six of us needed a quiet evening and an early night. Deb and I spent half an hour in the Crow's Nest reflecting on the last two days, and the last three months. The cruise may not have had the major "wow" factor of that first world cruise five years ago, but it had still been amazing, and we had loved every day as we ploughed across the oceans. It was really an honour to be able to see so much of the world in this gentle relaxing way.

Aurora was now heading north-east across the vast Atlantic Ocean. We had five days at sea, and the bridge officer told us we would probably see very few other ships before we arrive at our last stop in the Azores. The temperature over the next few days would be going down, so we had to make the most of any sunshine and warmth that remained.

Crossing the Atlantic Ocean
Thursday 13th April

The temperature crept up to 25°C today in the back garden.

The sea was quite calm but a Force 5 wind buffeted Aurora making us jiggle and bump along. This was the first of five sea days before our arrival in the Azores.

It took a little while to get to sleep last night. Our neighbours came in just as I was dozing off, and checked that every drawer in their cabin was securely shut before settling down. I woke as the daylight streamed through the curtains well before 6:00, but I managed to ignore that until 7:30.

Today was the penultimate medicine restocking day. There was just nine days left before we would wake up in Southampton, and the case of pills, potions, deodorants and toothpaste was almost empty. There was another sign that the cruise was coming to an end as Deb packed away some of her formal wear yesterday, along with various other clothes that wouldn't be needed again. There were lots of days left yet, but without a doubt the finishing tape was in sight.

Still time for lots to do yet!

Before 9:00 we were up on the open deck to absorb some more of the hot sunshine. Deb doesn't want to fade before we get home, and I continued to give my back a bit of colour to get somewhere close to that of my chest and legs.

After an hour we returned in doors and I sat with my laptop catching up again, while Deb went to the final port talk on Ponta Del Gardo. We have no tour there, and will simply stretch our legs and get a final souvenir or two.

When the talk finished, we met up back in the cabin and I asked if Deb wanted to go to the dance class. Today's dance was the tango, which is a dance we have never really tried to do. The next two days were concentrating on a basic set of steps and I was hopeful that my knees would survive.

By 11:45 we had had a real laugh after an introduction to the dance. It seemed to be going well, and although my knees were tired, they kept going. There was another lesson after lunch.

At midday the clocks took another leap forward and we were now on GMT-3. Of course, that meant the lunchtime activities all began with a bang, and Deb went to the Battle of the Sexes. I watched from the back and saw the ladies beaten once more. DJ Martin kept saying there was plenty of time left for them to catch up, but there were less than ten days remaining.

We had lunch together and then relaxed for a while on the balcony, before returning to the tango. It was another successful session and we continued to smile.

The evening entertainment was a comedian called Mike Doyle. We had seen him on a previous cruise, and although he had a good act we had no plans to watch him, especially as there was a late-night champagne waterfall that we wanted to watch.

It was a formal evening and the dinner table looked very smart with all eight of us showing off in our best. There were just two more formal evenings to go now, so no need to send any more shirts to the laundry.

The six of us did the early quiz and failed on the tie-break about the date of the rock group Queen's last tour. After that defeat we had a break in the cabins before meeting up, and losing the later quiz again.

We then scurried to the Atrium to watch the champagne glasses being carefully stacked to form the waterfall. It was a terrific sight as the champagne started to flow down over the sides and it required 72 bottles of fizzy wine (not champagne) to fill every glass. Several people helped to pour the wine, including Deb and Angie, to increase our photograph record of the cruise once more.

At the end we had the chance to drink a glass (well two actually) of the sparkling wine as each glass was very carefully taken down again.

This was a very nice end to the day before we crawled back to our beds. Aurora continued to bump and jiggle around quite a bit, but I think it was mainly due to the wind rather than rough sea.

We had four more sea days as we sailed north east across the Atlantic Ocean towards the Azores. We all knew the temperature was going to start dropping, and we expected the sea to become less calm. This really was the final few days of our adventure, so we had to make the most of the remaining time.

....

Friday 14th April

Oh dear, the temperature only managed to warm the balcony up to 23°C today.

The navigation page on the television described the sea state as 'slight', and the wind as force 4. The ship moved quite noticeably this morning but my brain and stomach remained happy. The temperature had dropped, but after breakfast we returned to the sheltered spot we found yesterday and absorbed some more vitamin D.

After that it was a chance to have a cup of coffee in Raffles, and that left just one cup each on the card. The cost for the card was £22, saving approximately 20% on ten cups of coffee. It was always a treat to sit in the comfy chairs as well.

Tango lesson number three pushed us a little further, with more new steps that confused many people with the staccato style of the dance. Yes, we struggled as well, but we persevered and were enjoying it.

Midday, and yet another clock change sent Deb rushing to Masquerade's for the Battle. I took her shoes back to a rocky cabin but went to watch the quiz to avoid the rolling that was very noticeable in the cabin. My stomach was still OK but I was getting concerned that my head felt quite confused with the motion now.

The ladies lost again, but Deb wasn't concerned and took it all as a bit of fun. It was time for lunch, and we had a full meal in the buffet. The other four from our dinner table group were on their final Round the World lunch, and this evening we planned to have a little party in our cabin. We had various nibbles to snack on, and lots of quiz wine to drink.

The afternoon brought the final tango lesson and I thought we had reached the peak of our abilities for now. The last move was a struggle but we did finally manage to grasp the twisting steps. My knees were still just about going, but my head was spinning from so much turning in the dance. It had become worse because I gave in to a white pill to stabilise my stomach, and that was trying to convince my brain that I needed to lie down for a while.

There was no time for rest as we had to shower and prepare the cabin for our little party. Deb and I still managed to fit in the individual quiz, but time was quite tight. As we were getting ready, Deb turned on the DJ Martin radio show and she won the music quiz. That meant another little golden sticker on her card for the end of cruise prize-giving.

Our party was a very boozy evening. We got through a lot of crisps, nuts, and sweets that had been stored away in our cabins, along with a bottle of Prosecco, spiced rum and sparkling red wine, to accompany the quiz wine. We had a 45-minute break for a quiz allowing our steward (Lloyd) to sort out the cabin, but we told him not to go too mad.

After another quiz failure we returned to wine and nuts and Richard played music to challenge us to guess the song and singers. That passed another couple of hours before we cleared the cabin (a bit) and went to attempt the syndicate quiz.

The quiz started with a wonderful moment. The first question was to name Britain's largest snake. By now Richard was seriously inebriated but looked up and said *"grass snake"*, before dropping his head noisily on the table, and falling asleep. We didn't believe his answer, and decided it was the adder. Richard never knew that his answer was correct, and he slept through a disastrous first five questions. After that we fought valiantly through our alcoholic stupors, and by the end we had managed to pull up very well, but not enough. We still hadn't managed to win this quiz. There were just seven more attempts remaining, and I didn't feel confident about our chances.

Not to worry, as we always had so much fun before bedtime with this session.

The entertainment that we missed tonight was from four young ladies singing classical and pop songs. They were called IDA and were rather good, according to Robin and Rosemary from our dinner table.

Aurora had settled down a bit, and the jiggling and rolling were not quite so noticeable. The Captain in his evening chat to the passengers suggested the weather would stay kind to us tomorrow, although the temperature would continue to drop.

....

Saturday 15th April

Sea day three of five on our journey north to Ponta Delgada, and the maximum temperature dropped a little more to 21°C on the balcony.

The sea definitely felt smoother this morning, and the wind had dropped to force 3. Aurora was less jiggly as we went to breakfast and it was a lot cooler on the open decks: I didn't fancy sun-bathing this morning.

At midday we would be having our Round the World lunch, so we would be full up and tiddly this afternoon, and fit for little except snoozing.

The clocks stayed the same today so we had a little longer to sober up, and get an appetite back for some sort of dinner this evening. Sadly, with the lunch at 12:00 there wasn't really time to go to the dance class, which was rumba this morning. We know the basics of this dance, but it would be interesting to look at what they were doing.

We went out onto Promenade Deck and walked a mile, and it was lovely. This was something we did regularly during the early sea days, but we had joined in with a lot more things since then and it was now a rarity. Perhaps over the last few days we would try and get out there more often.

Suitably glowing from our efforts, we went for a cup of coffee in the buffet. With well over an hour before we had to get ready for the lunch, we succumbed to the sunshine, grabbed our towels, and went up on deck. We thought it was a little cool earlier but now it was deliciously warm again.

I heard a rumour that there might be snow at home in Britain.

The lunch was a pleasant way of passing a couple of hours, but it was more about the chatter with our Officer host, and the other guests, rather than the food which was a little disappointing. First Officer Warren Payne (Bridge Officer) made pleasant conversation and talked about his career, and answered any questions we put to him. He had just finished an eight-hour shift and was probably more interested in going to bed, but he acted as the perfect host.

Our menu had a limited choice and wasn't overly exciting. On this cruise the weak points have been entertainment and the food. We had a choice to watch, or ignore the cabaret acts and make our own entertainment, but the food had let us down. In the past we'd always been able to enjoy the food but during the last year the menus changed, and perhaps on a short cruise it is variable enough to satisfy, but on this long cruise it had become boring, and the food didn't seem prepared as well as in the past.

Anyway, the wine with our lunch (house wine by the way) was enough to smooth over the cracks left by the food, and we went back to the cabin just before 2:00. It was time to relax and let our stomachs prepare for the next meal. I had a bath (yes, fell asleep) and then joined Deb on the balcony in the pleasant afternoon warmth.

The main entertainment that evening was from two pianists, quirkily called The Piano Brothers, who were very good according to our dinner table critics. As per usual, Deb and I passed on this opportunity of 45 minutes of music. Our evening was quiz-based again, and we returned to our cabin after 11:00, rather tired, and wine-less.

My bedtime reading had changed. All the books I had on my e-reader were finished and I'd started looking through all my book projects that were partly complete. There were at least five projects that may, or may not, get finished, and this was a good opportunity to read through them to get a feeling of whether they are worth continuing with, and also to remind me of how far they had gone.

Coincidentally one of them was about our cruises to the south, including a section on our next stop at the Azores.

Aurora continued to sail nearer to Britain and although the sea was calm, and the wind gentle at that moment, the Captain warned that we could expect less pleasant conditions in the coming days. I wasn't sure if that meant gales and rough seas, or if it was just an end to the delightful sunny and warm weather we had been enjoying.

There were two more days and nights at sea before we reach Ponta Delgada in the Azores. We had been at sea for almost 100 days now, but the adventure had seemed to have flown by.

....

Sunday 16th April
Brrr, it only climbed to 20°C on the balcony today.

This is our final Sunday at sea (on this cruise anyway) and everyone was doing their best to make the most of the last week, but there was an obvious atmosphere of things coming to an end. Aurora was just west of Lanzarote this morning, and the television navigation map showed Spain and France, just to rub in the fact that we were almost home.

Deb and I had a good night's sleep again and woke with another sunny, but rather cooler, day. It was only 20° on the balcony at 8:00 and as we walked across the Lido deck to breakfast, the thought of sun-bathing really seemed out of the question.

When we went to Reception after breakfast to grab the daily crossword puzzles we asked for some luggage labels. Because we moved cabins, our current labels were incorrect, and we needed some more anyway. We had already been notified that our disembarkation time was scheduled for 08:45 on Saturday morning, so we should be away quite early on our drive back home.

Sadly, this was confirmation that we were getting ready for the end.

It was time for some office work, before we decided how to pass the rest of the morning.

The clocks would be going forward by another hour at midday to GMT-1, meaning that we were just two hours behind home. We'd gain another hour tomorrow before getting to Ponta Delgada, and then just one more to correct ourselves to British time, during the final leg of the cruise.

While sitting in Anderson's with my laptop I could see a steady stream of windswept passengers walking past the windows as they pounded around the

Promenade Deck. The idea appealed and we gave up the office work. A mile later we were having a cup of coffee in the buffet, and feeling rather windswept. It was good to stretch the legs, and although the breeze was quite noticeable, the sea seemed quite calm.

The entertainment today saw the Piano Brothers back in the theatre this afternoon, followed tonight by Mike Doyle. There was also a classical concert this evening from the two ladies called Zeitgeist Duo in the Playhouse. And in Carmen's there would be the penultimate formal dress evening with a ball featuring music by Kool Blue.

Talks this morning included Ivy Partridge discussing the mystery of reading a music score, plus various enticements talks about spa treatments and overpriced jewellery. During the afternoon Daniel Davies continued his series of talks about cruising, this time it was all about the 'Golden Age of Cruising' from 1900 to 1945. I am sorry to disagree with him but I think that was an age when cruising was very exclusive to a small group of well-off people, or those emigrating.

Of course, throughout the day the usual bridge, art, dancing, and choir sessions, plus various quiz opportunities continued.

Oh, and for anyone really interested, there would also be further talks from the spa and shop about treatments and jewellery that we really, really, can't do without.

Many people on cruises are very negative about sea days, but there really is a wide range of things available as you plough through the oceans.

Or if you are like us, even after 100 days we were still enjoying the atmosphere and spending time with our new friends.

As expected, we ignored Mike Doyle's second act, and had a quiet evening with Richard and Angie. We actually won a bottle of wine in the late evening quiz and then shared it while we failed miserably in the syndicate challenge.

Deb and I returned to the cabin and after the usual read, we turned the lights off and snuggled into our pillows.

Just after midnight, we were both shocked awake by our neighbours playing loud music. It lasted about 30 seconds before Deb resorted to the boarding house primeval method of making our feelings known, and banged on the wall. It worked and the music went down to a more acceptable, if still annoying level, for that time of the night. I was now wide awake, angry, and concerned that we could be seen as the aggressor with our wall banging.

It was over an hour later when I finally settled again.

....

Monday 17th April
Another temperature milestone as it dropped to a maximum of 19°C today.

When Deb woke and got up to make the tea, it was after 8:00.

After breakfast I apologised at Reception for banging on a wall, but made my feelings known about the noise from our neighbours since they joined the ship in San Francisco.

It was cloudy and even cooler this morning, and as we took an early walk on the Promenade Deck we could see showers on the horizon. Aurora was now level with northern Spain and roughly on the same latitude as New York and San Francisco.

With a mile walked we had little to do. There was a talk in the theatre from a submarine officer describing an attempted rescue of a Russian submarine called the Kirsk. It got into trouble in 2000, and all of its crew were killed. It sounded quite interesting, but rather morbid, and we tend to avoid stories of maritime mishaps when on a cruise.

There was the final Around the World morning coffee sessions, and we also planned to go to the dance class. Today the instructors would be attempting to teach everyone a very popular sequence dance called the saunter together. We have had a go at this dance on several occasions in the past and failed to come to terms with it, but hopefully today would be more successful.

At 10:00 in the morning I was sitting with my laptop in Charlie's just outside of Anderson's. The single travellers' morning coffee was going on behind me in the Lounge, and in front was the usual mayhem with temporary shop counters selling the day's amazing deals. One of the racks was selling Aurora tee-shirts at £10 for two. These came from previous world cruises, and other old designs that no-one wanted. The corridor was quiet with just a handful of prospective customers squeezing the merchandise and hunting for price labels. I really believed that the shops had reached a point when there was nobody left who had not taken a look at the handbags, jewellery, soft toys, and old clothes.

Never mind, on Saturday evening they could start all over again with 2,000 new customers.

It was time to go and find Deb and get ready for our coffee morning and dancing.

Well, the coffee morning was well attended but as on the previous occasions, the cakes and biscuits weren't the most inspiring. At least we had a chat with someone different before we dashed up the stairs to our dance class.

The Saunter Together went very well, and by the end of the 50 minutes we were happily doing the first two thirds of it. The remainder would be covered in the afternoon.

Surprise, surprise, the clocks went forward again at midday which set us up for Ponta Delgada tomorrow. It was 100 days since we left a chilly Southampton and somehow three months had flown by with our global adventures. After our final stop at the Azores we will have just three days and nights to complete the voyage around the world, and begin normal life again.

As the clocks changed Deb went to her Battle of the Sexes quiz. I watched from the back, and still didn't help the men's side. They were quite a cocky band of people who took it far too seriously and often aimed some *'not very nice'* banter at the women. They did however have a fair degree of knowledge between them, and yes, they won again.

After a healthy lunch (not) of hot dog and chips, we had a rest in the cabin with a glass of coke and some chocolate.

Mid-afternoon we returned to Carmen's to finish the saunter together dance, and an hour later we had successfully mastered it. This may sound ridiculous but we started learning this dance some 35 years ago, and had finally managed to do it.

Having said a few not-so-nice things some weeks ago about the dance teachers (Roger and Anne), I have to say that I was warming to them. We now chatted with them, and were actually enjoying their teaching, and we had managed to learn a lot in the last ten days or so.

Late in the afternoon the sun came out and the sea became almost flat. It was quite a different picture to the dull and cool weather during the majority of the day.

Later during dinner, a shout went up as whales were spotted some way behind us. Being at a stern window in the dining room we had a good view of the water spouts, but no actual whale was seen.

Still no luck!!

This evening the theatre hosted a performance from the girl singers IDA, and in Carmen's the cabaret was from a Frank Sinatra tribute artist.

No thanks!

Ponta Delgada meant the final cabaret act would be joining the ship, plus we believed another girl singer would also be performing. She actually arrived at the same time as Leon St Croix became the Cruise Director, and they spend a lot of time together.

After a four-way tie break in the early quiz, (we lost again of course) we all met up later to continue our unsuccessful quest for wine in the late-night syndicate challenge. There were just four more chances remaining.

Wineless, but happy, the six of us made our way to the cabins for a good night's sleep. We had our final port day tomorrow and needed to be ready for it.

Tuesday 18th April – Ponta Delgada, Portugal

As I peered out onto the balcony, our little thermometer announced it was cool again, and it only struggled up to 17°C during the day.

We had arrived at the city of Ponta Delgada on the Portuguese island of San Miguel. This was the final port of our wonderful adventure.

Looking around at the scene, I spotted a smaller ship parked to the stern of Aurora called the Serranisima. Elsewhere this busy port was home to hundreds of yachts, from small family boats through to huge ocean-going palaces of millionaires.

We had been here on a cruise in 2006, but my goodness it had changed. Today we were parked in what appeared to be a very new harbour complex with a superb cruise terminal. This was connected by underground walkways to a vast shopping area that curved around to the main road, with numerous places to sit with a coffee or a beer. To our right we could see a large outdoor swimming complex with diving and other pools besides the main swimming area.

It was obvious that Ponta Delgada wanted to attract and make the most of cruise ship passengers.

What I did recognise was the buildings of the city that are virtually all black and white. This makes them stand out from the lush green hills in the distance. The only exceptions to this black and white theme were the powder blue balconies of what I assumed was a newly-built apartment block near the harbour, and far away between the hills there was another apartment block with yellow panels. Everywhere there were red rooves, with some a brighter red showing their newness, compared with the darker faded ones of older buildings.

After breakfast we did a bit of office work to allow time for the tours to get away, and for the bulk of the local shops to open before we ventured out. I was initially wearing shorts, but on reflection from the cool walk to breakfast, I changed into trousers, and dug out a jumper for when we went out.

By 9:30 the sun was beginning to make an appearance so we decided to get ourselves ready for a walk. It would be good to be on *Terra Firma* for a while, as we had been warned that bad weather was expected on the way to Southampton. We were in for a rocky ride to end our voyage.

We spent over two hours walking around the streets of Ponta Delgada, and it was delightful. The memories came back of the black pavements made of what looks like volcanic rock. They have patterns created by little white marble squares set against the dominant black. We had no plans to do or buy anything, but after noticing that the prices in some of the shops were ridiculously cheap, Deb became tempted and bought some clothes. We even bought a glass jar for 2 Euros which would have been nearer £10 back home. Clearly Portugal, and her islands, was going through harder times that I had expected.

There was little hesitation when I suggested a coffee break and we stopped for a rest in a little café. Here we had a cup of coffee plus a nata cake each, and the bill came to 2 Euros and 40 cents, which is less than £2. Of course, the cakes were delicious and another couple from the ship asked what they were, and ended up buying some. We could hear them sigh with delight at the taste.

Another pair of converts to these wonderful Portuguese custard tarts.

With our bags full of clothes and souvenirs we made our way back to the ship for a slightly later than usual spot of lunch. Deb was planning to spend an hour in the warm sunshine, but early afternoon saw the arrival of clouds, and the warmth disappeared.

With sunbathing forgotten, Deb put a final load of washing in a machine while the laundrette was unusually quiet. There was no urgency for this, but it gave us plenty to wear if needed during the final few days.

Many cruisers seem to insist on washing everything before they go home, but Deb is more of the opinion to leave the washing until we get home to use our far better washing machine.

The sun came out again late in the afternoon. We were not inclined to go out on deck, and just stayed on the balcony watching things going on below us. The harbour area was a vibrant scene with lots of people eating and drinking in the cafes. Although nobody was in the pool, several people were enjoying the water in a roped off area of the harbour just in front of us. There were some serious swimmers and some not so proficient. Some took longer getting into the water, than the time they were actually swimming, and a small group of boys were more interested in posing on the side of the water. They demonstrated various gymnastic feats and only once jumped into the water for a photograph.

Soon the trickle of passengers returning to Aurora increased, and as the last tour buses arrived the numbers climbing the gangway dwindled and stopped. Captain Dunlop came on the PA system almost immediately to announce we were about to sail for Southampton. His weather forecast was as suspected, and from tomorrow afternoon the wind was going to increase to gale force and the swell would be 4-5 metres. The sea state was expected to be 'medium to rough'.

To be honest we had had a reasonably calm passage for most of the three months, so our luck had to run out eventually.

The ropes were soon dropped and Aurora's departure was under the control of the Safety Officer, closely supervised by his seniors. He gave three long hoots of the horn as we moved away from the harbour, and then we quickly built up speed to head out into the Atlantic Ocean.

The entertainment tonight had a lady singer in Carmen's called Clare Bonsu, who was billed as The Girl from Tiger Bay, or putting it another way, singing in the style of Shirley Bassey. At the other end of the ship the Headliners were presenting their show called 'We'll meet again'. Of all the shows they perform, this is probably our least favourite.

At 10:30 the dance teachers were hosting an hour of sequence dancing in Carmen's to give us a chance of trying out yesterday's saunter together, and remind ourselves with some of our other favourite dances. We had already warned our quiz friends that we wouldn't be around for the syndicate challenge tonight.

For dinner we had a lovely meal in the Glass House with just three other couples arriving while we were there. What a waste of a beautiful room compared to how busy and vibrant in its previous life as Café Bordeaux.

Unfortunately, there was a slight annoyance.

The music being played when we arrived was rock and roll from the 1950s, and it was rather pleasant. Then a couple arrived and seemed to be annoyingly questioning how the waiter had set up the table. More seriously she complained about the music and asked for it to be changed. The waiter did so half way through the rock classic "Tutti Frutti" and replaced it with the Carpenters singing middle-of-the-road mood music.

I called the harassed waiter over and asked for the music to be changed back.

The waiter was worried and sent for the head waiter. He said that a customer had asked for quieter music, and I said I'd liked what we had been listening to for about 20 minutes, and didn't see why one customer should decide what the rest of us listened to.

The head waiter didn't have an answer, and the Carpenters continued.

We immediately asked for the bill, thanked the head waiter for a lovely meal, but made it quite clear that because of what had happened, we didn't want anything else.

Aside from that, we had some excitement when there was an order from the bridge for the fire crew to respond to an alarm in the Sindhu Restaurant. It turned out to be smoke from an overheating air-conditioning drive belt, but the result was a full response with breathing apparatus and hosepipes all over the corridor. The Captain soon told us that everything was OK, and apologised for any inconvenience caused.

It is so good to know the system works when an alarm goes off, and how well the officers kept us informed.

With our meal prematurely over we went to the early quiz and lost.

Well, we did go to the second evening quiz in Champion's, and along with Robin and Rosemary we actually came equal first on a challenge about recognising Eurovision songs. As Coral couldn't do the planned tie-breaker because she had let the band go, we gave the prize to the other team so we could leave for the dancing.

In Carmen's we had a go at six or seven sequence dances and were there for an hour. It was really good to spend time on the dance floor doing different dances rather than being taught the same one over and over again. I was dripping in sweat by the end of that very energetic hour.

It was bedtime, and I read my book for a while until my head had stopped leaking. Aurora was jiggling again, and the wind was sounding quite strong as it buffeted the balcony door.

Goodnight.

Wednesday 19th April – Re-immigration Day

The temperature was returning to what we would expect in Britain. It only managed to creep up to 15°C today on the balcony.

It had not been the best of nights as the wind increased and the jiggling turned to bumping. When we got up at 7:30 the TV navigation channel was reporting wind Force 6 and sea state 'moderate'. And this was just the beginning of the expected storm.

Aurora was ploughing through the sea and we were a little over half-way up the coast of Portugal. By the evening we would be entering the Bay of Biscay where the storm would be building to its crescendo.

I quickly took a white pill in readiness for nature's "welcome home" present.

With the temperature just 15° any final sunbathing looked to be over, and our thoughts turned to doing some further packing. It was also our final trip to the 'chemist suitcase', so our spare pills could be packed away, along with the remaining breakable souvenirs. They were wrapped and tucked away with some of the dirty washing.

There was one little task for everyone on the ship this morning. We had to line up in Masquerade's to have our passports checked by the UK Borders Authority. We were told to wait for an announcement for when it was our turn, but as I was updating the blog in Charlies, I saw people coming out of Masquerade's, and realised the process had started early.

Deb and I were in and out in less than a minute and I resumed work on my laptop for a little while longer. Deb returned to the cabin and continued with the packing, and put away another suitcase of unwanted clothes and 'bits' that we had collected.

After a while I gave up the office work and went for a walk around the Promenade Deck where it was almost deserted as the sea crashed and boiled around the ship.

Our only plan for the morning was a quickstep dancing lesson at 11:00, but the way the ship was being tossed didn't bode well for this session. In actual fact it wasn't too bad, and the dancing lesson gave us a really good reminder about the quickstep, and also highlighted a couple of bad habits we'd developed. Of course, our attempts at *slow, slow quick-quick slow* weren't helped by the ship adding its own *slow, slow,* to the left, and then *slow, slow quick, quick, quick* to the right.

The clocks leapt forward for the final time at midday bringing us back in line with home at GMT+1. Deb didn't have the Battle of the Sexes today, so the time change wasn't a serious issue with getting to events …. not for us anyway.

The amount of movement was increasing as the hours passed, and I was less than inclined to stay in the cabin for long periods.

In the afternoon we had the second quickstep lesson of the day, and despite the unpredictable movements of the ship, it was really good. Tomorrow the instructors planned to add in the *running steps* that make this dance so good to watch.

Dinner was a good get together again, and I sat with my back to the window to avoid having to watch the sea. It was getting rough, and the forecast was for worse to come. By now I had taken a further pill to reduce my discomfort, and I certainly had some concerns for the next few hours.

We all trooped along to the theatre tonight to watch a ventriloquist/comedian called Gareth Oliver. He started a little slowly with some weak jokes but when he went into his ventriloquist act, along with his wife, the show became absolutely brilliant. The couple did a double act that was technically superb, and then his final section with Brian from the audience had the theatre in stitches. Gareth Oliver was a finalist in "Britain's Got Talent" on the show with Susan Boyle, and proved that sometimes (but not always) talent can be discovered.

From the theatre the six of us split up, and Deb and I went to Anderson's for a drink. This was to be a mistake as I should have remembered that the pills I was taking for the sea-sickness responded badly to alcohol. Anyway, when we went to bed the ship was performing a sensational rendition of a jive, and along with the violent movement, every bit of Aurora's structure seemed to be creaking. The pitching motion was causing wild roller-coaster movements with deafening crashes as we head-longed into a Force 8 gale.

I couldn't sleep.

The alcohol had mixed with my pill and I had twitching and cramp in my legs. I saw that the clock was saying 2:00 am and it was probably an hour later, before I eventually fell asleep.

Thursday 20th April - 'The Storm'

The temperature dropped again and it was just a little over 12°C at the best.

Today wasn't a very comfortable or pleasant day.

I woke but my eyes didn't want to open, and my stomach was quietly telling me something was wrong. Strangely I still managed to go to breakfast and treated myself to a sausage sandwich.

From then on, my day was little more than existence, in what I think was the worst period of bad weather I have ever experienced on a ship.

As soon as I cleaned my teeth, I began a morning of moving from one comfortable and quiet seat to another while my pill took effect, and I attempted to coordinate my brain and the various senses that sea-sickness confuses. Deb stayed in the cabin and even managed to pack another case, but by mid-morning she was feeling her own symptoms of 'mal de mer'.

During the morning and into the afternoon the wind increased to Force 10 at one point, and the sea was described as 'rough' and curiously at one stage as 'high'.

The dancing lesson never did any more quickstep, and I couldn't have faced it anyway.

During the morning I went to the theatre, and watched a talk by Gervase Phinn with his stories from a career as a school inspector. It was superb, and I was looking forward to reading his book that I had downloaded yesterday, after seeing his name in the daily newspaper. Unfortunately reading would have to wait until my eyes were ready to stare at small print again.

Deb managed to ignore her discomfort and fulfilled her role as captain of the ladies in the Battle of the Sexes. After that we both had a little lunch, but in my case, this was just an automatic process, and not because I was hungry.

In the afternoon I tried watching a film, but having fallen asleep twice in the cinema, I joined several other people who trickled out of the room realising the film was pathetic, except as a way of snoozing.

Deb and I had another cup of tea and then I went to watch the choir give their final show. They were brilliant, and even the rocking and rolling couldn't stop them. The performance had to be moved from the theatre to Carmen's because of the ship's severe movement, so the audience were packed into the much smaller venue. I stood at the back singing under my breath the songs that I had taken part in. Although I hadn't joined in this sector, the choir had reminded me of the joy of singing, and hopefully I would find a choir when I got home.

Deb and I had decided that we wouldn't dress up in formal wear this evening, and not go to the dining room to eat. It was horrendously rough and even simply washing my hair almost tipped my stomach over the edge. During her lunchtime quiz Deb had given a request for DJ Martin Scott to say a big *"thank you"* to our new-found friends on his teatime radio show.

I had been quite negative about Martin, but that was all about the cricket. I saw the man in a different light since I stopped playing the game, and had much more positive views about him. He worked hard, like all the entertainment team, and posed some wonderfully challenging quizzes, that were so much better than the "questions supplied by Carnival HQ", that featured so many American-themed questions that they were a farce on this British ship.

Martin was also a great help to four passengers who had fallen foul of pickpockets in America and lost their passports. The ship's management did virtually nothing except kicking them off the ship, but Martin gave them advice and sympathy in what was a horrendous situation to be in. I must also say that the British Embassy did a tremendous job as well.

I know the ship had no option but to put them ashore, but there ought to be a softer way of reacting to this situation.

Well done Martin, for all the work you did, but I hoped he would have a slightly different approach to the cricket in the future.

The couples involved left the ship in San Francisco. After the embassy officials had sorted out new passports, they returned to Aurora in San Diego. They were temporarily looked upon as criminals, rather than victims. Their experience left them several hundreds of dollars poorer, and quite annoyed with the way they had been treated.

After our dinner in the Horizon Buffet, Deb and I joined up again with Richard, Angie, Robin and Rosemary. We just lost the early evening quiz, before going to the theatre to listen to a rock and roll band called The Bluejays. They were superb and deserved the applause and shouts for "*MORE*" at the end.

The entertainment at the end of the cruise had been so much better than at the beginning.

After the show we all went to Carmen's and succeeded in winning a bottle of wine. Then we moved to Vanderbilt's for the syndicate quiz. The other five drank the wine as I wasn't interested in upsetting my sea-sickness pill again. We lost in the quiz by two points which seemed to be our standard result.

Perhaps the sea had calmed a little, but when we went to bed it was obvious that the storm was still very bad, and the crashing, banging, rocking, and rolling wasn't going to help us get to sleep for another night.

We were in the Bay of Biscay by now and tomorrow would be our final day of this wonderful adventure. It was a pity that the weather had meant a slightly sour end to it, but we had so many amazing memories.

And the Captain had promised that the weather was going to improve during the night.

Friday 21st April – The Final Day

Oh dear, just 12°C on the balcony today, and it wasn't very nice in the back garden any more.

After finally falling asleep last night when my legs stopped twitching, I was rudely woken at 7:30 by a new day.

The storm had abated from the crashing and banging of yesterday into mere bad weather. It was still blowing at Force 7 and the sea was simply 'moderate', but after the last 48 hours this was a doddle.

There were blue skies as we set about completing the Biscay crossing. Aurora had speeded up from the crawl through the mountainous seas of yesterday when we were rarely much above 15 knots.

With breakfast over, Deb attacked the suitcases again, while I cowered from the bumpy weather doing my blog in Anderson's. When I returned to the cabin just before 10:00 it had turned into a second-hand suitcase stall. Deb had virtually completed squeezing everything into six of our suitcases and one holdall. There was another holdall to take the final remaining bits, and two smaller roller cases for the fragile items, wash kit, and things needed to hand in the morning.

I struggled to be of any serious assistance as the sea was still throwing my balance around, and packing always makes the problem worse.

We wouldn't be going to the dance session, as Roger and Ann were just recapping bits that the dancers wanted to perfect. We met them while walking along the corridor and thanked them for their time. We had really enjoyed the 'going back to basics' and ironing out some bad habits.

There was time for a cup of coffee and then we picked up the last of our photographs, and the DVD of this final sector. The photo package we bought at the beginning of the cruise had been amazing, and we had many lovely pictures to take home of us in a variety of formal clothing, with varying hair lengths and suntans.

Suitcases were already appearing in the corridors, many with tropical night flower garlands around the handles. Ours would stay in the cabin until after lunch, as had been requested: I sometimes think people never read the letters that give information and instructions about these things.

Deb completed her Battle of the Sexes captaincy and had some more stickers for this evening's prize collection, and a promise of yet another bottle of wine from Martin. She didn't really want the wine because we already had one in the cabin for this evening, plus another from Richard and Angie to say cheerio to each other.

There was a farewell cocktail party before dinner, where there would be yet more free drinkies. This party was postponed from yesterday because of the bad weather, and would be held in the Atrium rather than split between the Crow's Nest and Carmen's. Apparently, Captain Dunlop favours one big event for each sitting.

At 1:30 after our last lunch on board, the first three suitcases were sealed and put outside in the corridor. Three more cases and a holdall were also ready to go out when there was space outside our door.

The sea continued to calm down as we neared Ushant Island where the Bay of Biscay officially ends. That would be late in the afternoon and would just leave the Channel and Solent, before our expected arrival in Southampton at around 6:00am tomorrow morning.

There was an announcement during lunch to let people know the upper outside decks were re-opened, to allow the quoits and shuffleboard competitions to go ahead. They had been closed for two days because of the bad weather, and a lot of people wanted to have a final game.

Before 4:00pm the last item of our luggage was put outside the cabin door. We had spent a couple of hours up in the Crow's Nest reading our books. As had been a very common theme, my eyes became heavy and I was no longer reading words, but just looking at them. I put the e-reader down and settled into the comfy settee. I think I was instantly asleep, and when I woke, my confusion and the sounds of chatter around me, came as a flashback of when I regained consciousness after my hip replacement operation. This painful memory lasted for just a couple of seconds before I remembered where I was, but I must have slipped into a very deep sleep for a while.

All around us there seemed to be people with pots of tea, so I suggested that we go for one in the buffet. It meant a walk outside along Deck 13, and although there was a blue sky and sunshine, it was most definitely a late winter afternoon again. The memories of hotter days in the Indian Ocean when we had temperatures into the high 30°s, paid a fleeting visit from the depths of my mind into my consciousness. There would be many such moments in the coming weeks as we settled down in Herefordshire once more.

Back in the cabin our shoes were taken off, and we lay on the bed. The TV navigation channel showed we had crossed Biscay, and would soon be turning right around the Brest Peninsular and then into the English Channel.

This evening the entertainment in the Curzon Theatre was a triple bill of singer Claire Bonsu, ventriloquist Gareth Oliver, and the rock and roll group The Bluejays.

The six of us went along together to enjoy the final show, and afterwards we laughed our way through the last couple of quizzes, and drank all the remaining bottles of wine we had collected.

We didn't stay up too late. We had lost a lot of sleep over the last two nights, and we all had to drive home tomorrow. There were some sad goodbyes with promises to keep in touch, and a plan was already in place to meet up later in the year.

After one last loud goodnight in the corridor we went into our cabins. Our disembarkation time in the morning was 8:45, and there was a slight delay before getting into bed, while I programmed the phone number of the car parking company into my mobile.

The wind had reduced to an acceptable level for our last night on board. Tonight I was sure I would sleep, but I also suspected I would wake up to familiar noises, as we docked at the Mayflower Cruise Terminal early tomorrow morning.

The last 104 days and nights had been terrific, and I was very sad for it to be coming to an end, but deep down I was ready to go home, and looking forward to the comfort of our own bed, and Deb's tasty meals.

Goodnight for the final time from Aurora.

Saturday 22nd April – Time to go home
The temperature on the balcony today was of no interest to us.

As usual disembarkation day began a little strangely. The experience was like a dream where you are in a rush to do something, but you don't really want to do it.

I was awake long before we had to get up, and I listened to the familiar sounds of Aurora coming into a port. After the side thrusters had stopped roaring I began to hear noises of a dockside with fork lift trucks going back and forth, and the 'beeps' from the air-bridge being connected to the ship.

Eventually I couldn't put it off any longer, and left my comfortable bed and put the kettle on. There was no need to peek out through the curtains, I knew we were in Southampton, and it was time to go back home.

While the tea was brewing we had our washes and packed away the overnight bits. Deb grabbed the final account statement from outside the door, and we quickly confirmed the bill was accurate as we drank our tea. Breakfast was the usual stressful half an hour to grab something to eat and find somewhere to sit in the buffet. We still had time to chat to total strangers sharing our table, and wished them a safe journey home before we galloped back to the cabin.

We cleaned our teeth, emptied the safe of our valuables, and gathered up the necessary paperwork to get off the ship and find our car. Before 8:00 we had opened and checked every drawer and wardrobe shelf at least twice, zipped up our cases and were leaving the cabin.

Soon we were sitting in Carmen's where the early leavers were gathering. Angie and Richard appeared struggling with serious amounts of luggage, and then Rosemary and Robin also arrived. We had a final moment of cheerio with each other, with lots of hugs and kisses, and then the announcement invited us to disembark.

Now the crazy time began. At least the queue to get off wasn't bad, but the luggage area was the usual chaos of trying to find our red cases amongst the hundreds of other red cases. With two trolleys loaded precariously with our luggage, we squeezed through the crowded walkways and joined the line to leave the hall, and to exit out into the pandemonium of traffic coming and going.

We had already told our car parking company our estimated departure time and we knew where we were going, but getting there was frustrating. We had to cross the road to the short stay car park, but every time we found a way across the road, the terminal guides pushed us back and forced us to walk the longest possible route. Eventually we got to the car park with our unsteady loads and were greeted by the man with our car.

It was clean and unscathed, so after a final signature we loaded the suitcases and strapped ourselves in for the journey home. We gave a sigh of relief that was tinged with sadness. It took a few minutes to remember how to drive, but by the time we reached the dock gates my inbuilt autopilot clicked into action, and along with satnav reminding me of quite familiar directions, we were on the way.

Traffic wasn't overly bad, and soon we were away from the various interchanges around Southampton and settling into the journey. We didn't say much, and both just wanted to eat up the miles. After about an hour I suddenly realised the trees were in leaf. This may sound stupid, but the branches were bare when we left in January, and it suddenly struck me that we had missed the worst of winter and it would soon be spring.

We were home before 1:00pm, and our only stop had been a short detour into Ross-on-Wye, to get some essential foodstuff to last the first afternoon and evening at home.

It took half an hour to wake up the house again. The water had to be turned on, and that took a moment to remember how to do it. The electricity had tripped so needed to be reset, and that took a couple of attempts before it stayed on. The fridge and freezer were then switched back on. Meanwhile the suitcases were brought in and Deb took the one with the majority of the washing out to the garage and gave the washing machine its first of many loads.

We took a short break to draw breath and drink our first cup of tea.

The next hour or so was a well-drilled exercise of heaving the cases upstairs, opening windows to get some fresh air around the house, getting the heating going again, and sorting out the mountain of mail. By the time we had sifted through the two huge piles of mail, there were roughly just 30 items to file away, and only about five things that needed action. It seemed rather sad that having been away from home for a quarter of the year, there was so little within the hundreds of items of post that was actually of any interest or importance.

We had lunch around 2:30, by which time the suitcases were empty, and ready to disappear up into the loft. There were piles of books, and souvenirs on any available surfaces that needed to be found a home over the coming days.

Deb and I also took a break to explore the garden. Our lovely neighbours, Pam and Kim, had cut the grass in an attempt to takeaway that shock when we got home. As the grass had grown to more than 30 cm high, they didn't know exactly where the edges were, so it was still in need of a further cut, but that wasn't a priority today.

Apart from the grass needing cutting, the garden was full of weeds. They were so big, that it was difficult to instantly know if they were actually plants that should have been growing, or if they were interlopers. The apple trees were in blossom, the pears had small fruit on them, and the soft fruit bushes were loaded with sweet delights for the weeks to come. Sadly, the vegetable patch was bare, apart from weeds, and would have to be dug over and planted out very quickly to give us a harvest.

Almost as soon as we arrived home, I began to suffer from the strange phenomenon of 'land sickness'. This affects a lot of cruise passengers and leaves our bodies struggling to balance, and we wobble as if still at sea. By mid-afternoon I was really in trouble, and although the world around me was still, I was moving as if I was still on the ship during that three-day storm. I was dizzy and rocking, and Deb even suggested I took a sea-sickness pill to see if that would help. I knew that it would soon clear up, but this time it had been really bad, and I was still not totally back to normal two days later.

In the evening Deb cooked a delicious meal of steak and kidney pie, mashed potato and carrots. The taste was so much more intense than the majority of meals we had on Aurora. The ship meals may be adequate with unusual names and ingredients, but they can't always produce the same degree of taste when catering for hundreds of passengers.

After eating, we both had long deep baths, and generally relaxed on our familiar settees while discovering just how many television programmes we had recorded. There was enough to last for several weeks when nothing live took our fancy.

We were home, but our minds were still full of the adventures, the highs and lows, and the fun and laughter of our 100-day adventure.

Final Thoughts

It's a week now since our suitcases were put outside the cabin, and our adventure came to an end.

Deb and I slowly came down from the euphoria we had experienced for three months, and life reverted to a normal day to day existence. The holiday washing was completed, the suitcases put away in the loft, the cupboards had been restocked with food, and the freezer was filling up.

Our minds had come out of holiday mode, and plans were now about going to see our family, and what needed to be done around the house and garden.

In other words, we were back to the normality of life.

But when relaxed at the end of the day, it was too easy to be reminded of the experiences on our adventure. Those memories were still far too vivid to shove to the back of our brains for a while yet.

So, how can I summarise those 104 days, those 30 or so different countries, the 50 or more cities that we visited, the hundreds of amazing memories, and those thousands of smiles and laughs?

Of course, there were some bad moments, and this book has probably captured many of them, but have they soured the experience?

Most definitely not.

Had it been a good cruise?

Yes of course it was.

Was it better than the first world circumnavigation five years ago?

No, the buzz and excitement of the experience wasn't so intense.

Would I do it again?

Yes, in a flash, but I don't think it will happen.

I believe the experience would almost certainly be even less exciting. I fear it would become what I noticed on several faces of those passengers who annually repeat the winter world cruise as a habit. They don't see it as an adventure; it's just what they do to avoid the British winter. Hopefully in the future we will still take some longer duration cruises, but concentrate on visiting new countries and destinations.

So, what was different from our world cruise in 2012?

The level and quality of service has decreased as P&O (like other companies) are trying to maintain a healthy profit without significantly increasing prices. The market for cruising has exploded in the last decade, and the thousands of new cabins on the giant ships have to be filled. This has meant new people experiencing this amazing holiday product, and they don't notice that service and facilities have changed. Those passengers who have enjoyed life at sea for many decades are the ones that notice the little changes year on year, but we are in a minority, and though our voices are heard, our opinions don't seem important in the grand scheme of 21st century cruising.

Even in the five years since our first world cruise, there have been noticeable changes. Stewards who used to look after a dozen cabins have had their daily workload almost doubled, and no longer have the time to talk with us, and give us that *extra special* level of service.

The dining experience may look very similar, but the menus have been simplified. There are what they call 'always available' starters, main courses and puddings, but the daily specialities are rarely spectacular, or as tasty as many of us expected. On a short cruise I can understand that passengers would be excited with the food, but on a three-month cruise we repeated the options over and over again.

And yes, the waiters have to look after more tables. Sadly, that has meant the food comes to the table complete with vegetables and sauces. The days of being offered more potatoes, or waving away the carrots have gone. OK, so the waiters would always get extra or different vegetables whenever possible, but that means someone else on another table would have to wait longer for their food.

The select dining venues offer a far superior choice of food, with sensational taste experiences and service. But the surcharge cost of these restaurants has spiralled as more people try them.

Let's be honest, the cost of these venues has had to make up some of the profit margins lost by not increasing the cruise prices. Drink prices have also increased, and it is obvious that the drink waiters are pushed to increase sales. Their eagerness is often far too excessive, making it uncomfortable to refuse. Once again, a world cruise makes it difficult for them, as the majority of us do not drink as much as on a short trip around the Mediterranean. Five years ago, to see someone drinking in the theatre was unusual, but now it seems to be the norm.

Moving to the entertainment, it was certainly not as good as we remembered from five years ago. There were far too many vocalists, including at least four female ones that described their act as "a tribute to the divas". I am sure many people enjoyed them, but we prefer something to laugh at or be surprised by occasionally. The comedians, and speciality acts – magicians, conjurors and ventriloquist – were superb, but many jokes and tricks were repeated.

The on-board entertainment team were a let-down. Not because they were bad, but because there weren't enough of them for a major three-month cruise. For the first few days after San Francisco we had just two trained hosts plus the DJ, along with two absolutely brand-new girls. This pair had to be trained and prepared by the others before being let loose on their own. It meant we had no special events and even the syndicate quiz ran with just one host rather than two.

We deserved better!

So, after a lot of negative thoughts, how can I possibly say that the cruise was a sensational experience and worth the small fortune we paid for it?

Well, the ports of call and the cities were amazing. Even the places we had seen before were special because we made the most of what was on offer. We explored some cities on our own, but also had some wonderful organised trips.

We also enjoy life on a ship, well maybe not the rough weather, but generally we find the days at sea, the evenings of organised fun, and the pampering is a real treat.

And of course, we made some wonderful friends. The six of us who turned up on the first evening at the dinner table gelled. It took a day or two but we quickly shared our evenings together, and chatted or laughed as if we had known each other for a lifetime. We were comfortable with each other. Now the six of us have gone our own ways, but we will be meeting again.

So, what's next?

In three months Deb and I are off again with a short cruise on P&O's little Adonia going to Bordeaux and Bilbao. This was never planned, but an offer came along that just couldn't be refused. In the meantime, we will be travelling around the country to see friends and family.

We will be meeting up with the dinner table gang at the end of the year, for a couple of days. As well as a game of trivial pursuits, and a few glasses of wine, we will no doubt be planning our adventure together in January 2019.

The six of us will be departing Southampton on Aurora again for a trip to the Amazon and Caribbean, and we have all tagged on a second cruise at the end going to the fringe of the Arctic. It will be almost ten weeks at sea, and hopefully, we will resurrect our close friendship, the food will improve, and the entertainment will be more varied as we plough the Atlantic Ocean, and see more sunrises over new countries.

So that's it, and all that remains is to thank you for taking the time to read about our adventures as Deb and I sailed around the world. It had been sensational and I would truly jump at the chance to go again.

And as I said at the end of my first book about world cruising...

... there really is still an awful lot more of the world to see yet.

Bye for now

Other books by the author

Cruise Related
A Cornishman Goes Cruising

Around the World without Wings

A Cornishman Cruises to Venice

A Cornishman Cruises to the Mediterranean

Autobiographical
Time for Tea and a Cheese Scone

Would You like Some Plums?

A Cornish Boy Grows Up

You Need a New Hip

Printed in Great Britain
by Amazon